SEVERED

This book was
Designed by Connie Johnston
Cover design by Will Sultzaberger
Printed in the United States of America

Published by
V. Eric and Bonnie Kotter
3708 Canterbury Road
Harrisburg, PA 17109-1211
Order by Telephone: 717-379-6341

ISBN 978-0-692-24581-1

CONTENTS

ACKNOWLEDGMENTS

Our sincere appreciation is extended to Evy Kalbus who was an invaluable source to call upon while translating the voluminous amount of material necessary to complete this book. Her encouragement and experiential knowledge of the history contained herein were a constant support. Another cherished resource was Luule Pavelson whose personal friendships with many of those mentioned in the manuscript and whose firsthand historical perspectives have been inestimable.

This manuscript was made stronger by the comments and suggestions of Christine O'Hagan and Lynnet Reiner as they tirelessly read each chapter while we slogged along on our journey. We are also indebted to Hillar and Rita Kollist who provided some undocumented history from their own experiences with family members.

We will forever be grateful and amazed at the daily diary that was relentlessly maintained by Ilse Kotter during her years of confinement in Siberia, sometimes on mere scraps of paper. Meeta Kollist and Amalie Kollist are to be remembered, as well, for their scrupulous keeping of letters, documents, memorabilia and memoirs.

Finally, we would be remiss if we did not extend our thanks to the numerous people who either read our manuscript or heard the story and encouraged us to publish it.

PROLOGUE

In the late 1930's Nazi Germany expanded eastward in Europe. This brought concern to the little Baltic country of Estonia since Hitler had long had an interest in the Baltic area. The other concern was the Soviet Union because it began to look for ways to bolster its western border against a possible German attack, and the Baltic States were viewed as an important strategic buffer.

Secret negotiations between Nazi Germany and the Soviet Union culminated in the Molotov-Ribbentrop Pact initially agreed upon on August 23, 1939, which assigned Finland, Estonia and Latvia to the sphere of the Soviet Union. Lithuania was included into this pact on September 28 in exchange for additional territory in Poland which Germany desired. By late August of that year, Soviet troops were mobilized near the Estonian border, and by mid-September occupied eastern Poland. Approximately 160,000 Russian troops were massed at Estonia's eastern border. With the escape of a Polish submarine from the harbor of Estonia's capital city of Tallinn, the Soviets took advantage of the occasion to patrol the country's coast and to demand a pact that would allow for Soviet naval and air bases in Estonia, all the while assuring the country they had no intention of interfering with the neutral nation's internal affairs.

On September 27 an Estonian delegation arrived in Moscow to begin negotiations. They were met with the allegation that an unidentified submarine had sunk a Soviet ship off the coast of Estonia and V. M. Molotov, the Soviet commissar for foreign affairs, demanded the placement of more troops in Estonia under the guise of protecting the little country from being drawn into war and to maintain its internal order. As a result of these negotiations Soviet air and naval bases were established on the islands of Hiiumaa and Saaremaa off the west coast of Estonia and on the mainland at Paldiski, not far from Tallinn. Later demands from the Soviets created naval and air bases at Haapsalu and two air bases in the interior at Rapla. A reorganization of the Estonian government followed. Two members of parliament who had negotiated with the Soviets, Jüri Uluots and Ants Piip, became prime minister and foreign minister respectively. Simultaneously with these events the USSR was also negotiating similar pacts with Latvia and Lithuania.

In October of 1939 Germany called for all German people residing in Estonia to return to Germany. In November the Winter War between Finland and the Soviet Union began with Soviet planes conducting bombing missions from Estonian air bases—a violation of the mutual assistance pact agreed upon in negotiations. By June 1940 Soviet military leaders were no longer in communication with Estonian military leaders. The Soviet Army occupied Lithuania by mid-June and troops within Estonia began moving toward Tallinn with large quantities of additional forces being amassed at the Estonian-Soviet border. On June 16 Molotov accused Estonia of collaborating with Latvia and Lithuania to join in an alliance against the USSR. This alleged problem prompted a demand from the Soviets that a government be established in Estonia that would guarantee the execution of the Soviet-Estonian mutual assistance pact and also demanded that free passage be given to Soviet troops entering the country. As a result, at least 115,000 of the Red Army were firmly established in Estonia, and the country came under complete military control.

Within three days A. A. Zhdanov, a top associate of Stalin's, appointed Johannes Vares, an Estonian doctor and poet, as head of the new cabinet. Eventually President Konstantin Päts was forced to resign and Prime Minster Vares took his place. By late July political and military leaders of the former Republic of Estonia began to be taken into custody. General Johan Laidoner, commander-in-chief of the Estonian armed forces, was deported to Siberia as was former President Päts.

Estonia became a member republic of the Soviet Union, all land was declared to belong to the people and banks and large industries were nationalized. Estonian political figures that had been prominent during the independent era, along with military officers, were deported to Siberian prison camps. Between August 1940 and June 1941 political and economic Sovietization advanced quickly. Many of the elitists of independent Estonia were deported to the Soviet Union's interior.

CHAPTER 1

Prelude to the Crisis
Estonia 1941

Meeta Kollist said good night to her sister Ilse on the evening of June 13, 1941, with the familiar *head õhtut*[1] and walked up Seedri Street toward the center of Pärnu, Estonia, their hometown. Meeta had always enjoyed walking along this serene street. It was almost rural in nature since houses stood only on one side. Opposite the houses were birch bushes and an open field beyond that led to the Baltic Sea. But the formerly well-manicured yards were already beginning to show signs of a careless conqueror. Her body tensed as she heard a mother call to her child in Russian.

It had been little more than a year since the Russians invaded their Baltic country, yet tremendous changes had already occurred. President Konstantin Päts had been taken from office and deported to Siberia along with other prominent political and military leaders of the formerly peaceful Republic of Estonia. Under Soviet military control, the government had been reorganized with a prime minister appointed by a top associate of Russian dictator Joseph Stalin. Most businesses were now operated by the new Communist government.

In September of 1940 the Kollist family's leather tanning factory had been confiscated. Jaak, Meeta's father, was forced to work as a common laborer with his regular employees. Ilse continued working as bookkeeper and her husband Peeter Kotter continued as business manager, but all were now supervised by a commissar. Because Jaak was the former owner, the government imposed a heavy tax on him that he was unable to pay. For payment the family's furniture was taken from their home which was located next to the factory. They were left with only two beds, a dining table and a few chairs.

The currency changed from the Estonian kroon to the Russian ruble, and commodities sold at higher prices. This meant that the workers' real purchasing power was reduced by about 20 percent. The Kollist family could no longer afford a housekeeper. In addition, the State now controlled real estate and appointed trustees who regulated the use of large houses. A house next door to Ilse's had been taken over by the government for use by the secret police and had become an office for the NKVD.[2] Other homes and apartments had been forcefully taken for official use or to make room for Russians who were establishing themselves in Estonia. In such cases owners and apartment dwellers were given three days to vacate. Having no place to go, many took only necessities with them and left behind furniture, pictures, linens, utensils, and tools. The fortunate ones moved in with relatives or friends; others found themselves homeless.

Jaak, his wife Amalie and daughter Meeta were still allowed to live in their home, but a good portion of their nine-room house was used for an office, work rooms and a cafeteria for the factory workers. They were left with just two rooms and use of the kitchen.

Ilse and Peeter knew it was only a matter of time before they, too, would be required to share their home. The Russians had ordered just nine square meters of living space for each member of the house, and they had more space than allowed. So before they were appointed an unknown personage, they invited a congenial single woman to live with them. Miss Karlson was the cashier at the local movie theater where Jaak and Amalie used to play the violin and piano respectively together before the advent of talking movies to provide the dramatic background. So Miss Karlson was well known to the family. She was given a bedroom and the dining room to use as a living room with the bathroom and kitchen being shared. The entrance hallway of the house separated the two living quarters.

As Meeta walked, she mused about the different paths she and her sister had taken. Because of her great love of music and the piano in particular, Meeta had attended the National Conservatory in Tallinn[3] and graduated in 1938. The plan had been that Ilse, who was four years younger, would next attend a university of her choice, but events had changed those plans. Ilse and Peeter were married that year.

Meeta could still see Ilse's dimpled smile as she walked down the aisle of Saint Elizabeth's Lutheran Church in her long white gown. Though Meeta would never admit it to anyone, her secret thoughts recalled how she had envied her sister that day. Now at the age of 31, with no prospective suitor, chances seemed scant that there would ever be anyone to cherish her, and Ilse had once again outdistanced her by giving birth to a beautiful baby boy.

Perhaps I'm destined for loneliness, thought Meeta. Though the eldest of three children, she had never felt completely accepted even by her siblings. Ilse, the youngest, always seemed to be the ringleader of the children. Often Oskar, the middle child, would team up with her as she led the way to some adventure.

Meeta thought about the times as children when they studied their homework together around the large mahogany dining table. Suddenly Ilse would nudge Oskar and jar his writing arm. He would return the nudge until the two of them would interrupt the study time by running through their spacious house chasing one another. Meeta would not take part in the chase. Reading and studying were important to her. It seemed a waste of time to run about senselessly when there was so much to learn about the world in which they lived.

Though Mother would scold the two runabouts for their behavior, Meeta always detected a glint in her eyes when she addressed Ilse. Everyone seemed to love Ilse. When Peeter came to work at the factory, it was Ilse that attracted him, even though in regard to age Meeta would have been the more likely choice.

Meeta was in love once. Her life-long friend and roommate at the conservatory had introduced her to Eugen, and Meeta had fallen very deeply in love. She thought the relationship was mutual. They had dated steadily for three years. But one day her roommate saw him with another girl at a club in Tallinn. Meeta was devastated by the news. It was true they were not engaged, but she had fully expected that would come in time and felt betrayed and deceived. What had these three years meant to him? she thought.

The next time she saw Eugen he was waiting for her as she left to perform at a concert. He appeared serious as he spoke. "Meeta, I would like to talk with you this evening."

Meeta struggled to keep her voice from wavering for her whole body felt shaky. "Tonight is our yearly concert." She continued walking toward the concert hall as she spoke.

Eugen walked alongside her. "I know you're aware that I have been seeing another young lady, and I would very much like to talk with you about that. Would you please consider foregoing the concert tonight and spend the evening with me?"

Meeta's forehead creased and her voice rose to a higher pitch. "Eugen, how can you ask such a thing of me? This is the yearly concert in which all the students are involved. I'm scheduled to play."

"I guess it depends on how important this is to you, Meeta. Do I mean more to you than the concert?"

Meeta's mind became fevered. I have already been replaced, she thought. I will not beg or compete for his affection. To forfeit my performance at the concert would be turning aside from the very thing I still have and love. Firmness now entered her voice. "I *cannot*, Eugen. I am scheduled to play, and I will meet my commitment."

They continued walking in silence though the air around them seemed charged with emotion. When they arrived at the hall, Eugen stopped and turned to face her. "I hope the concert and particularly your playing will go well, Meeta."

That was the last time she ever saw him.

After the breakup she was unable to eat or sleep or even practice her beloved piano. She seriously considered consulting with a psychiatrist. At this time the son-in-law of her landlord was doing some painting in the house where she rented a room. He was a devout Christian and began speaking to Meeta about spiritual things. "Meeta, you need to satisfy the needs of your soul with God."

She was intrigued by his faith and actually began following him from room to room as he worked and continued talking. One afternoon he knelt with her and had a long prayer on her behalf. After the prayer he said, "Meeta, you need to talk to God about all of your concerns."

That evening she decided to try it. She took a streetcar to a seaside park. It was late and the park was empty, but the moon was bright and the balmy evening beckoned her. She walked the paths and talked aloud to God. As she spoke, her pain vanished and was replaced by a serene peace. She returned home and for the first time since the breakup slept soundly. This experience produced a profound, lasting impression upon her.

As Meeta continued walking toward the harbor, a breeze blew a strand of her short brown hair. Her fine European hair was a real problem these days. In better times it had been styled by a professional on a regular basis, but now it was combed straight back and secured with a clip. The style was not becoming because of her high forehead and prominent cheekbones. The style also accentuated the Mongolian fold of her eyelids. She was the only one of her family that had this characteristic. It was a recessive trait that stemmed from the Finno-Ugric origin of the Estonian people.

Meeta turned a corner and saw Elli Müllerson, a long-time neighbor and friend, walking just ahead of her. Quickening her pace Meeta caught up with her. "*Tere õhtut*,[4] Elli."

The elderly widow was always pleasant. Meeta often visited with her and her greeting was warm. "*Tere*, Meeta. I guess I shouldn't be surprised to see you. I'll bet you've been visiting Ilse."

"Yes, I just left her home. Peeter is in Tallinn on a business trip for the factory and Mamsi wanted me to be certain all of Ilse's needs are cared for in his absence."

Elli had known the Kollist children since they were babes themselves, and to think that now Ilse had a child of her own delighted her. "How is your sister? When we last spoke, she told me she was not feeling well and that Vello was losing weight because she didn't have enough breast milk to feed him."

"Ilse has been ill with a kidney infection since giving birth three weeks ago. The doctor has her on a meager diet that does not provide enough nutrients for nursing. She was able to locate another woman who is breastfeeding, and this woman is supplying milk for Vello. She still must sometimes supplement with formula, but the breast milk has proven a great help."

Elli gave an understanding nod. "She was fortunate to find someone willing to help."

Meeta and Elli approached the center of town and saw the Pärnu square crowded with vehicles of every description—from taxis to trucks. As they drew closer to the square, Meeta noticed a man standing next to a truck. For a moment their eyes met, but he immediately turned away. Meeta understood this gesture all too well. Within just a few months the normally friendly, hospitable people of her country had become quiet and suspicious. One never knew these days who might be speaking to you or who might overhear a conversation.

Meeta and Elli stood transfixed as they looked about.

"What do you think this means, Elli?"

"I don't know, Meeta, but you can be sure it spells more trouble for us Estonians. You know what happened the last time vehicles gathered like this."

"Yes. The *Metsavennad*[5] were hunted like wild animals and either killed or imprisoned. But the *Metsavennad* appear so weak now they pose no threat to the Communist government. Do you think they will try again to eliminate any remnant of them?"

Elli's voice grew intense. "I wouldn't be surprised. The Communists want no opposition. They have long desired decent harbors for their ships, and now that they have the Baltic States in their grip they will stop at nothing to keep them. What's more the Russians who have immigrated since the takeover think they have found paradise. Our medieval towns reflect more of western Europe than they've ever seen."

Meeta's face grew sullen. "Oh Elli, this is such a fearful time to be alive. Nothing is certain anymore. Father is no longer the owner of the factory he built and labored so hard to develop, and who knows how long we will be allowed to live in our home. Into this world of confusion my sister has brought a son. What kind of future will this child have?"

"It is indeed a fearful time, Meeta. We expected our freedom to last forever, and it lasted only 22 years. What a short time…a mere moment in history."

Meeta observed a deep sadness in Elli's face as she stared at the conflux of vehicles. Meeta knew the history of her country, but Elli had experienced some of that history.

Elli's voice softened; she spoke pensively as though oblivious of Meeta's presence. "The Danes, the Germans, the Russians, the Swedes—all have held us in their clutches at one time or another. What a sweet respite was ours after the First World War." Then almost reverently she added, "Freedom is such a precious a gift."

Turning once again to Meeta, Elli's voice was resolute but still low. "We will have freedom again, Meeta. I have dreamed many times in recent weeks that the red flag came down atop Big Herman[6] and the blue, black and white flag of Estonia once more flew aloft."

Meeta looked into Elli's thin face. "I hope for all of us that your dream comes true."

CHAPTER 2

Forebodings
Estonia 1941

Ilse Kotter sat quietly in her two-room apartment. She felt tired, and the medication she was taking made her mind seem fuzzy. Vello had fallen asleep just before Meeta had left for home shortly before 8:00 p.m., and Ilse took this opportunity to lay her head against the high-backed chair in the front room.

As she began to doze, the telephone rang. It was her next-door neighbor whose voice demonstrated concern as she spoke. "Ilse, I don't want to alarm you, but a man is hiding behind a bush across the street, and he's signaling someone with a flashlight. He's been watching your house for the past hour. I see him even as I speak to you. Can you see him from your window?"

"I'll go and look…just a minute."

Ilse turned toward the window before setting down the receiver and then heard her neighbor speak loudly into the phone. "Be discreet and try not to let him see you."

"I'll be careful," said Ilse.

During June and July "official" sunset occurs around 9:00 p.m. Being so far north, however, Estonians experience enough light to be able to read a newspaper outside in the middle of the night except for about two hours before dawn. It was no problem, therefore, for Ilse to see the man as she peered between her drawn curtains.

She returned to the phone. "Yes, I see him. He is looking at our house."

"That's why I thought I should alert you. I know Peeter is in Tallinn and you're alone."

"Yes, I would feel safer with him here."

"If you need us, call. My husband is at home."

Ilse checked the window several times during the next hour. Shortly after 10:00 p.m. she noticed the man was gone. Just then Vello began to cry and Ilse walked to his crib, which was located in the corner of the room.

Vello had weighed nearly nine pounds at birth but had lost almost two pounds because of her inability to provide enough milk. She was currently out of the breast milk provided by her benefactor, so she hastened to the refrigerator for some cow's milk to which she added water and a little sugar. While warming it she picked Vello up in her arms and stared into his handsome face. "There now, Vello, you must be patient. Your milk will be ready in a few minutes."

She made use of those moments by changing his diaper. "My, my, Vello, you do seem to be constantly wet." The baby followed his mother's motions with eyes wide. As she cooed and muttered to him, his lips parted into a smile.

Ilse fetched the warmed milk and then settled into the couch as she fed and talked to her son. "My little man, how very fortunate I am to still have you. If it had not been for your father's cool head, you wouldn't be here in my arms right now." She recalled how frozen she had become when her son choked and stopped breathing just a week ago. Fortunately Peeter was at home and quickly grabbed Vello, turned him upside down and slapped him on his back. "If you grow up to be as intelligent and controlled as your father, you will be quite a man." She gazed distantly and then added almost in a whisper, "I only hope the world you have been born into will allow you to be all you can be."

As Ilse fed her child, she heard the latch on the front door turn. Startled, she quickly rose from her chair and peeked out the door leading to the entrance hall.

"Peko!" Ilse nearly shouted. Peko was a nickname she had given her husband. "I didn't expect you home until tomorrow."

"I considered staying the night, but I was so eager to be with you and our son I couldn't force myself to remain in Tallinn." He kissed Ilse and then took Vello into his arms.

"So, my young man, you stayed awake to see your father, did you?"

Peeter was 5'6" and 45 years of age—18 years and nine months older than Ilse and just two inches taller. He was a trim man with medium brown hair that was a bit thin, blue-grey eyes and a prominent nose that slightly tilted to the right.

With one arm cradling Vello, Peeter picked up his suitcase and seated himself on the couch.

"Can I fix you something to eat, Peko?" asked Ilse.

"No, no. It's too late to eat. Come sit beside me." He patted the cushion next to him as he spoke, and Ilse quickly sat close to him. She felt complete and confident near him.

How thrilled she was that she had been able to provide him with a son. Peeter had a sad marriage as a young man. His wife became addicted to alcohol and finally committed suicide. She had left him childless, and he had not remarried until he met Ilse. Peeter thought he would never have a child, so when Ilse became pregnant after more than two years of marriage she nicknamed him Peko, a god of fertility. Peeter relished the title.

"Give me the bottle, Ilse, I would like to finish feeding my son." Vello's lips encircled the nipple and drew strongly from the bottle. "He'll gain his weight back in no time. Just look at the way this little fellow eats. I'd say he has his father's determination to get things done."

Ilse and Peeter laughed as they watched their son devour his meal.

"Ilse, you know Vello has your round face."

"Yes, but he has your nose." Ilse enjoyed watching her husband as he stared into the face of their son. "Vello is quite content in your arms. Look, he is already growing sleepy."

As Vello's eyelids began closing, Peeter rose from the sofa and placed him in his crib. Ilse stood by his side observing the tender manner in which Peeter laid his son down and placed a gentle kiss on his forehead.

"You are a doting father, Peko. Just look at you. You can hardly take your eyes off this little one. Your face has fatherly pride written all over it."

"Aha, I have been discovered. I am a proud man, proud of my son and proud of my wife." As he spoke, he wrapped his arms about her.

"I'm so glad you're home, Peko."

"Are you feeling weaker, Ilse?" Peeter's voice showed concern.

"No, I think the kidney infection is finally under control, but this medication clouds my mind. I have not yet felt well enough to register Vello's birth at City Hall. But that's not why I longed to have you home. It's because of a strange event that happened this evening."

Peeter's face grew serious. "What 'strange event,' Ilse?"

"A man was hiding behind a bush across the street from our house. He watched this apartment for several hours. I peeked at him periodically from between the curtains until about 10:15 when he apparently left. …What do you think this means, Peko?"

Peeter's body grew rigid, and he led his wife back to the sofa where they sat close together with Peeter holding her hand. "There is much apprehension and fear in Tallinn. Some people are talking about fleeing to Finland. Some who have gone on business trips there have not returned. My financial associate tells me all are expecting the worst from this new government."

Peeter looked intently at his wife. "Rumors are flying like autumn leaves, Ilse. The Russians have long wanted possession of the Baltic States. We are their 'window to the West.' Now that they control us they will suppress all opposition. Opposition can mean anyone who poses even a potential threat to them. I hesitate to voice this but you know my record, how I fought in the White Russian Army[7] against the Reds. Even if they somehow do not locate that information, I am the business manager of your father's leather tanning factory—a prominent citizen in this community—known by nearly everyone. If they do not link me with my White Russian background, they will try to solicit my allegiance to their Communist views. If they do link me to it, I will be considered a threat to the government. Either way the future looks tenuous for me. Perhaps the man you saw watching our apartment this evening is the prelude to whatever is to come."

Peeter rose from his seat, walked to his son's crib and stared at him in silence as Ilse remained seated, still digesting all that her husband had said. The atmosphere of the room seemed clouded and heavy.

Peeter turned slowly toward his wife, his face registering compassion as he walked toward her with his hands outstretched. She arose from the couch, and he surrounded her once again tightly within his arms. "My dear Ilse … my dear, dear Ilse." They held each other for several minutes, each of them lost in their own world of thoughts.

Ilse could not remember a time when her husband seemed so troubled. At last he spoke. "How I wish we could have escaped last winter after the Baltic Sea had frozen. We may have been able to make it to Finland on skis."

Ilse interjected, "By the time the sea was frozen enough, I was six months pregnant. It was unlikely that I could have made such a strenuous trek. Even your idea of possibly hiding in the coal bin of a ship would have been difficult for me in that condition."

"Yes...we both agreed it would have been too risky."

"I wanted this baby so badly, Peko."

"As did I, Ilse." They clung to each other more tightly as they spoke.

After several minutes Peeter broke the silence. "I have had a very long day, Ilse. I would like to lie down while you ready yourself for bed."

"Yes, of course. I'll tidy things up a bit and be along shortly." She forced the words, then moved slowly, methodically. Her body was tired, but her mind was alert to the prospects of their future.

It was near midnight before she entered their bedroom. Peeter was awake.

"Ilse," his voice was anxious as he reached for her hand. "I just had a dream." Ilse sat on the edge of the bed. There was still enough natural light to see the tightness of his jaw and his furrowed brow as he spoke.

"From Russia my godmother and godfather came to visit us." Ilse knew they both had been dead for many years. "I was so glad to see them. I kissed their hands, and I wanted to introduce you and Vello to them. I called you, but both of you were not at home so I ran out into the street to look for you. I looked in every direction, but I didn't find you. Then I awoke." Peeter paused for a moment and then continued. "This dream does not portend anything good." He drew Ilse's stocky body to him. "Will something really separate us?"

For a long while Ilse and Peeter lay clinging to each other as if their embrace could hold onto the life they had known.

Peeter once again broke the silence. "Do you remember the first time I saw you?"

That statement brought a smile to Ilse's face. "You've never let me forget it." She couldn't help but chuckle as she spoke. She well remembered how Meeta had announced that her best friend Tutti was waiting for her. Assuming she was in the dining room, Ilse came bounding into the room. But instead of Tutti she found Peeter, having just arrived from Tallinn and in the midst of a serious business discussion with her father.

"The way you leaped into the room shouting, 'Tutti'...It took all I could do to keep myself from bursting out with laughter...And that surprised look on your face was so priceless," laughed Peeter.

"Well, it was rather embarrassing to meet 'the crack accountant' that had been recommended by the Minister of Justice in such a childish manner." Ilse smiled as she reminisced. "That first evening after your arrival was so special. There was an air of confidence about you that we all sensed, and we gathered hope just being in your presence. The fearless way you demanded the financial records from Papsi's two business partners was impressive. But once you began delving into those books, we were all amazed at the way you worked. You had to be reminded about meals and worked late into the night. Mamsi said you 'worked like a hound who had found the scent.' When you finally had the evidence that the partners had embezzled funds, we were all thrilled with the way you conducted yourself before them. I hung onto every word as you spoke. You were so confident and unflinching."

Peeter broke into the conversation in a surprised tone. "You 'hung onto every word'? You weren't even there, Ilse."

Ilse chortled, "No, but I had my ear to the door of our living room where you met and heard everything you said. When you would make a point and reveal evidence to back it up, I would silently cheer."

Peeter began tickling Ilse. "Why you little sneak!" Then he kissed her and once again held her close to him. "That's what won my heart, Ilse, your impish, unpredictable ways."

Ilse smiled broadly and nuzzled Peeter as she spoke. "The ultimatum you gave those two thieves was terrific. I could hardly keep from squealing aloud." She lowered her voice and pursed her lips as she continued. "'Gentlemen,' you said, 'you have two choices. You can either relinquish your portions of this business partnership to Jaak Kollist, or I shall present this information to the authorities.'" Ilse smiled as she returned to her normal voice and said, "Papsi said they about fell over each other trying to sign their names to the documents you had prepared for them."

"I did do a supreme job, didn't I?" Peeter beamed.

Ilse feigned shock as she struck him playfully on his chest. "Why you egotist."

"Now, Ilse, you know that's what finally attracted you." Peeter smiled confidently and looked directly into her eyes as he spoke.

She couldn't deny that the cocky directness he was even now manifesting was part of his appeal. There was something comforting and secure about it. It gave not only Ilse but also others who came in contact with him a sense that this man would complete whatever task he undertook.

In self-defense of his penetrating look Ilse responded, "You won my father's heart far quicker than you did mine."

For a moment Peeter's voice revealed his shrewd business sense. "Your father is an intelligent man. He realized he didn't have the administrative skills needed to make his business succeed." Softening and reverting back to his playful mood, Peeter continued. "But once I became his business manager you couldn't resist me, could you?"

Still coyly defensive Ilse said, "May I remind you it took nearly three years before I was taken in by you."

Undaunted Peeter replied, "I had to wait until you grew up." Then rising on one elbow and hovering over her he said, "By the way, what do you mean 'taken in' by me?" He put his free hand on his chest and then gestured in an oratorical manner. "That's not saying much for my wit, my charm and my charisma."

Teasingly pushing him Ilse responded, "Oh you're impossible! I shall try to raise your son to appreciate humility, though I'm sure it will be an uphill battle."

Their laughter and light conversation felt good. During the past year they had times of laughter, but it had been superficial and fleeting. The loss of their country's freedom hung like Dionysius' sword[8] above their heads, and it felt good to remember the good times—the best times.

At last weariness overtook both of them, and they fell into a deep sleep.

***

The ring of the Kotter's doorbell shocked the morning air. The ticking alarm clock beside their bed read 4:30. Ilse's eyes stared wildly and her heart raced. Peeter reached for her hand, his face tense. The doorbell rang again. Peeter hesitated just a moment and then rose to open the door.

Men's voices filtered into the bedroom and with them came the stinging thought, Now they have come for Peeter. Ilse quickly grabbed a coat from a hook near the bed and walked into the living room. Two Communist soldiers carrying rifles with bayonets attached and two men dressed in civilian clothes stood with Peeter. One civilian was an Estonian, the other a Russian. Ilse vaguely heard instructions about packing within half an hour and leaving with them. Stunned, she sat on the divan. Could this really be happening? Perhaps this is only a dream—a bad dream. How could she endure life without Peeter? And what about their baby? Would he be raised without the father who adored him?

She watched as the Estonian took a seat behind their writing desk and then looked directly at her with expressionless eyes. His voice was devoid of emotion as he spoke. "Mrs., why are you sitting there? You're coming, too."

Ilse looked at the man as if unable to believe her ears. He had spoken the words so casually—as one would say, "It looks like it's going to rain." The man's features were sharp and appeared calm until she noticed his jaw muscles flex as he stared back at her from beneath a tan flat-crowned cap that covered half his forehead. Sweat appeared on her brow, and her body drained of any strength. She could not move. Questions and confused thinking controlled her mind: Why must I go? Where are we going? Why did I have a child? Who will take care of him? He will now die. What's to become of us?

As the man's words made contact with her intellect, she turned toward her sleeping child. Her eyes showed the fear of a stalked animal. Struggling for composure, she finally gathered enough momentum to speak. "May I telephone my parents?" None of the men responded, so she went to the phone and dialed the Kollist home.

CHAPTER 3

The Phone Call
Estonia 1941

Meeta had thought of calling her sister to tell her about all the vehicles she had seen at the Pärnu square on her way home that evening but decided not to impose another burden on her. She mentioned the large gathering of vehicles to her parents, and they wondered as she did, what this could mean.

After her parents retired for the evening Meeta readied herself for bed but found she could not sleep. Instead she sat on a chair in what used to be their living room but was now the eating area for the factory workers. Her thoughts reviewed the events of the past year. How much her country had changed in such a short time.

Her mind's eye saw her father and mother, Ilse, her brother Oskar and herself gathered together in this very room along with neighbors and friends, each with their favorite instrument —mandolin, zither, flute, violin, cello—and she seated at the piano playing song after song together. Music had been such a part of their lives, such a wonderful part.

We played beautiful pieces, she thought, the music of Chopin, Haydn, Beethoven, Strauss, Mendelssohn. On summer evenings people would walk the street in front of their home to listen. Some families would bring their boats to the bank of the Sauga River, atop of which the Kollist house was perched, to listen.

Meeta rested her head against the high-backed chair and closed her eyes. She could see Papsi, his round head completely bald bent over his violin. How he loved this instrument. Self-taught, he had excelled so in its playing that he amazingly became first violinist in the Pärnu Orchestra.

The corners of her mouth curled upward as she thought about the day six years ago when Oskar ruined 100 choice hides by mixing improper amounts of chemicals together. He had just completed his course work at an international school for leather technicians in Freiberg, Saxony near Dresden, Germany. There he had studied to become a master tanner and had learned to measure chemicals by weight. Papsi had always just smelled and tasted the chemicals to determine proper amounts.

When Papsi learned what his son had done, he remained outwardly calm but retreated to this living room where he picked up his violin and began playing. After playing a few measures, he stopped, shook his head and said, "A little boy is a little boy. What did he do? . . . 100 hides . . . How could he do that?" He went back to his playing for a few more measures, stopped again and mumbled, "A little boy is a little boy. What did he do? . . . He still doesn't know how to tan."

This scenario continued until the mumbling lessened and the playing increased. Finally only the violin was heard, and the family knew that Papsi's frustration had been carried away on the wings of a melody. When Oskar returned home that evening, Jaak spoke no word of condemnation to him.

Oskar's schooling eventually did pay off. The quality of leather produced at their factory became preferred over all Estonian leather, and her brother's hard work was largely responsible.

Meeta was glad that Oskar was now safely in Finland. How providential, she thought, that he left for vacation the previous summer on the last cruise ship the Russians would allow out of the harbor. Seeing the political scene in Estonia, he wisely chose to remain in Finland. No one was allowed to leave now without the strictest scrutiny.

It was long after midnight before Meeta went to her bedroom and fell asleep. It seemed as if she had only slept a moment before the ringing telephone awakened her at 4:40 a.m. She rose quickly hoping the call would not disturb her aging father. Nearly two decades older than his wife, Papsi needed rest at night. He was still working full time at the factory.

Meeta did not feel the usual drowsiness of being awakened suddenly. Instead she felt alert and apprehensive. She heard her sister's voice, tense and quivery.

"Meeta, we are being taken away."

"Where," asked Meeta.

Ilse ignored the question and continued. "Tell Mamsi and come over here quickly. Time given us is only one-half hour. Take a taxi."

The words caused Meeta's stomach to tighten. She opened her mouth to speak but Ilse had hung up.

Meeta stood like a pillar of ice for a moment, her mind whirling. Who was taking them? Where were they going? What did she mean by "We"? Had Peeter returned from Tallinn, or was she referring to Vello and herself?

Then her thoughts turned to the immediate. Should I wake Papsi also? . . . No, not Papsi. This news would be too hard for him.

She walked quietly into her parent's bedroom and, in as calm a voice as she could manage, woke her mother and whispered the message she had received. Meeta and Amalie dressed quickly without waking Jaak. They both agreed there was not time enough to wait for a taxi to arrive, but Amalie had an idea.

"Meeta, look to see if any fishing boats remain. If a fisherman can take us to the harbor, it will save us much walking time."

Meeta hurried to the bank of the river behind their home. It was an idyllic summer morning. The river appeared covered with diamond dust as the sun shone brightly upon its calm, flowing water. The lush green grass and full-leafed trees along the bank seemed to beckon her to come rest a while. Everything Meeta's eyes saw appeared to mock the inner turmoil she was experiencing.

If Meeta could signal a fisherman for passage to the harbor, it would save them almost two and a half kilometers of their otherwise four kilometer walk.

But all the boats were too distant from shore. Perhaps if they were lucky they could flag a taxi as they walked. They would have to go by foot down their street, across the Sauga River Bridge along Jannsen Street and across the 250 meter Pärnu River Bridge. After that they had to walk another two and a half kilometers to Ilse's house on Seedri Street. Could they make it before Ilse would be taken away?

Meeta signaled no to Amalie and began to run. Amalie was in good health and was accustomed to walking, as were most Europeans of her day, but she was in her 50s. For a while Amalie tried to keep pace with Meeta but finally resigned herself to a fast walk with an occasional spurt of running. Meeta alternated between a hard run and a fast walk. Her heart pounded against her chest wall and into her ears.

Meeta passed Elli Müllerson's house. All appeared peaceful there, but further down the street was an unfamiliar pick-up truck parked in the front of a neighbor's house. She hurriedly crossed the Sauga River Bridge and began her journey down Jannsen Street. She passed apartment houses and saw other strange trucks and vehicles parked in front of the entrances.

As she approached the Pärnu River Bridge she thought of Anna, her cousin, whose Danish boyfriend helped build this structure. Anna was safe as a resident of Sweden now.

As Meeta passed the marketplace, she noted that all was quiet with no one in sight. At this time of day one would normally see women walking with brooms in anticipation of sweeping and watering down the large square where later produce stands would open to sell their country-fresh products. Nearing the Pärnu square she realized that the vehicles she had seen the night before were all gone. But where are the taxis? she thought.

Meeta looked at her watch. It read 5:05 and she estimated she still had about two kilometers to go. The thought that she might not make it to Ilse's in time drove her to a hard run once again, and she breathed a prayer. "Dear God, please help me."

She ran past the post office and then turned right and continued down a series of side streets that led to Seedri Street. Her watch read 5:20. Her eyes scanned the long street. As she drew nearer her sister's home she could see a dark pick-up truck standing by the curb just in front of the iron rod gate leading to the front walkway. Her body felt hot and droplets of moisture dotted her forehead. Her face, already flushed, felt a surge of additional heat as she anticipated what it would be like entering the home. What would she find inside? Who was present in the house with her sister? Would entering the house spell danger for her and Mamsi?

Meeta hurried to the front door and tried the latch. It was open and she entered. A Russian soldier immediately stopped her. He held his rifle diagonally in front of him with the bayonet pointed to the ceiling. "Are you a tenant?" he asked her in Russian.

Meeta had become familiar with some Russian words and understood his question but was not capable of responding in the language. She began to speak in Estonian, "I am the sister of Ilse Kotter." The Russian motioned for her to stop and then called for the Estonian civilian to come to their aid.

Meeta once again began her response in Estonian. "I am the sister of Ilse Kotter. My mother will be here shortly. We have come in response to Ilse's telephone call."

The Estonian explained in Russian to the soldier, and Meeta was allowed entrance. She noticed that a second civilian stood against the wall between the entrances to the bedroom and living room. Another Russian soldier wandered about the kitchen opening cupboard doors as if searching for something. From the bedroom she heard her sister say, "Peeter why are you packing so many sheets?"

So Peeter is home, thought Meeta.

Peeter's response was strained. "You have a child, Ilse. You will need diapers."

Fear gripped Meeta as she thought of the child. Ilse can't nurse him. How will he survive?

Meeta entered the bedroom and observed her sister. Ilse was seated on the bed watching Peeter pack. She appeared bewildered. When she saw Meeta she rose from the bed and came to her.

"Meeta, I'm so glad you're here. Where is Mamsi?"

"We couldn't get a taxi and had to come by foot. I rushed ahead of her. She should be here shortly."

The Russian soldier whom Meeta had observed in the kitchen suddenly entered the bedroom carrying an enameled cup that Meeta recognized as the one she had given Ilse on her last birthday. It had the picture of a girl walking a dog on the front of it. He handed the cup to Ilse along with a package of cocoa which he had obviously located in one of the cupboards. He muttered something to Ilse in Russian.

"He wants you to take these along with you," said Meeta.

Ilse handed the items to Peeter and he promptly put them into her suitcase.

"They have ordered us to pack separately, no more than 100 kilograms each." She stood as if cataleptic while Peeter moved quickly around the room putting as many clothes as he could fit into her suitcase and filling a large piece of felt material with her winter coat and warm clothes. "I can't find my felt boots, Meeta. I can't remember where I put them, and we have been told to take warm clothes."

Once again the Russian soldier entered the bedroom. This time he handed Ilse a gold watch which he had found in the apartment and motioned for her to take it along. She pointed to the face of the watch because the glass was missing. The Russian nodded that he understood and pushed it once again into her hand.

Ilse put it on her wrist.

Just then Amalie burst into the bedroom and rushed to embrace her daughter. Sweat poured from her face and breathlessly she asked, "Where are they taking you, Ilse?"

"I don't know, Mamsi." Her forehead creased and her eyes were fearful. "Whatever will become of Vello?"

Without hesitation Amalie said, "Why don't you leave him behind?"

This was a new thought to Ilse. She immediately walked to the doorway of the bedroom and blurted out, "Can I leave my baby behind?"

The Estonian replied quickly. "Why do you want to leave him?"

Ilse burst into tears, "Because he will die!"

Silence fell upon those in the room, and for a moment all activity ceased. Peeter evaluated the lack of response as an affirmative. He quickly began unpacking the numerous sheets he had put into Ilse's luggage and replaced them with additional clothes for her.

With that important decision made, Ilse's posture appeared to relax somewhat, and her full attention turned to locating her boots. Meeta and Amalie joined her in the search, but the boots could not be found.

The Estonian civilian became impatient. "We must leave right now. You have already taken too much time." While they had been packing, this man had been making a list of all the Kotters' possessions and handed the list to Peeter for his signature. Then he pointed toward the luggage and said to Peeter, "Take these to the truck outside."

Peeter picked up two suitcases and walked out the bedroom door. At the doorway he stopped and looked toward the crib where his son slept. He walked to the crib, set his suitcases down and bent over to kiss his son good-bye. As Peeter left the room and headed toward the hall, the child began to cry.

Meeta observed this farewell and thought, Can Vello possibly sense this tragedy?

Ilse halted and looked toward her child, but the Estonian nudged her forward. She walked mechanically yet erect and tearless. The two Russian soldiers followed with the Russian civilian behind them. Amalie and Meeta were the last to leave the house. Peeter placed the luggage onto the pickup truck. Then Amalie embraced her son-in-law and daughter. "We will take good care of Vello, Ilse," said Amalie as she held her daughter close. Ilse stood stoic and expressionless as she returned her mother's embrace.

Meeta hugged Peeter about the neck and then held her sister tightly. "Goodbye, Ilse." The words sounded so final. "Write us just as soon as you can." Somehow these words lightened the parting. Surely she would be allowed to write, thought Meeta.

In a last-minute gesture, Amalie took off the head scarf she had worn that morning and put it into Ilse's hand saying, "You might need this."

Peeter helped Ilse aboard and they were both told to sit with their backs against the cab of the truck. Ilse sat sideways with her legs curled close to her body. Peeter sat beside her with his legs bent and spread in front of him. The two Russian soldiers took a seat opposite each other on the wheel wells with their rifles in their laps pointing toward the Kotters.

Amalie, who had been emotionally solid to this point, cupped her cheeks with her hands as the truck began to pull away. Then her brow furrowed and tears began to flow.

Meeta was too stunned for tears. She stared at her sister as the distance between them widened. My sister looks so valiant, she thought. There is actually a faint smile on her face. Surely she is relieved that Vello has been allowed to remain with us.

Meeta walked to the center of the street and watched the truck as it reached the corner and turned out of sight. She stood gazing at the empty street. It looked so normal, so ordinary, so peaceful, and yet where a moment ago she had embraced her sister, now there was nothing.

CHAPTER 4

Separated
Estonia 1941

As the truck pulled away from the Kotter home, Peeter looked at Ilse and asked, "How do you feel about Vello remaining here?"

Ilse smiled slightly. "I feel like a rock has been rolled away from my heart." She took a deep breath before continuing. "Now perhaps he will live."

The truck continued to the end of Seedri Street and then turned right. When it passed the local prison where Ilse thought they might be taken, she knew they were going elsewhere and cast a quizzical look toward Peeter. Nothing more was said between them until they reached the Papaniidu Railroad Station where a train awaited.

Many people were disembarking from various vehicles. Ilse and Peeter recognized one of their factory workers named Toots carrying and loading some of the luggage of those being escorted to the train. A trusted worker, he had been Oskar's right-hand man. Peeter called out in a friendly tone, "Toots!" and waved. Toots' eyes filled with fear and he nearly dropped the suitcase he was holding. He quickly turned and rushed to distance himself from them.

Men and women were now separated from one another. Peeter embraced Ilse briefly and then they were directed to separate wagons. All seemed surreal. People were amazingly calm and followed the orders of the soldiers. Many relatives of people being sent away stood about weeping quietly. Some had brought food and other items they felt their loved ones might need and passed them to their family members as they were ushered onto the trains.

Ilse, along with 17 other women and children, were ordered into one car. Normally used to transport animals, it was lit by only a small louvered opening located near the top of the car. Although June 14, 1941, was a sunny day, the train car was shadowy and dim.

There were no seats, so each person sat on the luggage or bundles they had brought. Ilse situated her large fiber suitcase and her bundle tied in a felt cloth beside a woman who had four children. She surveyed the family and wondered how this mother was going to feed them. Their bag filled with clothes and footwear was already heavy, and Ilse felt certain she could not have packed much food. No one appeared to be well supplied with food items.

Those aboard sat quietly without much speaking. All seemed stunned trying to make some sense of their situation. One woman who appeared particularly fearful asked, "I wonder if we're to be used for prostitution." Another woman tried to allay her fears by suggesting, "Perhaps this will be a short trip for the purpose of using us for a building project or road construction."

As the sun rose higher in the sky, the train car grew very warm and people began nodding and dozing on their luggage.

Ilse learned that the person seated next to her was Elsa Reim. She had three daughters: Mall, eight years old; Hell, age seven, and Tiiu, six. Her fourth child was a three-year-old boy named Mart. At first her children sat close to their mother clinging to her, eyes wide, scanning Ilse and each person confined to the boxcar. As time stretched on past noon, the children became restless and hungry. Several women began to bang on the side of the car calling for bread.

After a while soldiers gave each detainee a loaf of bread. It was extremely hard, and many did not want to eat it. Ilse tucked her loaf beside the pack of cocoa which the Russian soldier had encouraged her to take from her kitchen. One family had relatives who lived near the train station. Somehow a pail of butter mysteriously arrived for them. Since soldiers would not allow people near the trains, it was assumed that a family member had bribed one of the guards.

Later that afternoon the train began to move. Ilse noted the towns that the train passed through: Turi, Paide, and then it stopped at Tamsalu. The route so far had been on a narrow-gauged rail, but at Tamsalu it became a wide-gauge and the cars were twice as large.

All of the people were ordered out of their current cars and into the larger ones. An additional 18 more women and children were added to the car in which Ilse was now placed, making a total of 35 people. The larger cars had four louvered windows. They were small openings and high up on both sides of the car, two at the front and two at the back. At each end of the car were three-tiered plank shelves about two meters deep. Families were given the two lowest bunks, so Ilse climbed to the highest tier under the ceiling. Though more difficult to navigate, it did provide her with a window.

In the middle of the floor of the car but situated close to the wall opposite the entrance, was a hole for toilet purposes. Two young ladies expressed a need to use the "facilities," but they were too embarrassed to use the hole in such an exposed manner. Some of the women ingeniously hung sheets suspended from the ceiling around it to provide a semblance of privacy.

At Tamsalu a woman about 40 years of age boarded the train. Her husband was a lawyer in Pärnu. She had two daughters with her, ages 10 and 13. Learning of Ilse's separation from her infant son, the woman became vehement. "How could they separate you from a recently born child? What a wicked deed." Ilse did not comment. Although her heart ached for Vello, she knew that caring for a baby under these conditions would have been impossible and felt relieved that he was in the care of her mother and sister.

Some of the older ladies on the train had gone to school during the years of the czars and knew the Russian language. Somehow they learned where the men were located and kept pestering the Russian soldiers to open their car's door so they could get out to see them. Finally the soldier guarding Ilse's car conceded.

All was quiet as they stepped from the boxcar. Ilse walked to the car where her husband was purported to be. Peeter stood before a louvered opening of his car calling out, "Does anybody know where Mrs. Kotter is?" The louvers inhibited him from seeing her.

Ilse stood in front of the other women. "Can't you see me, Peko? I'm one of the first ones standing right in front of you?"

Peeter quickly repositioned himself so he could see her and said, "Look, Ilse, there on the grass is a bag with sugar cubes and two packs of margarine. Bring them here to the car. Take one pack of margarine for yourself and half the sugar."

Ilse looked behind her and saw the items Peeter had mentioned about 10 steps away. There was not time to ask him where they had come from. Knowing the ingenuity of her husband she assumed he had thrown money to someone passing by. Perhaps the person feared coming near the train carrying supposed prisoners and just dropped the goods. Ilse picked up the products and brought them to Peeter. He was allowed to push the train's door open and received one pack of margarine. Then they divided the sugar.

"Where will I put the sugar cubes?" asked Ilse.

"Put them in your bra."

Ilse verbalized a thought that came to her. "Too bad we didn't take along two of our enameled soup bowls."

"I will write home," said Peeter. "Perhaps someone can bring them to us."

Before they could converse further, the soldiers pressed the women to return to their own train.

That night was spent in the boxcar. During the middle of the night, the car's door was thrust open with a great clanking noise. A light mattress with clothing, a package and the owner were thrown in. The woman and her items landed on top of others already situated on the floor of the car. Seeing her predicament, Ilse called her to come up to her third-tier bunk where there was still some space for her few possessions.

Lisette Silm was a 53-year- old housewife. Ilse learned that she and her husband owned a chicken farm and grain mill. "My husband was not at home when they came for us, so I alone have been taken," Lisette sobbed.

"The first day is very hard," said Ilse. "But you will see, tomorrow will be easier. You will overcome the shock." Somehow by consoling Lisette, Ilse's own pain seemed to lessen.

The following day the train left Tamsalu and stopped in Tartu, a university town, and then continued to Orava where the train remained for a longer time while more detainees were added. Within the border of Estonia, the local people brought food for those aboard. One of the women in Ilse's boxcar, Emma Ristna, was very aggressive. When anyone carrying food came close enough to their train car Emma called out, "Give it to us." She was successful at the Orava station and obtained a dish filled with pancakes.

On the morning of June 17 the train left the Estonian border and entered Russia. Ilse looked at the gold wrist watch the Russian soldier had insisted she take along; it read 11:02.

At one sweeping turn in the track Ilse could see the whole length of the train from her slatted window. Her heart pounded and her stomach knotted as she realized the men's cars were no longer attached.

CHAPTER 5

A Frightening Order
Estonia 1941

In the days following Ilse's departure, the Kollist family tried to develop some modicum of normalcy. Jaak daily worked at the leather tannery, Amalie busied herself with household chores and the care of little Vello, and Meeta continued working as an accountant for the Bester Undergarment Factory in Pärnu. But a heavy pall covered not only their city but also the entire country of Estonia. News spread rapidly that hundreds of families had been disrupted on the early morning of June 14 just as theirs had been.

Each succeeding night found Meeta listening to passing cars and trucks. The screeching of brakes or the grinding of gears on Haapsalu Road outside their family home caused her to awaken in full alert. Her parents were in a depressive state.

Since the night of Ilse's phone call Meeta had been concerned for her father and how, at age 74, he would deal with this tragedy. His life had experienced so much loss. As one of 10 children born to a humble grain miller in the hamlet of Karksi, he had shared with her how devastated he was when his older brother Ants had died of smallpox—the dear brother who had introduced him to his beloved violin. She had heard him express the horror he felt the first time he looked into the mirror and saw his own face after recovering from the same disease.

She knew how at 18 his desire to become a leather tanner led him to Ruhja, Latvia. There he served as an apprentice under an established tanner. Then for 16 years he developed his skills as an apprentice and journeyman working throughout Finland, Sweden and Germany gaining all the technical knowledge available to him.

Finally, in 1900 at the age of 38 Jaak had saved enough money to begin his own business. But five years later, in need of additional capital, he entered into partnership with two brothers who took advantage of his naïve trust in people and by 1909 forced him out of the partnership.

That same year he married Amalie Katarina David. Her mother helped financially, and they began another business with a new partner who even became the godfather of their first child. But this partner also betrayed Jaak. He embezzled funds from the business and gained financial control.

His third and fourth attempts had to be aborted because of building rental issues, so his current factory was his fifth attempt. He once again entered into a partnership and found joy in concentrating on good quality leather while trusting his two partners to handle the financial end of the business. Amalie, however, sensing all was not well became suspicious of his partners and convinced Jaak to have the records investigated.

When Peeter Kotter entered the scene, he provided the ingredient Jaak had been missing for so many years. Jaak's desire for a quality product had been enhanced by the skills his son Oskar had learned to apply. Now a first-class product coupled with Peeter's strong accounting skills and ability to negotiate good sales and purchasing agreements developed the factory into the third largest leather tannery in the country. Just when all of Jaak's dreams seemed to have become a reality, the country was invaded, his factory was out of his control and Peeter and Ilse had been stolen away. How, Meeta thought, could her dear Papsi endure?

Despite her fears, however, Jaak had once again manifested his resilience with quiet albeit tearful resignation and even found some joy in having his grandson a part of their home. As Meeta evaluated the past few days, she concluded her family was as normal as a family could be in an abnormal environment.

One evening at nine o'clock, about 10 days following the deportation, Meeta answered the telephone. After identifying herself, she was startled to hear, "This is the city administration speaking. You and all able-bodied workers at the leather factory are to be ready at seven o'clock tomorrow morning prepared with a food supply to last a few days. Bring with you shovels, axes and spades. A truck will be sent for you."

"What is our destination, and what are we going to do?"

The caller became enraged. "It's none of your concern." Then as abruptly as it had come, the call was ended.

Meeta stood numb with the receiver still in hand, her face drained of color. Will I be the next to be sent away? Why shovels, axes and spades?

Jaak had heard his daughter's side of the conversation and saw her rigidly standing beside the phone staring but not seeing. "Meeta, what's the matter?"

Meeta struggled to gain some composure, but fear almost overwhelmed her. She hesitated as she spoke but explained to him what the caller had said.

Jaak's bald head bowed and his stocky body tensed, but he did not say a word. After a long silence, Jaak spoke. "Meeta, we are in the hands of Providence. I will contact the workers and alert them immediately."

Meeta walked outside, but her legs felt weak. Lost in thoughts of gloom, she suddenly became aware of the fragrance of peonies. Many times she had gathered bunches of these flowers and put them in clay vases on the floor, in windows and on the tables of their home. She loved the smell permeating the house as the summer breeze blew in through the windows. But today it was all wrong. That was another life—another time. Today one must think about survival.

A restless night turned all too quickly into morning for the Kollist family. Amalie and Meeta packed loaves of dense Estonian bread, hard cheese and small cans of sprotts[9] and placed them in a large canvas bag. Jaak organized the necessary tools that Meeta would be taking with her and mingled with neighbors who had received similar calls the night before.

One particularly distressed neighbor approached Jaak. "*Herra*[10] Kollist, rumors are spreading among us that we will be taken to the forest to dig our own graves and then be shot."

Jaak sought to calm his neighbor's fear. "This is a troubling time for Estonians, but let us be reasonable. You have been asked to take food for a few days. I think we can rule out the possibility you have mentioned. You have not been asked to take along additional clothes, an encouraging sign that this is not another deportation. It is likely that you will be used for some project."

Despite Jaak's attempt at projecting optimism, his bright blue eyes filled with tears as his strong arms wrapped around his daughter beside the waiting truck. "Go with God, Meeta."

Amalie could not stifle her tears as she bade her last child good-bye. She had lost two children as babes: one a stillborn, the other at the age of one from dysentery. A week and a half ago Ilse had been taken away. Oskar escaped to Finland more than a year ago, and now she was seeing her last child taken to an unknown location.

Nausea gripped Meeta as she boarded the large truck, and she swallowed several times to suppress it. The truck crossed the two bridges that Meeta and her mother had walked only days before to reach Ilse's home. The memory of that morning came back vividly to Meeta; once again the nausea returned. She forced herself to change her focus. Heikki, one of the factory workers, sat next to her. He was a thin middle-aged man but wiry and strong. She looked at his exposed forearms and hands. The muscles were rippled and the veins stood out like tributaries. I wonder how many hides those hands have tanned, she thought. Though they did not speak as they rode, being seated beside him gave her strength. He sat calmly with a shovel and an ax resting diagonally on his crossed legs. He wore a slightly soiled flat cap atop his thinning hair. A weathered face peered out from beneath it revealing determined blue eyes that squinted in the morning sunlight.

The truck traveled down Riia Street, a long road that led from the center of Pärnu into the countryside. Fear erupted within Meeta as the truck turned onto a lonely dirt road and began to enter the forest. Her thoughts were now rampant. If this is a project as Papsi suspected, why are we entering such a secluded area?

Deep into the forest the truck came to the bank of the Pärnu River and stopped. The Communists had chosen people who were lower-level workers to become supervisors of more prominent citizens. In their new role they often proved to be demanding and sometimes abusive of their power. Brazenly the two Estonian supervisors commanded the people to descend and begin digging a trench all along the bank toward the city of Pärnu as they stood watching.

When Meeta and her fellow workers broke the soil, they began hearing planes approaching. Heikki, who was shoveling beside Meeta, nudged her and looked up in the sky. She followed his gaze and suddenly her heart pounded inside her chest cavity. Soaring above were German reconnaissance planes. So that's the purpose of this trench, she thought. This is a defensive measure against a German invasion from the sea.

CHAPTER 6

Enroute to Siberia
Russia/Siberia 1941

Almost immediately after Ilse's train crossed the border from Estonia to Russia, the landscape and buildings changed significantly. The land was devoid of forests, and the countryside was generally desolate and monotonous. Houses were undecorated and built of logs. No bushes or flowers surrounded the homes, and crops consisted only of tubers such as potatoes, beets, turnips and carrots. It was later learned that grains were only permitted to be grown on the *kolhoos*.[11] A family was allowed only one cow, a pair of pigs and chickens. Most families, however, had a goat instead of a cow because they were easier to feed. The people were poorly dressed in rough, well-worn clothes. Most wore *fufaikas*, quilted coats made of cotton.

The train traveled through Pskovi, Porhovo, Staraja Russa, Bologoe, Bezetski, Robinski, Jaroslavi, Danilovi and Bui. At one of the railroad stations a girl approached Ilse's car and offered the women one-half liter of milk in exchange for some bread. At another station a boy of about 12 years of age begged bread from the prisoners. The deportees now realized that the Russian people did not have sufficient food. Therefore, those who still had bread with them from Estonia decided to dry it.

On June 25 somewhere before Revda in the Ural Mountains the train stopped, and all of the people were permitted to leave their cars. The sun was shining and the day was pleasantly warm. Ilse breathed deeply and swung her arms as she walked, trying to loosen her cramped body. This was the first time she had seen a forest since leaving the Estonian border, and it made the landscape appear more welcoming. Alongside the rail she saw a forest road where the trees had been cut down. Ilse wondered why the stumps were about a meter high, some even higher, and commented about it to the woman walking beside her. The woman looked toward the stumps and then replied, "In Siberia the snow does not melt until spring, so during the winter the trees are cut at the snow line."

"Oh, I see," said Ilse. Sensing the woman was interested in talking and seemed knowledgeable, she commented on her other observation. "It's good to see forest again. I haven't seen any since crossing the Estonian border."

"Do you know why?" asked the woman.

Ilse's blank expression caused the woman to continue. "It's because the Russians cleared them so those destined for the prison camps could not jump from the train and escape into them."

Ilse felt a chill as she pondered the woman's statement. Her mind reeled. Is that where we're headed—a prison camp? Was this woman just trying to frighten her? Or was she despondent herself? Ilse was not sure how to evaluate the statement, so she said nothing.

After about 40 minutes Russian soldiers gave the order for people to return to their respective cars. The journey continued for two more days. When they traveled through Sverdlovsk on June 27, they learned that Russia was at war with Germany. The following day they came to the station at Kamōshlov where their train was pulled off the main track to allow a westward train to pass. It was filled with Russian soldiers and war equipment headed for the front line.

Emma stood looking out Ilse's window at the passing train. A Russian guard stood outside the window close to their car. Emma spit on him, and then quickly turned away from the window, leaving Ilse alone. The guard turned and saw Ilse. Thinking she was the one who spit at him, he muttered something to her. Emma, who spoke fluent Russian, translated for her. "He said, 'Soon you won't have any spit to spit.'" Ilse had not expected a kindly comment, but this statement penetrated to her core. She interpreted his words as a harbinger of what was to come.

While waiting at the station, Emma cried out to one of the guards, "vadō, vadō," which means "water, water" in Russian. Thankfully, the guard responded to her cry. Some of the women aboard had brought buckets with them, so when the door was opened two ladies were allowed to get water. In those days every train station had a water tower where one could get cold and hot water. They were able to obtain not only enough water to drink but also to lightly wash themselves. They also took this opportunity to wash around the hole used for toilet purposes. While the train was moving air flowed into the car from the louvered windows, but when it stopped the smell of urine became offensive.

Ilse was thankful that Peeter had packed a thermos bottle in her suitcase. She filled it with cold water from one of the pails and took a long drink. Then she poured some in her hand and splashed her face again and again, letting the cool water run down her chest. What a precious gift water is, she thought, as she refilled her thermos. When her turn came at the bucket with hot water, she took a towel from her packed bundle and saturated it. Then she unbuttoned her dress and rubbed her body, underarms and feet. After 14 days without a bath, she was thankful for this refreshing moment.

Later that same day they arrived in Tjumeniss where for the first time they received food from their captors. The two ladies with the pails were sent to get soup. The soup actually turned out to be watery millet porridge. Those who still had food products from their homes only tasted it and then poured the rest down the hole in the floor and onto the railroad tracks. Ilse, though unaccustomed to such porridge, ate it because she had no other food.

The dry food and lack of water and exercise produced a constipation problem for many aboard the train. This was especially true for the children. At Emma's request laxatives were brought to them.

On Monday, June 30, the train arrived in the large city of Omsk where for the second time they received something to eat. Again two women, accompanied by a soldier, were permitted to get the food. This time millet mush was provided. The Estonian bread that had been dried by the women still had to supplement the meager rations.

It was interesting for Ilse to observe the behavior of the women and children aboard the train. She noted that generally people began to accustom themselves to their new situation. They were peaceful and didn't whine or complain—except for Elsa Reim's three-year-old son Mart who whimpered almost constantly. He was a beautiful boy with big eyes and long eyelashes. His mother tried desperately to quiet him by telling him stories and playing finger games so he wouldn't trouble the others. But her attempts ultimately failed.

On one occasion a young girl of about seven years of age said, "You are an eternal monkey." Mart's large eyes opened to their full size as he replied, "No, I'm not a monkey. I'm beautiful." That response produced an explosion of laughter from everyone on the train.

In contrast to Mart, Ilse took note of five-year-old Jaak Süber who remained peaceful and undisturbed by anything. Even when his mother reprimanded him for some small offense he did not cry or whimper.

On the evening of July 1 the deportees arrived in Tshainsk located about 250 kilometers from Omsk. Here the women and children were commanded to get off the train and to take their luggage and packages with them. Pigs and chickens wandered about and even accompanied them as they walked the main street. The deportees were led to a schoolhouse, surrounded by a fence with armed guards, where they were to sleep for the night. The room was so small they could not lie stretched out on the floor, so they slept sitting upright with their backs against the walls as their heads nodded.

The following day the train continued to Tshainõi, a large town where everyone was commanded to disembark the train with their belongings. They were led to the edge of town. As they walked they passed a kiosk selling *pirukad*. [12] The guard allowed the prisoners who had money with them to purchase the food. Ilse found the kiosk and the *pirukad* to be dirty, but hunger caused her to purchase some anyhow.

Their destination was an empty marketplace outside of town surrounded by a fence. In the farthest corner was a roofed section that covered a counter and some benches. The rest of the area was an open lawn. Most of the people put their belongings under the roof, either on the counter or benches. Ilse found the grass more comfortable and spacious, so there she put her luggage and bundle.

Folk now freely mingled with others from different boxcars. Ilse began speaking with a young woman named Linda Männik who was also from Pärnu. She complained that in their car they had not had enough water to drink. She had two small children with her, Kaie who was 18 months old and another baby girl named Marta who was only about one month old. Linda had an ear infection that was giving her much pain, and Kaie was sick with a fever.

As evening drew on, it became apparent that the entire group would be spending the night in the marketplace. Ilse put her bundle next to her suitcase and lay on top of them. Then she covered herself with her spring coat. She felt warm beneath it, and enjoyed breathing the cool, fresh, evening air, a welcomed relief from the malodorous boxcar.

Awaking in the morning, Ilse walked toward the covered area where other members of her group had spent the night. A man about her age began walking in her direction. He looks like a relative of ours, she thought. She had not seen Endel Kalbus for some years and questioned whether it was him, but walked toward him to see if he would recognize her. When they reached each other, she said quietly, "Endel?"

He looked at her in amazement. "Ilse, is it you?"

"Yes, Endel. How is it that you are here?"

"I was with my father at our farm in Kaljapulga when the authorities came for us. Mother and my brother Arvo had not yet returned from a trip to Tallinn, and Juta, my sister, was at Tartu University. When Mother and Arvo returned and discovered that we had been taken, they quickly prepared a food pack for Father and me and rode to Petseri Railroad Station. The food pack was given to Father, but he and I were separated into two different cars." He paused and then added, "Unfortunately, I didn't get any of the food."

Endel looked quizzically at Ilse as he finished his explanation. "And what of you, Ilse? Mother told me you now have a child."

"Yes, Endel, that is true, but fortunately I was able to leave him behind with my mother and sister. Peeter and I were also separated into different cars. Perhaps he and your father are together somewhere. Peeter can read and write Russian and speaks the language fluently, so I feel he will get along well." Peeter had been born in Königsberg, Russia, but of Estonian lineage.

Ilse and Endel continued talking as they walked to join the others under the roofed area. As they arrived, a Russian man of apparent authority came to them and began organizing the people into various groups. Those who had been together with Emma Ristna on the train joined in a band and were the first to be sent to a truck where they placed all their baggage on the truck bed and then sat on top of the luggage.

They were driven to Orava Village where there was a settlement of Estonians begun 100 years earlier when the Estonian farms had been controlled by German barons. The Czar had promised Estonians that they would be given property and could become landowners if they would settle in Siberia. Those who accepted the offer had left the Village of Orava in Estonia and established the same named village in Russia. Here the truck stopped for a time. Ilse and the others took the occasion to stand and stretch their bodies.

A group of Orava people stood near Ilse. One old man walked up to her, made a fist and shook it in front of her face saying in Estonian, *"Paras teile,"* which means "You deserve this." Startled by his demeanor, she thought surely he must think I'm a German baroness being taken as a prisoner. The clothing the Estonians wore was of fine material, in contrast to the rough clothes worn by the people of Russia. Ilse assumed he thought because of her attire she must be a lady of influence. She did not respond to this man but turned to the others with him and explained, "We are Estonians, not Baltic baronesses. This man has been left behind in time."

That night at about nine o'clock they arrived in Vengersk region at a *kolhoos*. Ilse was placed in a hut with Elsa Reim and her four children. The shack did not have a bathroom, and their bed was the floor covered with bedding straw.

In the morning the group was assigned work in the *kolhoos*. The establishment had a dining room where one could buy cooked pearl barley, the only food available. Next to the village was a flowing stream. Ilse took off her shoes and waded into it. To her delight it had a sandy bottom. For a moment she was a girl again wading in the waters of the Pärnu beach, enjoying the wet sand oozing up between her toes. Relishing the cold water swirling around her feet, she splashed like a child.

The next day brought another unexpected pleasure. The Russians allowed them to enjoy a sauna. Ilse and the Reim family went in together. Not knowing the sauna was free, both Ilse and Elsa tipped the woman attendant.

Later Ilse began to experience diarrhea. Emma Ristna had brought some spirits with her and gave Ilse a brew of it with pepper added. Ilse took a swallow, but it was so strong it burned her throat. Gasping for air, she ran outdoors. After several apprehensive minutes, normal breathing returned, but the supposed remedy proved ineffective.

Two days later, still suffering with abdominal problems, the order was given to Ilse's group that they were to quickly ready themselves to continue the trip. Being weak from her illness, while packing she accidentally knocked her thermos bottle off of the windowsill; it smashed into pieces. She stared at the broken bottle, shocked by what she had done. Now she had no container to store water and no opportunity to buy a new one since thermos bottles in Russia were almost nonexistent.

Ilse and her group traveled by horse and wagon back to Tshainõi where they again spent the night and departed the next morning on another cattle car. Once again bunks were located on both ends of the train. But there was no hole in the floor of this boxcar for waste, and she was still suffering with loose bowels. Before the train left and while the door of the car was still open, she had a great need. She jumped from the car and relieved herself right beside the Russian guard. Thankfully, after this event the diarrhea stopped, but Ilse was still very weak and had to lie down during the trip.

Lying next to Ilse on the train was Jette Gordin, a grandmother of 73 years of age. She was extremely ill, and Ilse wondered if she would make the trip to their next destination. The train departed at 9:00 a.m. for Novosibirsk.

The next day a starving baby boy named Allan died. He was four months old. The mother, Kaare Põltsam, had no more breast milk and no way of nourishing him. When he died, Kaare turned her back toward Allan and would not look at him anymore. Some of the women wrapped him in a cloth and sewed it shut. When the train arrived at Novosibirsk at noon, they informed the soldier in charge of their car about the death of the child. The soldier opened the door and commanded the dead one to be brought out. A woman named Marta Kuusner took the baby and stepped out of the boxcar.

Kaare still sat frozen in place. Ilse approached her saying, "Go to the door and see where they will take your child." Kaare arose and walked robotically with Ilse to the door, but as they reached the opening Marta returned saying, "Behind the fence in back of the railroad station stood a truck. They ordered the child to be placed on it."

Kaare's eyes seemed glazed. She returned to her seat in silence. The attitude of those in the car was one of resignation. No one cried out or screamed. Allan was the first in their group to die.

Ilse thought of her own son. The little breast milk that remained in her bosom had dried up on the second day of her journey. How thankful she was that Vello was at home with her parents. But angry thoughts raged in her mind concerning Allan. What crime had a four-month-old baby committed that he had to be deported? No one would even know where or if he was buried. In war, she thought, when an unknown soldier dies, a stone of remembrance is placed where he is buried, but little Allan has nothing, nothing at all.

CHAPTER 7

Surprise Invasion
Estonia 1941

Meeta worked digging the trench along the Sauga and Pärnu Rivers for three days and two nights. The first night the workers slept on the damp sand along the bank of the Pärnu River. The second night Meeta found herself close to a friend's house and spent the night there. The third day she was assigned to digging a trench on the opposite bank of the Sauga River from her own home. At the end of that day she was released from her work.

Her return home was a joyous occasion. When she told her parents the reason for the trench was in anticipation of a German invasion, her parents were excited. "Perhaps if the Germans invade, they will be able to stop the deportation trains," said Amalie. This hope grew in all three of their hearts.

By June 22 the Germans had amassed a huge army of approximately three and one-half million men. The army assembled along a front of almost 3,000 kilometers (over 1,800 miles), the longest military front line in history. It extended from the Baltic Sea to the Black Sea and was code named Barbarossa. Troops crossed into Soviet dominated territory in three locations. The southernmost flank of the army advanced to the oil fields around Kiev. The middle section headed to Moscow, and the northernmost troops progressed toward Leningrad. In order for the northernmost troops to reach Leningrad they had to go through Estonia, and they advanced rapidly to the border.

Meeta and a fellow employee at the Bester Undergarment Factory went to lunch together on July 8 at a diner near the large bridge that crossed the Pärnu River. As Meeta and Salme ate their meal, the sound of gunfire erupted. Knowing that the bridge had been mined by the Russians, they quickly exited outside and entered into the basement of the building for protection in the event the bridge exploded.

Sounds of gunfire and shouting were heard as they huddled together. Meeta began reflecting on an old man named Jarva Jaan who some people in town considered a prophet. While the Pärnu Bridge was being constructed, he had predicted "when it is finished, a great war will break out." The bridge was completed in 1939. The accuracy of his prediction caused Meeta to wonder if he truly was a prophet. She thought of him now and wondered if he were still alive what he would have to say about the outcome of this war.

After some time the gunfire ceased, and Salme ventured outside to see what was happening. She returned quickly quite out of breath and excitedly called, "Meeta, come and look!" When both of them arrived at ground level, they were delighted to see the whole breadth of Jannsen Street crowded with smiling

German soldiers, their shirt sleeves rolled up and collar buttons open in the warm summer air. Their boots clattered as they walked down the cobblestone street, and twigs flapped from their camouflaged helmets.

Women ran into the street and hugged the soldiers. Soon flowers were being showered on the German tanks, trucks and even bicycles of the soldiers by the Estonians. Meeta well understood the jubilance. If their country had to lose their freedom to any ruler, Estonians were much more comfortable with the Germans than the Soviets since they had had significant influence in Estonia for 700 years. Meeta and Salme, too, were glad and walked along the street absorbing the jubilation.

They stopped by one of the store owners who had set up a stand and was distributing lemonade to the troops. "Sir, please tell us how this all happened so quickly," implored Meeta. The man could barely control his exuberance as he replied, "You didn't see this? It was amazing. German soldiers suddenly appeared; it seemed out of nowhere. They so quickly advanced down Jannsen Street that the Russians didn't even have time enough to detonate the bridge." Then he chortled, "Good thing, because the Russians needed the bridge to escape. You should have seen them falling over each other horror stricken." He interrupted their talk to hand out more lemonade and to congratulate the soldiers.

Meeta and Salme continued walking and being jostled by the crowd that had gathered all along the street. They also observed other stores distributing food and cigarettes to the troops. But Meeta noticed that most of the soldiers were exhausted. Many of them slept in the trucks as they passed, and even the cyclists swayed with fatigue.

Suddenly they heard a shout. "The NKVD headquarters is burning! There are Estonian political prisoners in the basement!" The cry was quickly taken up by the crowd, and soon German soldiers were running toward the house that had been used for that purpose. The crowd followed as did Meeta and Salme. Three soldiers went into the building, and soon the prisoners were joining the street celebration. One grey-haired prisoner ran into the street and began dancing.

Salme appeared ecstatic as she said, "This is so amazing to watch, Meeta. I can hardly believe my eyes."

"It is unbelievable, Salme. I can barely tear myself away, but we really should go back to the Bester factory and see what's happening there." Meeta's watch read 3:05 p.m.

On the way to their place of employment Meeta and Salme saw two Russian soldiers who were unaware of the recent events, nonchalantly riding their bicycles along the avenue. They were headed directly toward the German troops. Meeta nudged Salme. "Salme, should we give warning as to what awaits them?" Salme gave Meeta a questioning look, but both remained silent, and the soldiers passed by talking to each other in a relaxed fashion.

Meeta and Salme continued toward Bester and found the employees gathered in the garden just outside of the underground shelter of the factory. German soldiers who were stationed on the Pärnu River Bridge had a clear view of the garden from their location. Soon Meeta heard a clicking sound on the wall behind her. The worker next to her jumped down the shelter steps. Meeta watched naïvely, but as the tapping sound continued it dawned on her that it was the result of fired bullets. She quickly rushed down the stairs to the shelter thinking the soldiers must have mistaken them for enemies.

That evening when Meeta arrived home, there was a mixture of joy and dismay in the family. Jaak had begun adding a two-story addition onto the factory before the Russians took control, and the work was allowed to continue under their supervision. Jaak told his daughter what had taken place that day.

"Sometime late in the afternoon the workers, learning that the Germans had arrived, went up to the unfinished roof of the new extension for a better view of what was happening by the Pärnu Bridge. German pilots judged the people on the roof as enemies, and one plane passing overhead dropped three bombs on them. One bomb fell in the river, another exploded on the bank across the river, and one dropped in our yard. Fortunately, no one was harmed, but the force of the explosion of the bomb that landed in our yard broke all the windows of the factory nearest the explosion and left a gaping hole in the wall of the nearby washhouse."

Meeta shared with her parents how the workers at the Bester Undergarment Factory had also been mistaken as the enemy.

Jaak looked intently at his daughter as he spoke. "Ah, yes, Meeta, despite the celebrations of today this is an anxious time. Yet, if the Germans can intercept the deportee trains, it will be worth it."

CHAPTER 8

Introduction to Siberia
Siberia 1941

Novosibirsk is situated on the powerful Ob River and is one of the largest cities in Siberia. The Ob River is very changeable. In the spring it floods the shores for several kilometers and is about three to four kilometers wide. The current of the river is exceedingly fast, especially where it makes turns. Where the water hits the high shore it causes the earth to erode, and the opposite shore grows larger and larger. By the end of the summer, however, the water recedes and narrows to one and one-half to two kilometers in width. Then low spots in the river floor can be seen where willow scrubs begin to grow. One must then navigate between the sandbars.

On the evening of July 12 Ilse and her fellow deportees were brought to the Novosibirsk harbor preparatory to being placed on a barge normally used for transporting produce and especially logs. The barges were extremely large with flat bottoms that permitted them to pass over the more shallow portions of the river. Some had no roof, but the one they were to board was covered. On the back part of the deck was the cabin where the arm-like steering apparatus was located. A motorboat was fastened to the side of the vessel filled with deportees; they were Moldavian women and children—lots of children. Ilse noted that all had black hair and brown eyes.

As she waited on the dock, she was surprised to meet Hilda Pavelson. Hilda and her husband Voldemar were close friends who had traveled through Hungary together with Ilse and Peeter in 1938, shortly after the Kotters were married. Hilda told Ilse that she, Voldemar and their nine-year-old daughter Luule were arrested in much the same manner as they had been on the very same night. Voldemar, too, had been separated from them, but now Hilda had another concern that she shared.

"Luule became ill on our journey here, and by the time we arrived in Novosibirsk she was unconscious. She was taken to a Novosibirsk hospital and was diagnosed with meningitis, but they would not allow me to stay with her. Now she is in the hands of the Russians who consider us enemies, and they are placing me on this barge to who knows where. What will they do to my little girl?"

Ilse's heart ached for her friend. She wondered if she could be of help. "It may be that they would allow me to remain with her since I'm not closely related. I'm going to ask."

Ilse located Emma Ristna to translate for her and then approached the officer giving orders who seemed to be in charge. She explained the situation to him and requested that he grant her permission to remain with the child until she was well. Then she offered him her gold watch as an incentive. The officer's face turned red, and the veins of his temple enlarged. "You want to bribe me?" he screamed at her. Then he called for two soldiers who, at the officer's bidding, promptly took hold of Ilse and threw her onto the barge like a sack of flour along with her luggage.

Fortunately, Ilse landed on the hard wooden deck with only a hip bruise. She and her fellow travelers were directed to a trap door where they descended by steps to the hold of the vessel. It was dark. The only light was that which streamed through the trap door. Ilse situated herself and, as her eyes adjusted to the dim light, noticed that the Reim family was not far from her. She estimated that there were about 600 to 700 people aboard. That night was spent on the barge.

Early the next morning, 18-month-old Kaia, daughter of Linda Männik, died. Her small body was handed up to a soldier through the trap door; that was the last anyone saw of the child. Ilse marveled that Linda's two-month-old daughter was still holding on to life. In this environment living infants were the exception.

Later that morning they departed. As they journeyed, Ilse was dismayed to learn that their raw sewage was released into the Ob River at the rear of the barge while their drinking water was retrieved upstream at the front.

After two days the barge stopped for a long while in Kolpashevo, and people aboard learned that sugar was available in the stores. The barge, however, did not dock and those aboard could not buy any. Some women began throwing money to boys on the shore asking them to bring sugar to them. Ilse noticed one boy who had already gone to the store twice for sugar and had brought it back to the women. She wrapped some money in the silk head scarf her mother had given her the day she had been arrested and threw it to the boy, but he did not return with the sugar. She thought perhaps he liked the silk scarf and didn't want to return it.

On Thursday, July 17, at three o'clock in the afternoon the barge arrived at Grishkin. By seven o'clock collective farmers from the surrounding villages appeared with horse-drawn wagons. Lisette Silm, who had shared Ilse's bunk on the train from Tamsalu, was paired with her, and they boarded a horse-pulled wagon. Their collective farmer was a German originally from the Volga River area whose name was Aman. Since Ilse spoke German fluently, she was able to speak with him.

Aman pointed to the surrounding fields and said, "When we were sent here 12 years ago this was but a dense forest between the tundra and steppes. We were simply brought here and dropped. We uprooted the forest and made it a field. There were no houses or building materials. We felled the trees and built our own houses with them. You are fortunate; you have houses already existing." Later that evening Aman's mother showed them some upright boards behind which they had first lived. Now it was used for an animal pen.

The village that was to be their new home was Maiga, about 30 kilometers from Grishkin. The houses Aman spoke of were rough-hewn log cabins with grass sod roofs. The furniture inside was made of tree limbs. Wood cots cushioned only with straw were used for beds. The hut had no indoor plumbing, but there was an outhouse where one could at least have some privacy for necessities. Though rustic, compared to the train and barge this appeared a palace, and Ilse was delighted to at last have a resting place. Their hut had a woman overseer, an elderly Russian woman who soon earned the title of the Old Woman. She made certain the residents were kept in line. In Ilse's hut were Lisette Silm, 53; Ella Nirk, 51; Jüri and Aino Nirk, fraternal twins, 16, and the Old Woman.

On July 24, just as the deportees were acclimating to their new surroundings, they were told the grandmother, Jette Gordin, who had lain ill beside Ilse on their train journey to Novosibirsk, died. Here, however, the Estonians were permitted to have a burial service for her and to place a stone of remembrance on her grave.

The work at the *kolhoos* was physically strenuous, and Ilse was unfamiliar with farm work. Her life had been one of relative ease until the Russians entered her country. Now she found herself working in fields, sometimes walking many kilometers to reach a field. Cutting hay was done with a scythe, and soon her blistered hands became calloused.

Each month brought a new learning experience. September required the harvesting of flax which she pulled by hand; next came the rye and wheat harvests. Many days found her beating grain until dark in the building where it was to be kiln dried. Workers were plagued with ticks and were told to take saunas to kill them. But at least they now had food to eat and a place to lay their heads at night.

Two more deaths occurred: an elderly lady and a young boy. Ilse and her fellow Estonians became painfully aware that the rigors of this life were too much for the elderly and very young; they were the first to succumb.

The first snow appeared on October 16 which demanded the need for more wood. Each hut was heated by a wood stove which also served as a cook stove. So Ilse and her roommates began cutting trees, chopping them into stove-sized logs and then hauling and stacking them.

Not being official members of the *kolhoos*, they worked only as their help was needed. Payment was in food or sometimes rubles. When there was no work for them, they had to find ways of providing for their own basic needs.

By November 12 the temperature was 20 degrees below zero Celsius,[13] and food was becoming less available. The *kolhoos* quota had to be met, and Russia had a military to supply with food. As the work in the fields diminished, the Estonians began visiting the villages surrounding them bargaining the clothing and items they had brought from Estonia for food. For one linen towel Ilse received a half pail of onions; for one pair of silk stockings, three kilograms of onions. One old woman gave her 40 kilograms of potatoes and one pail of onions for a sweater. The Russians were eager to obtain such clothing because these things were not available to them. Some of the food Ilse received she sold for rubles or exchanged for food that would give her a more varied diet.

During the month of December Ilse sold her gold wrist watch in Podgornia, 30 kilometers away, for 200 rubles. She now understood and was thankful for the insistence of the Russian soldier that she take it with her as he wandered about her home the morning of her deportation.

That month the officer in charge commanded those who did not read and write Russian to have regular classes in his office where they would be taught the language by the teacher of the community school children. They worked taking inventory of supplies and food for two days. The following day they were made to sort barley outside in the yard from eight in the morning until noon though the temperature was minus 46 degrees Celsius.[14] They covered their skin with clothing as best they could, wrapped rags around their shoes and worked as rapidly as possible to try to maintain their body temperatures. But Ilse's feet were numb by the time they finished.

December 21 was the birthday of Jüri and Aino, the twins who turned 17. It was also Stalin's birthday, but there was no celebration.

The evening of December 23 Lisette solicited Jüri's help to bring a Christmas tree to their cabin. They had nothing with which to decorate it, but Lisette had hoped it would at least provide some semblance of the holiday.

It stormed the next day so the workers remained in their homes. The man in charge of the pigs, whom they called the Pig Man, and another farm supervisor nicknamed Wooden Leg because he had an artificial leg, went from hut to hut gathering clothes for the Russian army. The Old Woman gave a new, white, man's shirt. The Pig Man eyed the Estonians in the room waiting for them to offer some clothes, but none moved to do so.

He spat out words of disgust to them. "You don't have anything to share? You who celebrate Christmas tomorrow? You Christians who promote sharing! Ha, this old Russian lady has contributed what she could. Where is your generosity? It's all talk, isn't it?"

Lisette moved toward her luggage, but Ilse put her hand out to stop her. The Pig Man glared at Ilse and then stomped out the door followed by Wooden Leg.

That night Ilse and her cabin family sat together mostly in silence as the Old Woman washed clothes. It seemed all wrong for Christmas Eve.

Ilse's thoughts were of Peeter. Where was he this night? If only she knew. Surely he would be thinking of her and the baby boy he so loved. Vello was seven months old now. The thought raised some questions in her mind. When would she see him again? How would he know she was his mother? How would he look? She ached to hold her son and share this first Christmas as parents with Peeter and her family. What would Christmas be like at home this year with two empty seats at the dinner table?

Her mind viewed Christmases past. Miila, her parents' housekeeper, would always bake raisin bread for the celebration. Now, as her stomach rumbled, Ilse could almost smell the delicious aroma. After baking the bread Miila would wash the kitchen floor, and all would be sparkling by six in the evening when most of the town's people would go to church. Following the service members would gather in the church fellowship hall to sing Christmas songs. Meeta would play the piano, Papsi and Oskar violins, and Ilse the cello. At home a decorated Christmas tree with real candles awaited them. Now she stared at the naked evergreen standing alone backed by the rough log wall. Instead of Lisette's tree bringing the spirit of Christmas, the bare spruce mocked the holiday and promoted an atmosphere of sadness.

CHAPTER 9

Hope Rises
Estonia 1941/1942

The arrival of the German army brought a new sense of hope to the people of Estonia in light of the massive deportations recently conducted by the Soviets. They were a people with whom they had some common history.

Germans had entered the Baltic region by the end of the 12th century. Even though the Danes were theoretically the administrators in Tallinn during the mid-1200s, some 80 percent of the vassals were German and "gradually acquired more power as a political body." Eventually, in "each of the urban centers a city council *(Rat)* emerged in which power was held exclusively by the richest German merchants."[15] Gradually serfdom developed. Despite an Estonian peasant revolt in the mid-1300s and the attempts of Denmark, Russia, Sweden and Poland to vie for control of Estonia throughout the centuries, the Baltic German nobility always emerged.

Now that the Germans were once more in their country, Estonian partisans who had fled to the forests to escape deportation fought with the German army to rid themselves of the Soviets.

Jaak retained control of his factory without supervision of the current government thanks to a fellow classmate of Oskar's who was placed in charge of these affairs by the Germans. Estonians in general experienced some sense of freedom under this new power. As some normalcy returned to their city, the Kollist family once again hired a housekeeper whose name was Anastasia but was known by Tasja. She adored Vello and became his chief caregiver.

Meeta was fluent in German and found employment with the German Civil Administration as a translator and typist. Because the German army blitzkrieged into her city, the Russians were unable to destroy their military records and she was privy to them. One day as she sorted through the files she found the names of those who were deported on the same day that her sister and Peeter had been arrested. It was a shock to learn that several thousand of her countrymen were included. She knew it had been many hundreds, but the realistic magnitude of this deportation overwhelmed her. She sat in stunned silence digesting what she saw before her. Reading on she discovered that another deportation was planned for a later date. Suddenly her hands began to shake and her face paled. Included in the list of names for this second deportation were Jaak Kollist, Amalie Kollist and Meeta Kollist.

The realization that without the invasion of Germany she and her parents would have been the next deportees left her numb for several minutes. She sat contemplating what could have been; her thoughts raced. What did the Russians have in mind for us Estonians? Were their plans to annihilate us and repopulate our land with their own people? As she realized the implications of this, her heart swelled with gratitude as she thought, The Germans have been our saviors!

Her next thoughts were of her sister, Peeter and the many friends and acquaintances she knew who had already been sent to Russia. What will the Russians do with them? She shuddered to let her mind dwell on the subject and found herself crying out, "Oh, God, help the Germans retrieve our loved ones and return them to us."

***

Now that the political situation had changed, the Kollist family hoped to regain the furniture and household goods that had been in Ilse's and Peeter's apartment. Customarily, the Russians distributed all such goods. One Saturday morning Meeta and her mother Amalie walked to Ilse's apartment and spoke with Miss Karlson who lived in the other half of the home at the time Peeter and Ilse had been arrested.

Amalie addressed her. "Miss Karlson, do you have any idea what happened to the furniture and other household items that were in my daughter's apartment? We would like to locate them. We are, of course, hoping the Germans will put an end to this war soon, and when Peeter and Ilse return they will need their furnishings."

"Mrs. Kollist, I was so troubled when I saw people coming to take your daughter's things. I thought, What can I do?" She paused and then asked them to step inside. "Wait here just a moment." Miss Karlson disappeared into her bedroom and shortly emerged with a list. Handing it to Amalie she said, "This is a list of the names and addresses of those who have taken the Kotters' goods and the items they should have in their possession."

Amalie and Meeta praised the woman for her foresight and thanked her profusely. Jaak solicited two of his factory workers to help him retrieve his daughter's belongings, and over the next few days reclaimed most of the personal property. The list was an invaluable document confirming the items belonged to the Kotters.

While in Finland, where Oskar had fled before the Russians had prohibited passage there, he voluntarily joined league with the Finnish army which was actively engaged in fighting the Russians in defense of their own country. He continued to do this although he held a job as technical director of the Hellman Leather Factory. Unbeknown to his family, shortly after the Germans invaded Estonia, he and other army personnel crossed the Finnish Gulf and headquartered in Tallinn. One day in late August, Heinrik, one of Jaak's factory workers, saw Oskar walking in Pärnu. "Oskar, what are you doing here?"

Oskar stood tall and erect in his Finnish army uniform. His hat shaded his eyes from the afternoon sun, but an impish grin could be clearly seen. "I have just arrived from Tallinn and must register at the Ranna Hotel. The Finns are establishing headquarters there, and then I will be going home. I had thought I would surprise my family, but seeing you has given me second thoughts about that. Perhaps they would appreciate some time to prepare for my coming."

When Heinrik returned to the factory, he told Jaak about his chance meeting with Oskar who shared the information with his wife and daughter. That evening the family waited anxiously for him. Several times in the midst of preparing a meal for his arrival, Meeta ran to the stone wall at the front of their home to watch for him. Finally, she saw him approaching their gate and ran to meet him, threw her arms around his neck and hugged him tightly. "Oh, Oskar, it is so good to have you home. We have wondered if this would ever happen." She held his hand, and they walked to the doorway where Jaak and Amalie were waiting. Oskar greeted his father with a firm embrace and then turned to his mother. Amalie held Vello in her arms, so he kissed her cheek as he cradled the opposite side of her head with his hand. Then he stood absolutely still and stared at Vello for a long while. No one spoke or even attempted to break the silence. Vello was a stark reminder of the loss they all sensed but could not express.

After supper that evening Vello could be heard saying, "ngoh, ngoh." Oskar looked toward the crib and asked, "What does that mean?" Amalie laughed as she rose from her chair and walked toward the child. "Vello is very cute. When he gets sleepy, he says, 'ngoh, ngoh,' and starts rubbing his nose. That's his way of letting us know it's his bedtime." She lifted Vello from the crib, placed him on his side in his baby carriage and put a pacifier in his mouth. Then she pushed him into the bedroom.

Jaak smiled at Oskar and said, "Vello is a good baby but he wets a lot." Meeta chuckled. "It's hard to keep enough diapers ready for him. When the weather is bad and we can't hang them outside, we must iron them dry. I call him Tiny Pee Vello." Oskar laughed and then walked toward his luggage. "I brought Vello something from Finland. I will attach it to his crib tomorrow." He pulled out a line of small toys. In the ensuing weeks as the child grew stronger, Oskar was amused by Vello's attempts to catch those toys with his toes.

By late October of 1941, Estonia was entirely under German control. Estonians who had cooperated with the Russians were taken out of power, and Communists or supposed Communist sympathizers were executed. With the Germans firmly in control, Oskar felt safe remaining in his home country. He knew his father needed his help, especially now that Peeter was no longer a part of the factory. He continued the work that Peeter had done, namely negotiating purchases and sales agreements for their leather products, and the business prospered. Oskar's work often took him to Tallinn where he met a girl, Ave Neumann. He continued courting her during his various business trips, and the relationship began to blossom.

During the Russian occupation the Kollist home had been reduced to two rooms and a kitchen. The remaining rooms were used for factory purposes.

With Oskar now home and a baby to care for, their quarters were not sufficient. It was decided that Oskar would continue living in the remaining space of their original home while Jaak, Amalie, Meeta and Vello would locate a more spacious residence. That fall they settled into an apartment on Vilmsi Street consisting of five large rooms plus a kitchen, bathroom and cellar. It was located in the heart of Pärnu across the street from the girls' high school that Meeta and Ilse had attended in their youth. The area held warm memories of a time when Estonians were enjoying freedom from the occupation of any foreign ruler. Hope for the future was high then, and the nation was prospering. Meeta loved walking in this part of town. It was near Egg Mountain, actually just a hill in the midst of a park-like setting where as children she and her siblings had enjoyed sledding in winter.

As spring approached, Vello's face and body broke out in an itchy rash which caused him to be very restless at night. A doctor acquaintance told Amalie, "It's because the child is overfed." Amalie retorted abruptly, "No, the problem is that the child has not received enough varieties of food." She was noticeably upset and later complained to Tasja. "I have raised three children and was never accused of overfeeding them. With this war going on, we certainly are not overfeeding Vello. But where does one get a variety of foods?"

Tasja empathized with Amalie and voiced her frustration. "We give him carrot juice and cranberry juice for vitamins in addition to his milk and porridge. That's the best we can do right now." Then she offered a suggestion that might calm his itching. "Why don't we try a linseed bath. During the day he is active and doesn't scratch as much. A linseed bath at night before his bedtime might soothe the itching and allow him to sleep." The baths seemed to be the balm he needed, so each night the linseed bath became a part of his regimen.

The Monday following Easter Sunday, April 6, Vello was baptized by the Lutheran minister Reverend Nuudi in the Kollist apartment at 4:00 p.m. Since Reverend Nuudi had been the homeroom teacher of Ilse while she was in high school, he did not charge a fee but only required payment for the carriage and horse that brought him to their home. More than 20 relatives and friends attended the event, and they planned to sing some hymns following the baptism. "You watch," said the reverend, "as soon as you start singing, Vello will start crying." However, Vello surprised everyone by screaming during the baptism and listening very closely to the music during the hymn sing.

The Kollist family celebrated Vello's first year of life on May 20. It was a joyous occasion with friends and relatives once again gathered together. The birthday boy was propped up in an armchair at the head of their dining room table and clapped his hands on the table top as he received his gifts. When family members began playing music, Vello started moving his body and hands in rhythm. Mr. Schmidt, a banker friend who had been chosen as Vello's godfather, presented him with a playpen. Guests also gave him toy animals, clothes and a blue hydrangea plant.

Now that Vello was one year old, the family began supplementing his milk and porridge with more solid food. They added potatoes with butter, meat broth, white bread and eggs. Gradually his rash disappeared.

June 14, 1942, was a sad day for the town of Pärnu; the entire town was decorated with half-mast flags commemorating the deportations that had occurred on that day the previous year. Tasja brought a bouquet of flowers to the Kollist home in the morning and placed it before a picture of Ilse and Peeter. Later the family attended a special service in honor of the deported at the Niguliste Lutheran Church. That evening radio programs were dedicated to those who had been cruelly snatched away.

A gloom pervaded their living room as Jaak spoke. "It would ease the pain if we could receive some word from Ilse." Amalie responded, "It must be extremely difficult for her also. If she is still . . ." Amalie would not allow herself to finish that sentence. "She knows nothing of her son . . . ." Her words trailed off in her emotion. She composed herself and then continued. "She is missing all the stages of his growth."

Meeta knew all too well her mother's feelings. They had no idea if Ilse and Peeter were still alive. No correspondence was passing to or from Russian territory. The silence was unbearable to families with missing members, and it was impossible to escape the thoughts of what might be their fate. Family members just acted out their lives as best they could from day to day, hoping and praying that this war would have a positive end for their little country.

The warm days of summer did bring some solace to the community. In July Meeta enjoyed walking in the midst of the linden trees. Their sweet fragrance brought back lovely thoughts of the times she and her friends enjoyed ice cream together as they chatted by the sea. She recalled the summer concerts and folk dances in the park.

It was during one of these reminiscent days that Meeta happened to run into a distant relative named Liina.

"Liina, I haven't seen you in such a long time. What have you been up to?"

Liina was close to Meeta in age but a petite lady with sparkling blue eyes and energy enough for two. "I've been selling books, Meeta . . . religious books."

"Is this your job now?" asked Meeta.

"Well, you might call it that." Liina smiled broadly as she spoke. "I consider it a calling."

"A calling?"

"Yes, Meeta. Some months ago I finally discovered that my God is truly a God of love."

"Whatever do you mean, Liina? I always thought God was a God of love." Meeta's brow furrowed as she pondered Liina's statement.

Liina looked deeply into Meeta's eyes. "I've always struggled with how a God of love could confine countless millions, perhaps billions, to eternal torment in hell fire." Fervency was in Liina's voice as she spoke. "How do you reconcile that with a God of love, Meeta?"

"I guess I never really gave it much thought. I just have always accepted it." Meeta's interest was now piqued.

"You're a tender soul, Meeta. Could you stand by and willingly watch anyone—even an animal—being intentionally tormented?"

"Oh, no!" Meeta protested.

"If you can't endure such a thought, how can anyone ascribe such a thing to a loving God?" Liina paused a moment and then continued. "Meeta, you have been confirmed as I have been in the Lutheran Church. Do you remember the Bible text that was central to all that we learned about Jesus?"

Meeta thought a moment. She really couldn't recall a Bible text. Though her family sporadically attended church on Sunday, it had been a number of years since she had actually read the Bible. She felt embarrassed as she responded. "No, Liina, I can't."

"If I begin quoting it, I'm sure you'll remember . . . It's 'For God so loved the world . . . '"

Meeta immediately joined in, "'that He gave His only begotten Son that whoever believes in Him should not perish but have everlasting life,' John 3:16."

Liina smiled. "I knew you'd remember that. I believe it was the very first Bible text we learned, and probably the one most quoted by Christians everywhere. But do we really understand what we're saying when we repeat that text?"

"What do you mean, Liina?"

"The text says . . . 'whoever believes in Him should not perish but have everlasting life.' There are only two choices, Meeta. We either 'perish' or we accept Jesus Christ and gain 'everlasting life.' When the Bible says 'perish,' that's exactly what it means. The whole gospel is spelled out here in this text, and Jesus is the one who spoke these words. If anyone should know what the gospel is, shouldn't He?"

"Yes, I guess so. But I'm confused. Isn't the soul immortal? Doesn't it live on after we die?"

"The Apostle Paul tells us that God 'alone has immortality.'[16] And in First Corinthians 15:51 to 54 he tells us that 'this mortal must put on immortality' and makes it plain that this does not happen until the Second Coming of Christ. If we already had immortality, why would we have to put it on?"

Meeta stared at Liina. "My, these are all new thoughts for me. They're so different than what I've understood."

Liina's eyes showed sincere compassion, and her voice softened as she spoke. "Meeta, I know this is a lot to absorb right now. Let me give you a piece of literature that will give you many Bible texts pertaining to this subject. Look them up for yourself. All I ask is that you pray before you begin studying your Bible, and ask the Holy Spirit to reveal the truth to you. Will you do that?"

"Yes, I will," promised Meeta. She took the leaflet, tucked it into her pocket and bade Liina good-bye.

When Meeta arrived home that evening she shared with her mother the conversation she had had with Liina, but Amalie was not impressed. "We are not able to understand the Bible, Meeta. It requires scholarship. You will do better to leave it to those who have gone to seminary." Abruptly ending the conversation, Amalie stood up from her chair and went to the stove to check the porridge she was preparing for Vello. "Meeta, why don't you feed Vello while I begin setting the table for supper? Jaak will be home soon."

Meeta walked to the playpen located in one corner of the kitchen. Vello smiled as she approached him and reached out his hand toward her. "Ati, Ati." It was a child's attempt to say *tädi*, which means "aunt" in Estonian. Interestingly, the name stuck and became his relentless title for her and a nickname of endearment.

After supper that evening Meeta retrieved her grandmother's Bible from a closet shelf and cloistered herself in her bedroom. Despite her mother's comments Meeta felt compelled to read the pamphlet Liina had given her. What's more, she took seriously her promise to Liina to pray for the Holy Spirit to guide her as she read the Bible.

Seated at a small desk, she took the pamphlet and began looking up the Scripture texts pertaining to what happens when someone dies. It was not easy for her to locate some of the books in the Bible and sometimes had to refer to the Table of Contents to get the page number.

The first text she read was Ecclesiastes 9:5-6: "For the living know that they will die; But the dead know nothing . . . Also their love, their hatred, and their envy have now perished." She was fascinated by what she read and continued reading to verse 10. "Whatever your hand finds to do, do it with your might; for there is no work or device or knowledge or wisdom in the grave where you are going."

This was so different from the concept she had of death. The words "the dead know nothing" and "there is no "knowledge or wisdom in the grave" challenged what she had always believed. She looked up the next text in Psalm 115:17. "The dead do not praise the Lord," and Psalm 6:5, "For in death there is no remembrance of You [God]."

She had been taught that the righteous go directly to heaven at death and are in the presence of God and that the wicked go immediately to hell, but in the Bible she was reading something quite different. Her mind raced. What does happen at death? Do we just cease to exist?

A passage in Job 14:10-15 got her attention. What is this "set time" when God would "remember" Job after his death? What is the meaning of "You shall call, and I will answer You; You shall desire the work of Your hands"?

The answer came as she read the next referenced passage in I Thessalonians 4:16-17. "For the Lord Himself will descend from heaven with a shout, with the voice of an archangel, and with the trumpet of God. And the dead in Christ will rise first. Then we who are alive and remain shall be caught up together with them in the clouds to meet the Lord in the air. And thus we shall always be with the Lord."

Now more questions arose in Meeta's mind. When would "the Lord . . . descend from heaven"? Who are those who "are alive and remain" until the coming of the Lord? What happens to the wicked that she had been taught were in hell? She had to know more. She had to talk again with Liina.

CHAPTER 10

Life in Maiga
Siberia 1942

Ilse and her fellow Estonians spent much of January 1942 winnowing oats, wheat, and barley and cutting down trees for cooking and warmth. Ilse became friends with some of the Russians in the village, and on January 6, Three Wisemen's Day,[17] she was invited to the home of the Kopseva family for a sauna.

When Ilse entered the home, which was a rustic hut, she immediately noticed what appeared to her as a luxury. The rough-hewn wooden table had a tablecloth. It wasn't elaborate—red with some embroidery work, but it seemed so long since she had seen something decorated that she found herself staring, not wanting to take her eyes off of it.

Mr. Kopseva, an elderly man with kind eyes, shared a bit of news he had received. "In Novosibirsk 200 prisoners a day are being released. That could be good news for you and your fellow Estonians, Ilse. Near Tomsk, north of Novosibirsk, there is a camp of 1,700 people."

Ilse listened intently wondering if all this could be trusted. So many rumors were circulating that it was hard to know fallacy from fact. Most, however, agreed that the war would not last longer than a few months. When a Russian soldier had expressed concern that the war would continue for four years, Ilse had labeled him "stupid" to her fellow Estonians and they had agreed.

In the days that followed, more and more child war refugees were brought into their village, which meant more mouths to feed and the need for more clothing. Once again the Pig Man and Wooden Leg made the circuit around the village collecting clothing and other items. Now they needed three pairs of felt boots, five fur coats for the military, and an abundance of things for the orphaned children. Since the Russian people had none of these, they once again solicited the Estonians. But this time Estonians were offered potatoes and turnips for whatever they would give. Ella did some bargaining and was able to exchange a sheet for 20 rubles and one pail of turnips.

The afternoon of January 11 the Old Woman took everyone in her hut, along with two other Russian women, to the schoolhouse to see a children's program. It was about a man whose two sons were angels wearing swastikas. A group of soldiers entered the stage. The first two men carried a dummy of a headless soldier on a board. The soldiers sang as they presented their cargo. "Communism is light brought to all the farmers. Capitalism is destroyed." Ilse remained silent during the program and said nothing as they returned home. But in her mind she was thinking, Some children's program!

The next day Ilse learned that two Estonian women had been imprisoned for submitting a petition requesting food. She feared for them because the prisons were hotbeds of disease, and rape was not uncommon. Ilse also learned that a 35-year-old Estonian mother was dying. She will leave behind two small children, thought Ilse. Later she learned that one of those children also appeared to be dying. She pondered this latest news with deep sadness. Lack of food, heavy labor and cold temperatures are taking their toll on our people, she thought.

On the evening of the Russian New Year, January 14, the Old Woman once again took her cabin family to the meeting hall. There God was denigrated and scenes of brutality were shown being conducted by supposed Christians. A film of German espionage was also presented.

The next day two more Estonians were added to Ilse's cabin family: Alma Mürk, age 33, and her son Leo, 16. This brought the total of residents in their cabin to eight. "We are lined up together like matches in a matchbox," laughed Ilse.

Late in February, a fellow Estonian named Raha visited Ilse's cabin. She claimed to be a seer and brought a dish which she inverted on a sheet of paper surrounded by the alphabet and numbers. The inverted dish was placed in the center of the paper. A mark was painted on the dish. Raha said that the dish could tell the future. She placed her hands upon it and asked when the Estonians would be released. The dish began to float beneath her hands and spelled out the month of March and the number 16. Later, when Alma came home, Ilse told her about Raha's visit and the date the dish had given for their release. Alma's naturally rosy cheeks became inflamed as she listened, and her forehead creased. "Beware, Ilse. This is the Devil's work. The Bible calls this 'witchcraft' and says that 'all who do these things are an abomination to the Lord.'" [18]

But Raha's visit had given Ilse hope. Though she weighed what Alma had told her, the desire to be set free to return to her homeland caused her to question. Four days later she visited Raha and asked how the dish could give them this information. She did not reveal who had questioned its source but said, "Some people think this is the work of the Devil."

Raha bristled at this and immediately responded. "Not so, Ilse. There is a magnetic field around each of us. If we tune into it, that magnetism causes the dish to rise and directs it. There is nothing spooky about it. It's extrasensory perception. It's just that most people don't ever develop it, but I have. And you can, too. Let me show you."

Ilse was skeptical but said nothing as Raha brought out the dish and placed it on the table. "I can see you're dubious," said Raha. "If you don't believe me, ask it a question to which you know the answer and see if it answers correctly. This time we will both put our hands on it."

Ilse placed her hands on top of Raha's and felt the dish lift of its own volition. At first she felt surprise. She had never experienced anything like this before. Raha noticed Ilse hesitate and encouraged her to ask the question. Ilse gave the last name of an acquaintance of hers and asked the dish to tell her the first name of that person. Slowly the dish spelled out the letters "E M I L." Ilse was astonished. "That's right!"

In Ilse's mind this correct answer gave new credibility to the date of March 16. When she returned to her cabin, Alma was there. She had been given some cigarettes and was enjoying this rarity as she sat at the table when Ilse entered. Ilse pondered telling Alma what she had done but decided to give Raha's explanation of how the dish worked to get her opinion. Meekly and with some trepidation, Ilse unfolded the whole event to Alma.

Alma took a long drag on her cigarette as if trying to calm herself and then said, "Ilse, you are getting into something you should not touch. You will end up like Saul with the witch of En Dor.[19] He began as a king eradicating witchcraft and ended his life involved in it." She looked directly into Ilse's eyes as she spoke. "You must make the choice to believe Raha or me. But mind you, if you go the way of Raha there will not be a happy ending."

Alma's words temporarily startled Ilse. As she mulled over the situation, however, she rationalized that there could be such a thing as extrasensory perception. So a few days later, as Ilse grew eager to know more about their supposed soon departure, she visited Raha's cabin.

"Raha, can you tell me anything more about when and how we are to leave for home?"

This time Raha picked up a deck of cards from a small wooden table. "The cards may give us details," she said.

"Cards?" asked Ilse.

"Yes, Ilse. They work on the same principle as the dish but can give more detail to us than the dish. Come sit down. I'll show you."

Ilse questioned in her mind this new avenue of telling the future. She had heard of fortune telling back in Estonia but had never frequented such places. Alma's voice of warning was still echoing in her mind, but she said nothing.

Raha took a seat with Ilse at a table centered in the room where meals were eaten and began putting the cards down in a horizontal row and then building vertically on each column. As she laid the cards down one by one, she began to read their tale. "The news is that soon we will return home. Further, Estonia and Finland are in league with each other against the Communists." Raha raised her head and looked at Ilse. "That's all the cards are revealing."

In Raha's cabin was a young girl who appeared to be very ill. Ilse asked about her.

"Leili is 13 years old; she is burning with fever," said Raha. "Another woman in the village, Marta Krull, who is 46 years of age, is also very ill with edema. The swelling has begun to spread into her back. Twelve days ago we requested a horse, a sleigh and a sledge to take Leili and Marta to the hospital in Grishkin but were told that no horse was available. We have no way of getting them to Grishkin which you know is about 30 kilometers north."

A few days later Ilse learned what had finally happened to these two sick ones. The day after Raha had talked with Ilse the horse and sleigh arrived, but the horse was an emaciated nag. Leili, who was now delirious, was placed on the narrow sledge along with Marta. Both were tied on so as not to fall off during the journey. Leili's mother, Herta, and Raha sat in the sleigh as the horseman drove. The journey took them four hours. Just as they neared Grishkin Hospital, Leili cried out in her delirium, "Buy the ticket for the home ride," and threw back the upper portion of the blanket covering her body. They pulled to the entrance of the hospital and began unwrapping the sick girl, but she was still and pale. Her pulse was very weak and two blood streams flowed from her nose.

It was a few moments before a doctor could be summoned, but when he examined her she was pronounced dead. Herta stared at her dead child and in a low, haunting tone said, "She's only 13." The doctor frowned and addressed Herta. "Why didn't you bring her earlier?" The doctor's words brought anger in the place of sadness to Herta's voice, and her face flushed. "We had to wait nearly two weeks for a horse!" The doctor stood awkwardly silent as he stared at the deceased girl.

A nurse in attendance assessed the situation and quickly intervened to invite Marta to see the doctor for her own malady. She was ushered into the hospital and examined. The doctor referred her to the pharmacist on the premises who searched with great effort to find a medication that would remove the water from her body. Among his scant supplies he finally found a medicine he felt would help her. She then asked for medication for the rheumatism in her legs. The pharmacist said he had nothing that could help in that regard but prescribed taking hot steaming baths and the use of birch whisks to beat the troubling area. Birch whisks were flimsy branches often used in saunas to encourage circulation. With that the sad entourage returned to their village of Maiga, the lifeless Leili still sharing the sledge with Marta.

The funeral was held on March 5 in the hut where she had lived. Leili was wrapped in a blanket; a tablecloth was cut in half and put under her head. The young girl was gently placed into a rough-hewed coffin, and Alma read a Psalm from the Bible. The coffin was then put onto a sledge and pulled by horse to the cemetery. The mother and her remaining 17-year-old daughter followed on foot along with other Estonian mourners up a slight hill to the cemetery.

The grave had been dug a bit short so the coffin had to be held at an angle with a rope while the hole was being filled. A pine-branch cross was placed at the head of the grave, and a hymn was sung. When the service ended, the mourners laid pine branches atop the grave as they departed.

It seemed strange so soon after a funeral, but the following day Alma baked a cake for the daughter of Raha who was turning 18 that day. She put beet jam, a little sugar and cranberries between the two layers of the cake, and the members of their makeshift family took it to Raha's residence. Sixteen-year-old Marvi, the daughter of Marta Krull, came along with them to celebrate. Everyone sang and tried to make the day a happy occasion for the celebrant, though it was whispered that Mrs. Krull was very ill. During the afternoon Raha slipped away from the celebration to be with her suffering friend.

Early the next morning Ilse's cabin family was awakened by the brigadier seeking Leo and Jüri to dig a grave for Mrs. Krull. Upon hearing the news of the woman's passing Ilse felt a heaviness in her chest. Death, celebration, death— is this to be our new reality?

Raha came over immediately after the brigadier left. She had been with Mrs. Krull when she died. Her eyes were red and filled with tears as she shared her experience. "I have been unable to sleep this night remembering the events of yesterday and last night." Raha sat stiffly in a chair, her round face contorted as she spoke. "Marta was in terrible pain all day yesterday. When she could not stand it any longer, she called for me and two other of her friends to come to her side. We were with her until 8:00 last night when she died. It was terrible." Raha wiped her tears on her sleeve and continued. "The poor soul cried so horribly; it was awful to hear. She said, 'Why don't you kill me? Animals are not permitted to be tormented like this.' I gave her a drink of water, and she was in such pain she chewed off a piece of the glass. We sent for a doctor to come from Grishkin, but they sent only a nurse who arrived after she had died." Raha buried her head in her hands and wept. "It is so unbelievable that while my daughter was celebrating her 18th birthday my friend was dying!"

It took two days for Jüri and Leo to dig Mrs. Krull's grave because the ground was so deeply frozen. Ilse and Alma tried to gather pine branches from the forest for the grave, but the snow was hip high. Their legs became heavier with each step and their feet numb from snow invading their shoes as they struggled to cut branches. With sheer determination they managed to gather a sufficient amount. At the ceremony the following day Ilse took note of the exceptionally beautiful pine-branch cross made by Alma and placed at the head of the grave. One of the mourners at the funeral told Ilse that the dish had predicted the death date of Mrs. Krull.

Ilse went to her home thinking that if the dish was right about Mrs. Krull's death date, it must be right about their departure for home on March 16. But March 16 dawned without a whisper of the Estonians leaving for their homeland. Ilse's sadness was profound. She confessed to Alma, "The dish disappointed me, and the desire to return home haunts me at every turn. With the predicted date having passed I feel sadder than ever."

Alma put an arm around Ilse and squeezed tightly. "Ilse, that is what the Devil does. He gives false hope and delights when he creates sorrow."

"But the dish predicted the date of the death of Mrs. Krull! Someone at her funeral told me that," said Ilse.

"The Devil is crafty. He can anticipate things and hit it right sometimes. Don't be fooled. He is a deceiver."

After this disappointment Ilse's thoughts turned more earnestly to survival. She decided the only thing she could depend upon was what she could do for herself. She began sewing a blouse from a pink slip she brought with her from Estonia. The blouse could be sold to the Russians for money or food. Thankfully, Raha had been able to bargain for a sewing machine and allowed Ilse to use it.

En route to Raha's home one day she talked with some fellow Estonians returning from Gogolvka where they had been trying to sell items for food or rubles. "While in Gogolvka we witnessed an auction of two Russian families' belongings. The women had nothing left but the clothes they were wearing because their husbands had deserted to the Germans. Tomorrow four more families will lose their possessions in the same manner and for the same reason."

Later Ilse shared this news with Emma Ristna, but Emma had some news, too. "When I went to Novogorotk to sell some items, I discovered there is a fear of typhus; it is forbidden for strangers to stay overnight. And in Guslarov I hear most of the inhabitants had to have their heads shaved to get rid of lice in hopes of avoiding an outbreak there."

A few days later Ilse's long-time friend Hilda Pavelson visited from Guslarov where she had been settled. An Estonian friend accompanied her and they told Ilse, "The report of lice in Guslarov is true. We are some of the few that still have hair on our heads."

Ilse was concerned if Hilda had heard any more about her daughter Luule, who had been stricken with meningitis, separated from her mother and taken to a Novosibirsk hospital. Hilda smiled broadly as she responded to the inquiry. "The Russian doctor who was treating Luule took a personal interest in her and brought her to his home to care for her. She remained there for two months but was returned to me last October. She has recovered but will have a limp in one leg."

"We can live with a limp," responded Ilse with a gleam in her eyes. To her it was good news in the midst of the gloom that surrounded them.

In late April flooding began from the melting snow. Muddy clay caused walking to be almost impossible. It was rumored that Moscow had been taken by the Germans and that in Novosibirsk people were dying of starvation.

With the coming of spring Alma and Ella bought an old cabin from the Volga German Aman for 300 rubles, and Ilse planned to move with them. That meant that Alma and her son Leo, Ella and her children Aino and Jüri, and Ilse would be together in the new location. The Gordins, a Jewish family consisting of a mother and four children who were formerly living in Aman's cabin, were to move in with Lisette.

The cabin in the new location was not in the best of condition. The floor was uneven, and the oven needed to be repaired. But it was a bit more spacious.

Until recently Ilse and her cabin family had been able to get water by melting snow, but the snow had gone. They now had to walk about five minutes to reach a well and then pull water up with a wooden bucket. The first time they tried they got one pail of water from seven attempts. After a while they became more proficient, but it was not a task they relished.

A Jewish woman in the village received a letter from her husband who said he was doing forest work near Sosva where nearly 400 men were being held. Ilse got the address of this woman's husband, and she, Alma and Ella sent a letter to him asking if their husbands were there.

The next day an Estonian woman received a letter from a friend who gave the locations of the men's concentration camps. It read, "Some men have been brought to the Amuur River to work in coal mines, some to Archangel for logging, but the greatest numbers of men, approximately 800, are in Sverdlovsk." Once again Ilse and her friends sent letters to these camps trying to locate their loved ones.

Jüri and Leo were sent away to do log rafting which was generally reserved for deportees. The better jobs were given to the locals. The work consisted of transporting logs tied into rafts that were connected with ropes made of hemp. The logs making up the rafts were between 4 to 7 meters long. The united caravan of rafts usually totaled about 167 meters and was navigated by oars. Navigators were housed in huts atop the logs as they traveled.

The morning of May 20 found Ilse feeling sad. It was Vello's first birthday. How she longed to see her little boy. So many questions crowded her mind. Was he still alive? Was her family able to get enough food to nourish him? What did he look like? How would he respond to her when she saw him again?

Some good news lifted her spirit in late morning, however, when the brigadier announced, "Estonians who want some land on which to grow food must all come tomorrow at 6:00 a.m. to help clear the forest in Guslarov." How wonderful, she thought, we can now have gardens to grow our own food supply. Perhaps this will bring an end to our constant begging and bartering.

Ilse, Lisette and Alma were on time the next morning along with about 25 Estonians and Jews. An equal number of Russian women also came. They walked to Guslarov, about nine kilometers to the north, where they cut down trees, trimmed off the branches and then dragged the branches to an area where they burned them. The work continued for two days; each worker received 1.25 rubles per day for their effort.

By the end of May no one had approached them about the land they were to receive for a garden. So Ilse, Lisette and Alma went to the office to ask for the promised plot. Ilse received 200 square meters of land, but there seemed to be no equality in determining how much land each person received. Lisette got 400 square meters and Alma received 1,000. The final surprise—they must find their own seed!

The next day they traveled to Guslarov to buy and barter for seeds. On the way they searched for mushrooms which they could sell or use for food. While in Guslarov they learned that almost all the Estonians there had joined the *kolhoos* and were receiving 600 grams of food per day.

When Ilse arrived back in Maiga she sought work at the *kolhoos* but was told they had none to give. While there two men arrived whom she thought at first were Russians because they spoke Russian fluently. However, when they heard her speak Estonian with some other women, they approached her. "We are Estonians who have escaped Leningrad."

Ilse was surprised but somewhat excited to be receiving news about what was occurring at a greater distance. "Tell me what you know about how the war is going."

One of the men, who appeared to be in his 40s, looked down at the ground for a moment. "It is very bad there. The battle for the city rages, and there is great hunger. People are eating their pets and even the bodies of the dead." His eyes filled with tears as he continued. "Some members of my family are still there."

Ilse was shocked at the thought of such hunger. She and her fellow Estonians had become weak from lack of sufficient food, but they were still able to get enough to survive.

The other man interjected seeming to try to change his friend's sad tone. "You have food in this village. The rural areas are faring much better than the cities. We feel as though we are on a vacation here. We have come to buy potatoes."

Ilse refrained from saying anything about her plight and the condition of the other Estonians in their village. She suddenly felt blessed in the face of what these men had witnessed. Instead, she said, "I wish I had potatoes to give you."

CHAPTER 11

German Victory Questioned
Estonia 1942

It was Saturday, an idyllic afternoon in late July 1942. People strolled leisurely along the tree-lined walkways of a beautiful park situated alongside the Baltic Sea. Meeta sat on a bench near the Pärnu Sanitarium located within the park and just off the beach. The Sanitarium was known for its massage therapy and mud baths that were extolled for their ability to relieve arthritis and other bodily aches and pains. Meeta had arranged to meet Liina at 2:00 p.m. and had arrived a bit early. The Bible she had brought with her rested on her lap.

Seated on a bench facing the sea, she waited for Liina thinking of the many times she had swum there. The ladies' beach was just off to her right, protected and reserved exclusively for women. There they could swim without bathing suits. She loved the unrestricted freedom of the water against her body and the feel of the warm sun basking over her entire frame as she sunned herself.

She remembered the first time Ilse had come with her as a child. Ilse was three years old then and she was seven. Mamsi had taken them to enjoy a day at the ladies' beach. She thought of how excited Ilse was to have such a "big bath." The water was shallow for at least 250 meters out into the sea, and the two of them had enjoyed walking hand in hand until the water had reached Ilse's shoulders. Then suddenly she stepped into an impression and ended with a nose and mouth full of water. Meeta instantly pulled her up, but Mamsi, speaking with another mother some distance away, was not pleased when she heard Ilse crying and came quickly.

"Meeta, you know better than to take her into such deep water!"

Meeta tried to explain what happened, but Amalie wasn't listening. "You are such a dreamer! You need to keep your mind on what you're doing instead of constantly daydreaming."

The scolding she received and the outline of her mother's handprint on her thigh for her supposed neglect of duty hurt even today. Her intention had been to have Ilse enjoy the thrill of the water rising slowly so as not to frighten her. She had wanted that first experience to be memorable and fun. Yet, as so many other times in her life, her mother had judged and labeled her "a dreamer."

True they were different personalities. Mamsi was quick-minded, practical and sometimes impulsive, while she was more pensive, analytical and pondered alternatives when making decisions. But why, she wondered, did she relive this particular event today? Was it because Mamsi was even this day calling her a "dreamer" because of her recent interest in studying the Bible? Her mother believed in God, but to her He was a distant God, not one interested in daily activities. Meeta pondered this. I long for a personal God—a God I can talk to and know He hears me. What I have been studying has brought Him so much closer.

Meeta's contemplation was interrupted as Liina came into view east of the Sanitarium. Her small frame moved energetically as she walked toward Meeta waving her hand in greeting. Her thin face always seemed to glow with an accompanying broad smile. They exchanged greetings and Liina sat beside Meeta. "I see you have brought your Bible with you, Meeta."

"Yes, you certainly have piqued my interest. I have checked out all the Scripture portions the pamphlet suggested and have read even further."

"What have you discovered?"

"It seems to be as you say, Liina. But I have many questions."

"Such as?"

"What happens to the wicked?"

Liina reached into her large handbag, pulled out her Bible, and directed Meeta to the Gospel of John 5:28 where Jesus said that there would be a resurrection of both the good and the evil. Liina paused after reading the text with Meeta and said, "Please note that the good are resurrected to the 'resurrection of life,' but 'those who have done evil, to the resurrection of condemnation.' If you turn to the last book of the Bible, the book of Revelation, you'll find what that condemnation is.

Liina directed Meeta to chapter 21, verses 7 and 8 and waited until she had read it for herself before she continued. "This tells us the end result of the righteous and the wicked. The righteous 'shall inherit all things,' and the wicked will suffer 'the second death.'" Meeta's eyes were totally focused on the passage as Liina continued. "Now look at the beginning of this chapter, Meeta. Verse one says, 'Now I saw a new heaven and a new earth. For the first heaven and the first earth had passed away. . . .'" Meeta followed the words eagerly as Liina continued reading through the chapter to verse four. "'God Himself will be with them and be their God. And God will wipe away every tear from their eyes: there shall be no more death, nor sorrow, nor crying. There shall be no more pain, for the former things have passed away.'"

Liina stopped there and looked at Meeta. "This says there will be 'no more death, nor sorrow, nor crying' and 'no more pain.' When God says 'no more' that's just what He means. How could we enjoy everlasting life knowing that somewhere out in the universe someone, perhaps even a relative or friend, is still suffering pain? Heaven wouldn't be a place of rest for us. The wicked will 'perish' but will not continue suffering for eternal ages."

A serene expression rested on Meeta's face as she pondered the words she had just read. "That brings peace to my heart, Liina."

The two talked for some time, but finally Meeta asked Liina if the Bible had anything to say about the current war.

"No," said Liina, "but it does tell us that no one will be able to unite Europe under one sovereign as it appears Germany would like to do."

"Really!" Meeta's eyes opened wide as she spoke. "Where?"

"You'll find it in the book of Daniel." With that Liina turned to the second chapter of Daniel and began to explain to Meeta a prophetic dream that was given to the Babylonian King Nebuchadnezzar in the sixth century B.C. "The dream was of a large image with a head of gold, chest of silver, belly and thighs of bronze, legs of iron and feet of a mixture of iron and clay. In the dream, 'a stone was cut out without hands, which struck the image on its feet of iron and clay and broke them in pieces. . . . And the stone that struck the image became a great mountain and filled the whole earth.'"[20]

Meeta followed along in her Bible as Liina went from verse 31 through verse 45 where Babylon is identified as the head of gold and explains that following Babylon another "inferior" kingdom would conquer Babylon. A "third kingdom of bronze" would appear next and a "fourth kingdom . . . as strong as iron." Liina explained that historically Babylon was followed by Medo-Persia, then Greece and finally Rome.

"Please notice," said Liina, "as the feet and toes of the image were 'partly of potter's clay and partly of iron, the kingdom shall be divided.'[21] That's exactly what happened to the Roman Empire, Meeta. It divided into what we know as Europe today. Look at what verses 43 and 44 say. 'As you saw iron mixed with ceramic clay . . . they will not adhere to one another, just as iron does not mix with clay. And in the days of these kings the God of heaven will set up a kingdom which shall never be destroyed . . . and it shall stand forever.' So you see, Meeta, according to the Bible, Europe will never again be an empire ruled by one man. Instead, 'in the days of these kings,' or separate countries, 'the God of heaven will set up a kingdom which shall never be destroyed,' and the Bible adds in verse 45 that this 'interpretation is sure.' So I can confidently tell you that Germany will never gain complete sovereignty of Europe."

This information became foundational to Meeta, and she began to occasionally meet Liina to study more of the Bible prophecies. The more she studied the more certain she became that Germany would be defeated. The things she was learning were so exciting to her that she spoke openly about them to her fellow employees.

Early in November of 1942 Meeta was confronted by a Nazi party man. "Meeta, what is this I hear of your disbelief in an eventual German victory. We are making great strides and have a superior army. We are well on our way to the oil fields in the Caucasus, and we have even now surrounded Stalingrad."

The study of the Bible had given Meeta a new confidence she had not known before, and she unflinchingly responded to the man. "You may not wish to hear this, sir, but in my opinion the German nation has discarded Jesus Christ and has deified a godless leader. I believe the Bible predicts that Europe will never be politically united under any one leader. Besides, no matter how superior you consider the German army to be, it is too small to be stationed in all the countries they wish to control."

The man's face reddened, and he turned unexpectedly and left the room without saying another word. After his hasty departure, Meeta wondered at her forthright manner. It was not like her to be so direct. But something had compelled her to speak. She had spoken what she truly believed, and now offered a quiet prayer. "Oh God, I leave the result of my outspoken behavior to You."

Meeta wondered if there would be repercussions for her because of what she had said. But all was silent. The next time she saw the man who had confronted her was three weeks later. By then word was circulating that all was not going well for the German army in Stalingrad. Some of the Axis forces had surrendered, and still others had to withdraw. Meeta wondered if what she had said to the man was taking root in his mind.

* * *

By mid-November Vello added some new words to his vocabulary. He called his grandfather "Apa," Uncle Oskar "Aka," and Tasja "Aja." Tasja and Meeta taught him how to wink, and Tasja found it humorous to demonstrate this new ability to Jaak and Amalie. As she winked her eye at him she said, "Watch his expression. He makes such a sweet, sly face when he winks his eye." Amalie laughed out loud. Jaak's face broke into an easy smile as he spoke, revealing two deep furrows which once were dimples. "It looks like we have a little lady's man among us."

Vello was now walking and seemed to enjoy music. Whenever he heard his grandfather playing his violin in the living room, he would go to the entrance and call loudly, "Apa, Apa." Each morning when Estonian border guards passed by their apartment, singing as they went, Vello would hurry to the window.

On November 20 the Kollist family celebrated his one and one-half year birthday. For the event Oskar bought a package of candy. Tasja was able to find some yeast, so the family enjoyed a treat of freshly baked white bread.

Following supper one evening in early December, Oskar and Jaak sat together in the living room as Meeta and Amalie washed dishes in the kitchen. Oskar began sharing his concerns with his father. "Papsi, as you are aware, it appears the Germans have no intention of returning our independence to us. Though life is far better than under Soviet occupation, the fact remains that we are an occupied country and an inequality prevails."

Jaak's bald head bent downward as he pondered his son's words. "What you say is true, Oskar. I'm well aware that Germans are paid more for their work than Estonians, and Slavic workers are paid even less. We also know that some Jewish acquaintances have disappeared." Jaak now looked directly at Oskar. "One thing we can be thankful for is that to date no Estonian young men have been conscripted into their army. That was not true of the Soviet occupation."

Oskar's forehead wrinkled as he spoke. "That's true for now. But you know that the German advance in the Caucasus has been stopped, and the battle for Stalingrad is not going well. It is my fear that, if the war goes strongly against Germany, Estonian men will be conscripted. And that would mean me. I don't mind fighting for our independence, but I have great difficulty imagining my fighting in defense of our occupation."

Jaak was pensive and chose his words carefully. "I sense your anxiety, Oskar. But we must be careful not to borrow from tomorrow's problems. Though many people have thought the German army to be invincible and are surprised at this setback, it may be only temporary. We must be wise and patient. The winter season is upon us. There will not be too much fighting done in the midst of a Russian winter. We must also keep in mind that the United States has now entered this war. They are a freedom-loving people. It is too soon to evaluate in which direction this war will lean. Let us wait until spring and see what may develop."

Jaak looked at his son and smiled. "Rest your mind for now, Son. You have a much more pressing issue to deal with—that being a lovely young woman in Tallinn who is preparing for her soon-to-be wedding."

On December 25 Oskar was married to Ave Neumann in her parent's home in Tallinn. It was a small wedding attended by both families and just a few close friends. The couple stood beside a lighted Christmas tree as they took the vows given by the attending minister. The Kollist family was gone a few days for the occasion, and Vello stayed in Pärnu under the care of Tasja. It was the first time the family had been separated from the child since his parents had been deported, and Amalie was anxious to return. She commented to her new in-laws, "The only times I have been away from Vello are when I occasionally go to the cinema with Jaak, and then I hurry quickly home to my boy." While in Tallinn she purchased Vello a toy truck and a white fur hat and collar which she presented to him for his Christmas present when they returned home.

The newly married couple remained in Tallinn until January 6 when Oskar returned to Pärnu with his bride. He was a serious-minded man and kept constant vigil as to how the German army was progressing. The continuing news of trouble in Stalingrad caused him serious concern, and his concern was not unfounded.

CHAPTER 12

Mosquitoes, Bedbugs and Snow
Siberia 1942

Ilse and her cabin family began earnestly to till the respective plots of land that had been given to them for gardens. But they found tilling the land difficult. No plowing was done, so the ground had to be worked only with shovels that they borrowed from Russian neighbors. The ground was hard, and they were weak from lack of food. But they were driven on by the thought that one day they would have their own supply of food and would no longer have to barter and beg.

Ilse planted onion seeds, garlic, turnips and potatoes. But the mosquitoes were fierce. She put on borrowed boots, a coat, heavy pants, a woolen kerchief on her head, and a cloth over her face. It was tremendously hot, but the mosquitos did not get her for a meal. The planting finished, Ilse could not help but remark, "I have planted this garden only by the strength of God."

The summer brought additional work for them for which they were paid. The work included digging ditches and leveling roads. Sometimes they had to build a shelter from poles and cover them with sod. They slept in these shelters on the bare earth. When it rained they slept on the wet ground until the project was completed. Though they were sometimes cold and wet, there were lovely days in summer when one could, during rest periods, enjoy the beauty of nature. On one such day while leveling a road, Ilse nudged Alma. "Remarkably beautiful flowers grow here." Then pointing her finger she said, "Look, on the hill over there are peonies!"

That evening the two washed on the shore of the river and basked in the beauty of the landscape which caused Ilse to comment again. "When the weather is dry and warm, living here in the open is quite pleasant." Taking a deep draft of the fresh evening air she continued, "Nature is very beautiful." Alma nodded as she lifted her head and gazed at the lush greenery about her. "The busyness of our days almost makes us forget the loveliness of creation. Now that I think of it, the gurgle of the river brings peace to my heart. There is a rhythm in nature. Sitting here quietly right now, I feel in tune with it."

Sometimes in the evening the Estonians would gather after a hard day's work and sing songs of their homeland. One evening they sang *Far, Far Away, Where Is My Home?* and concluded by standing and singing their national anthem. Somehow this gave Ilse a sense that their homeland was still within their reach and that one day they would return to it. The others must have felt something similar because they instinctively began shaking hands around the circle. Then they respectfully dispersed to their humble sleeping quarters.

Summer work also included cutting hay by hand with scythes at Kassakaso-vis, a day and a half journey from Maiga by foot where they lived in huts. Horse-flies were so dreadful there that the workers could not stop for a rest but had to keep moving or be bitten mercilessly. A horse was so severely attacked by them that she died.

At night mosquitoes thronged them. To avoid them one had to sleep completely covered beneath a blanket. But the heat was stifling. So sleep came hard.

Food was scanty and insufficient for the energy required for the work to be done. Their birch-bark shoes wore out, and they hardly had time to make new ones for themselves.

Finally, in late July they returned to Maiga where they were delighted to find raspberries in season. They ate some and exchanged some for bread. They also had their gardens. But during her absence the village cows had come into Ilse's patch and ate all her turnips. Nature again came to their aid in mid-August when black currants could be found in abundance, if one knew where to look. They could be traded for bread or sold for rubles.

September's arrival brought the harvest of flax and oats. During the day workers could toil in just a dress, but at night they froze and were thankful that the fields were within walking distance of their cabin. However, their house was in desperate need of repair and did not afford them much warmth. The floor was rotted, one window was missing, and the roof of the entrance had fallen in. When returning from the fields at night, each had to be careful lest in the darkness they step on rotten wood and fall through to the storage cellar below. To make matters worse, one evening Alma felt something crawling on her. She lit a match and saw swarming bedbugs. She immediately arose and went to sleep on the floor. Ilse, too, lit a match and saw bedbugs of all sizes on her pillow. She also arose and slept under the table. Soon Aino and Ella joined them on the floor. Fortunately, Leo and Jüri were logging along the Ob River and did not have to deal with these critters. The next day they were thankful to be able to get some insecticide from the office with which they sprayed their cabin.

They longed to have time enough to repair their cabin, but each day they were commanded to go to the fields to work. Finally, in late September Aino, Alma and Ilse were able to get some boards from the mill to repair the floor. While they were working, the supervisor came by to tell Ilse, "Tomorrow you will be sent to Tshainsk to repair the brigadier's office and living quarters." After he left, Ilse looked at her cabin mates and said, "Can you believe I'm being sent to repair the brigadier's quarters when our own home is in shambles?" Aino and Alma flashed looks of disgust but said nothing.

The next day Ilse was teamed with another Estonian woman in her late 40s named Reet. They took food with them and walked three hours to reach the town. It was a mild, sunny day. As they walked they were taken by the beauty that surrounded them. Fire red aspen backed by dark green silver fir trees were breathtaking.

The women worked for two and a half weeks whitewashing, patching and making general repairs of the brigadier's office, living quarters and sauna. They were rewarded by having a warm sleeping room and most days were given food, though on two days they had to work too late to make it to the cafeteria.

It was mid-October before Ilse and her cabin family could repair the roof of the entry way of their house. They also mounded dirt on the outside of their cabin to seal cracks and help keep it warm. Milk was now scarce because of the quota that had to be given to the government, so sometimes at night they would go secretly to the cow barn and milk some of the cows.

One morning Ilse awoke to an upset stomach and diarrhea. She was commanded to winnow that day, but she could not because of her condition. Raha, who did not have to work because of a severe heart condition, came to visit. Her seer talents had begun to be appreciated by the Russian women in the village, and they provided her with gifts of milk, pails of potatoes and other food items in payment for her predictions.

During her visit with Ilse she put down her cards on Ilse's behalf.

"You will have no more children," said Raha as she placed the cards atop one another. "And there is black blood regarding your husband."

"What does that mean?" Ilse's eyes squinted as she spoke and her face tensed.

"I can't be certain," said Raha, her hand tapping the table with the remaining cards as she spoke. "It could mean some of those who surround him are ill. It could mean that he is ill." A few more cards were placed upon the table. "A trip is in your future, Ilse."

Ilse's eyebrows rose and her eyes opened wide. "A trip? Where to?"

"I don't know. But the cards do reveal a trip for you. There will be some kind of misunderstanding with a man, and the trip will be with men. You are going on the trip against your will."

Ilse felt her stomach tighten. "My heart is heavy. I'm afraid I will suddenly be taken away again."

By early November both Jüri and Leo had returned from logging. The snow began falling and the nights were long. Hoarfrost appeared in the corners of the room. The small primitive oil lamp hanging in their cabin was very dim, and it was hard for them to do any sewing or mending at night. Ella borrowed a spinning wheel and began spinning flax into coarse thread, but even this was difficult in the dim light. The setting caused Alma to fantasize. "Our house is like an old-fashioned farmhouse. The spinning wheel is in front of the oven. The benches, the table and the walls are made of round logs. This is like stepping back into history."

Because of the long nights the cabin family began awaking in the dark. This gave them time to cook during the dark hours so they could save the light part of the day for sewing gloves, making birch-bark shoes, and mending coats and clothes needed for warmth.

It was too cold to use the outhouse at night so a large metal pot was used for that purpose and was emptied each morning. But by morning the odor was unbearable. Ilse at one point could stand it no longer and emptied the container at 2:00 in the morning. The house rule then became: "The last one to use the pot at night must dump it outside."

The radio in the Maiga cafeteria had not given any news from the war front for weeks. But one Sunday evening a teacher from Moscow came to the meeting hall in Makarov and gave them a brief overview of the war. Her most important nugget was "the Germans have not yet taken Leningrad or Moscow."

A newspaper was published occasionally, and in mid-November it briefly stated, "Germany is fighting in France." These snippets of news were all they had of the outside world other than rumors that flew from time to time.

On November 20 Ilse thought of her child. "Vello became a year and a half today. He must be running by now," she mused as she wrote in her diary. "Oh, how I wish I could see the various stages he is going through. It has been so long since I've seen him; his face is fading from my memory." She desired so much to write home to request a picture, but no mail was allowed to pass beyond the Russian border.

Later in the day each person received 400 grams of salt. This was a great occasion because salt had become a rare commodity.

In early December Ilse took a sled and walked with two other women to another village trying to buy or barter for food with some socks they had. Ilse was able to buy 110 kilograms of cabbage, fresh and well cleaned. The sack of cabbage was put atop the sled and dragged back to Maiga. A large portion of the journey had no road, only tractor tracks, and they strained to pull the sled. As they approached Ilse's cabin, they exhausted their remaining strength and managed to bring the cabbage inside. Some frost had already attached itself to the produce, but it was promptly divided between the women. Ilse stored her portion in the cellar.

On December 10 Ilse commented to Alma, "Today is Papsi's birthday. He is 76 years old and Oskar is 31 today. Their birthdays were always such a joyous occasion with father and son celebrating the same date." She reminisced about the parties they would have with friends and family gathered in their living room singing and playing their instruments of choice. "How far away and long ago it all seems now," said Ilse. Quickly she tried to focus her attention on a blouse she was sewing to hopefully sell for food. One must not allow such warm memories to linger long, she thought. The pain is too great.

The following day Rosa Gordin, the Jewish lady now living with Lisette, breathlessly entered Ilse's cabin. Ilse was alone at the time. "I have received a letter from the camp where Peeter is being held." It had been mailed on October 20 and had just arrived. Rosa handed the letter to Ilse and pointed to the words, "Alma Mürk's connection with her husband is established. He is in the same camp with Peeter Kotter."

Ilse's heart raced, "At last I have an address. It has been a year and a half…" The excitement caused her to lose her breath, and she could not finish the sentence. She quickly wrote down the address and thanked Rosa. Later she shared the news with an equally excited Alma. The urgency of meeting their immediate needs, however, kept them from writing at once.

On December 17 the snow began falling so hard that even the neighboring cabin could not be seen. Alma took note. "The weather is getting bad. Today is a good day to seal these cabin walls." Aino and Ilse braved the blizzard to get straw. But Ilse was not happy. "Aino, I can't even see the road that leads to the piles of straw. I am a bit upset that in this weather we are making renovations." Aino raised her hand to shield her face from the snow as she responded. "We might as well do it today though, Ilse. We may not get another opportunity, and this is a foretaste of what is to come."

All worked together and made a mixture of clay and chaff and put it on the walls between the logs. The clay was a little cream colored and Ilse thought it looked quite nice. With the walls now sealed, Ilse later noted in her diary, "The cockroaches seem to be less."

By December 21 their flour supply was running dangerously low, so despite the temperature of minus 50 degrees, Ella, Ilse and another friend walked the seven kilometers to Tshainsk in hopes of selling or bartering some items for flour. They did not go to the office to get permission because the *kolhoos* had not given their quota of flour to the government. When anyone was found with flour, it was taken from them.

In Tshainsk Ilse was able to trade the blouse she had recently made for three kilograms of flour. However, they were caught by the Maiga police on the way back home and were taken to the meeting hall at Makarov. There a Communist wrote down their names, confiscated their flour, and commanded them to go home.

By December 23 the entire cabin family was depressed. "We will be in the midst of the holidays without flour," said Alma. Despite their depression, they brought in an evergreen tree and sang "Silent Night, Holy Night."

On Christmas Day Ilse wrote a letter to her husband Peeter. She struggled with what to say and how much to tell him of her situation. Ella and Alma helped her edit what might cause him to worry about her. Then they took the letter to the postal clerk. In the evening they sang Christmas songs and burned some stubs of preciously saved candles on the Christmas tree.

Another funeral marked the end of the year. An Estonian lady in the village died of tuberculosis.

CHAPTER 13

Tide of War Changes
Estonia 1943

Oskar was now general manager of the factory. His newer methods of tanning improved the quality of their already exemplary leather, and the number of customers increased significantly. Amalie now kept the accounting records for the business and was meticulous.

As business prospered Oskar and his father purchased new machines from manufacturers in Germany which made the work more efficient. Soon the supply of inland raw hides was not sufficient to meet the demand for their product, and they found it necessary to purchase additional hides from Poland and Denmark. This meant that Oskar was traveling often in order to consummate these contracts. As he traveled, he learned more of how the war was progressing,

In mid-October of 1942 Adolph Hitler had ordered all Eastern Front offenses to cease with the exception of Stalingrad and the Caucasus. He ordered his troops to prepare for winter defense in anticipation of destroying the Russian Army in the spring, but Joseph Stalin was as determined as was Hitler. The German army was stopped short of reaching their goal of Grozny in the Caucasus, and by early February of 1943 the last of Hitler's besieged army was forced to surrender in Stalingrad.

The inability of Germany to take Stalingrad was an enormous defeat. Additionally, Allied forces had major successes in North Africa during the autumn of 1942, and Germany's Field Marshal Rommel had rapidly retreated to Tunisia. By March of 1943 mobilization of non-German men began. This had been avoided earlier because of the "Nazi ideology regarding 'inferior' peoples."[22]

In early May, after seven months of battling for Tunisia, the British controlled the city of Tunis. General Omar Bradley led the U.S. II Corps 1st Armored Division to take control of the Tunis to Bizerta railway line and cut off supplies to the Axis armies. On May 12 the Axis resistance in Tunisia came to an end with nearly 250,000 prisoners captured by the Allied army. Yet, despite all of this, life in Estonia continued fairly normally.

As Vello approached his second birthday, he was developing a personality. In the morning when he awoke in his grandmother's room, he would first throw his pacifier into her bed. Next came his pillows and both the dolls, Malle and Kalle, with which he slept. Then he would call out, "uppa, uppa," until Amalie would bring him to her bed where he would play until Tasja had breakfast ready and took him to eat.

When Jaak played the violin, Vello would either turn in a circle or stomp the rhythm with his little feet. Jaak taught him how to make a *kratzfuss*[23] when greeting someone. Each time Jaak would leave the apartment, he would say good-bye using the *kratzfuss* and Vello would copy him in mirror image.

He also began mimicking Meeta when she would talk to her friends by telephone. He found a boiled egg holder and would put it to his ear as he said, "alloo, alloo." Then he would laugh and pretend he was talking to someone.

During the winter Amalie pulled Vello in a sled to give him fresh air and sunshine, but by the middle of April when the streets were dry and clean she began taking him for walks. Sometimes German soldiers would pass by singing, and Vello would hurry after them singing in a loud voice. In time the Kollist family became friends with some of the soldiers. One of them was Sergeant Bublitz. Bublitz noticed how Vello liked to imitate his grandfather. Since Jaak always walked with a cane, Bublitz made Vello a beautifully carved one which Vello proudly used on his walks. Groups of German soldiers grew accustomed to seeing him and would smile as they passed and say, *"Das ist das Kind mit dem Stock."* 24

A birthday party was held for Vello's second birthday. Although it was officially on Thursday, May 20, it was celebrated the following Saturday afternoon when Meeta, who worked until shortly after noon, and other invited guests would be available to attend. Ave and Oskar were among the guests as was Mr. Schmidt, Vello's godfather, and his two little daughters. When it was time to leave, the two girls each made a curtsey as they said good-bye and Vello returned the curtsey. Finding this humorous, Ave curtsied several times just to see him follow suit. Amalie bristled as she watched. "Stop trying to make my little boy a little girl, Ave." The words came with such a commanding tone that Ave immediately wilted.

In spite of the superficial normalcy, by the middle of summer tension in Estonia was mounting. In June the Allies had begun a major offensive against Italian strongholds. By July 10 the invasion of Sicily began, and it was becoming increasingly clear that the Axis powers would be defeated. Oskar watched, listened and evaluated all the information he could glean and once again spoke with his father.

"Papsi, I feel my fears are becoming reality. Things are not going well for the German army, and they have begun mobilizing Estonians. Right now conscription is for young men between the ages of 19 to 24, but if things continue as they appear, the age will be expanded. Ave and I have spoken much about this, and we both want to raise a family in a free society. Even if events turn in favor of Germany, Estonia will still be an occupied country. It is clear to me that Germany has no intention of relinquishing control. On the other hand, if the war continues as it is now and the Russians return to Estonia, the executions and deportations will begin again." Oskar's face tightened as he continued. "More families will feel the loss that we have experienced with loved ones being torn from them. I for sure will be one of them since I have fought with the Finns against the Russians. It is my wish to fully liberate Estonia from the grasp of any country so that we may once again have our independence."

Jaak's face seemed drawn as he responded to his son. "What are you trying to say, Oskar?"

"Ave and I feel we should find passage to Finland. The Finns are fighting against the Russians for their freedom. Perhaps I could again unite with them against the Red army. Many of my friends feel the same. Some have already left for Finland, and still others are making plans to do so."

Jaak looked deliberately at his son. "And if the Finns fail?"

Oskar's six-foot frame slumped slightly, and his eyes turned away from his father. "We will be that much closer to Sweden. If events shift, we will try to flee there." Oskar then turned to look at his father who stood erect but with his head bowed in his characteristic thinking mode. Then without a word of remonstrance Jaak spoke. "How do you plan to reach Finland? The Finish Gulf is being monitored heavily."

"By fishing boat." Oskar's body seemed energized as he spoke. "I know a fisherman who has agreed to take us. Our plans are to depart sometime this September before the cold weather begins."

Jaak focused intently on Oskar. "I can see your mind is made up. If I were as young as you I would possibly feel the same, but I have struggled many years to build this business and I am hopeful. Perhaps I'm an old fool, but my hope is that the Americans will aid us in obtaining our independence. We gained it in the aftermath of World War I. Perhaps Providence will smile on us once again."

CHAPTER 14

He's Alive!
Siberia 1943

The New Year was greeted with a celebration in the Makarov social hall. The young people enjoyed the time together, and some budding romances were observed. Russians, Estonians and Volga Germans all joined together laughing and dancing to accordion music. Ilse thought, Why can't it be this way all the time? She even commented to her friend Emma Ristna, "I have never received so many New Year's kisses as today." Emma giggled as she said, "Watch out, Ilse, a Russian lady recently found her husband in a horse stall with another woman. One of these men might have his eye on you."

The following day was Leo's 17th birthday. There would be no flour this year for a birthday cake, but Alma made potato porridge and *pirukad* filled with sauerkraut and carrots. Wild chamomile tea also appeared—a real treat.

Later that day an Estonian woman received word that her husband had died of tuberculosis in one of the labor camps. It was also reported, "the Russians are advancing toward the west." Jews in the village rejoiced at the news, but the report upset the Estonians.

The next day was Sunday, and Ilse went to see Raha to have her inquire of the cards again. "Raha, I have the feeling that we will be going home soon. What do the cards see for our future?"

Raha, always eager to accommodate a request, promptly began laying the cards down on the table. "Soon you will receive a letter from your husband, and your heart will remain happy about home." The news was scant, but it was enough for Ilse. Her spirit remained positive even when she returned to her cabin and found it in complete darkness due to the lack of petrol for their one dim light. It helped also that there was enough wood to keep their dwelling as she said, "hot as a sauna." She and her cabin family had worked hard to cut trees from the forest, chop them into logs, and then laboriously haul them to their cabin. When Ilse shared with Raha how hard they worked to get logs, Raha said that she and a friend had found an easier way. "Wood is piled outside the village office, so one of us goes to speak to the overseer while the other steals the wood." Ah, thought Ilse, life in Siberia teaches one many things.

The next morning the village was astir with the news, "the front is 10 kilometers from Moscow." Then Aino brought word that Kolja, their supervisor, had been sent to war. "He was a kind man," said Alma. "We Estonians will miss him. He was fair in his dealings and tried to be equitable."

The Russian custom in the village was that family members would cry aloud when one of their own was sent to war. Outside Ilse heard them chanting in anguished tones. Kolja's mother was damning the Germans while his sister was loudly shouting, "My dear brother, my dear brother, what have they done to you! I will never again see you." Unfortunately, she was no doubt correct in her appraisal. Russian soldiers were succumbing in mass at the front.

Suddenly Leo opened the door to the cabin and stood in the doorway, tears streaming down his face. Alma hurried to her son's side. "Leo, whatever is the matter?"

"I am being sent to do forest work 120 kilometers from home along with three other teenaged boys." Alma stared at her son hardly able to believe what she had heard. She knew all too well the extremely hard work this required, and it would be done in subzero January temperatures. She and Leo also knew that recently a local veterinarian, who had been working in another town, was found frozen to death on the side of the road unable to make it back to Maiga before succumbing to the frigid Siberian cold.

Alma embraced her son and held his head next to hers as their tears intermingled. "When must you leave, Leo?"

"In two days."

Ilse, Ella and Aino stood helplessly watching. Finally, Ilse spoke in as positive a tone as she could. "We have two days! Let's get busy and make preparations for Leo."

Ilse's determination to prepare for Leo's venture turned the household into manufacturing mode. They solicited Raha, an excellent seamstress, to cut out three pairs of pants for Leo. Then Alma, Ella and Ilse sewed them. The office had given Leo five kilograms of flour and nearly 66 kilograms of potatoes to take with him. So Alma baked bread for his journey.

The morning of Leo's departure was a solemn occasion. Mother and son embraced one another, and their tears flowed. Ilse, sensing what Alma was experiencing, thought of the questions she would be contemplating if it were her son. Would this be the last time she saw her only child? What ordeals awaited him? Would his superior be gracious or formidable? What kind of shelter would he be given? Would food be sufficient once he arrived at his destination? How long would he be gone? So many questions for which there were no answers.

Leo mounted an emaciated horse and was barely out of sight before they were approached by an official who informed them that a war payment was to be paid by Estonians. "Each house is to give 75 rubles. Each person must give a minimum of five rubles."

"What if our household doesn't have 75 rubles?" Ilse asked.

"Then borrow it from someone who does," was the curt reply.

One Estonian woman, who had no other way of paying the amount, gave up her wedding ring in order to meet the requirement.

The following day Ella entered the cabin excitedly reporting, "Today the radio in the cafeteria announced that peace has been made."

Her enthusiasm was quickly deflated, however, as Ilse incredulously responded, "That was announced several days ago. One never knows what to believe. What I can believe is that my store of potatoes is now depleted, and I don't know whether I will be able to exchange something to get more."

On January 20 Ilse's thoughts, as it was on every 20th of the month, were of her son. Today Vello is one year and eight months old. She took a small red flag from a sack beneath her bed and displayed it on the table to commemorate the day. I wonder what he looks like now. He must be walking and saying words. How I long to see him. His face has grown dim in my memory. If only I had a picture of him. She forced herself to continue working on a blouse she was making. One must not dwell too long in the realm of the unattainable, she thought. The heartache is too great.

Material for the blouse came from a grey slip she had brought with her from Estonia. Selling items or trading them for food was her primary method of obtaining nourishment in winter while the kolhoos was not active. Two days later she and Ella traveled to a nearby town to sell the blouse. The journey was unfruitful since everyone was straining to pay the war tax.

Bikaalov, the new foreman, received a letter from his son who was serving at the war front. He wrote, "Soon there will be peace." Based on the hope of that news, that night in their cabin they imagined what it would be like to return home. Ilse said, "I will telephone from Narva and ask, 'Who is at the Kollist Leather Factory? Are Vello, Mother, Father and Meeta still living?'"

Alma tried to be a bit more playful in her approach. "I will go to the Tamsalu Train Station and sleep there the first night. The next morning I will have the station hold my packages while I go out to beg for food. When someone gives me bread with butter, I will say, 'My stomach cannot digest this. It will be helpful if you can give me an unpeeled potato with some salt.'" Everyone laughed realizing only those who had been through what they had could truly appreciate what she had said.

The great sport at night began after all conversation had ceased and the cabin family was finally in darkness; the bedbugs started coming out. Someone would light a splinter of wood from the fire in the stove and use it as a match to find the bugs and kill them. Sometimes they were even able to catch a few cockroaches.

The second week in February they awoke to the sun rising like a red wheel and no wind. This promises to be a beautiful day, thought Ilse. She contacted Elsa Reim to go with her to a village called Selpo where they hoped to sell or exchange some items. They left at nine o'clock and arrived at noon. The cafeteria there had only sauerkraut and tea, so they went from house to house seeking food. Finally, they knocked on the door of a schoolteacher's residence who gave them some milk, a chunk of bread, potatoes and sauerkraut. But Ilse's greatest joy came when the teacher offered her two notebooks and two pencils. Heretofore, Ilse had been keeping a daily diary on whatever scraps of paper she could glean from trashed sheets at the village office writing between the lines of the used paper.

Later, after she and Elsa returned to their respective homes, Ilse began to write in one of her new notebooks: "Now the sun is setting. Aino is the only one here, and she is sleeping. I am writing and looking out the window. We have a view of the whole of Maiga. In the distance on a hill is a graveyard where some of our people are buried. The expanse goes on to snowy, open areas, hemmed in by the forest, and then to the faraway shores of my beloved homeland. Home, home—for all of us the dream of dreams."

The following evening Leo came home. It had taken six days of travel instead of the projected five. His eyes appeared sunken with dark circles beneath them. His tall frame was bent and gaunt. As he walked through the door, Alma hurried to greet him but paused to stare at him. "Leo, you look half starved."

"The food was very poor, Mother, and the work very hard. I was sent home because I am too weak to work. The *kolhoos* does not have much hay, and even the horses were so weak they could not accomplish the norm."[25]

Alma led her son to a chair near the table. "Sit here while I make you something to eat."

Ilse, Aino and Ella stood silently assessing the situation. Ella was the first to speak. "Leo, I do believe you are infested with lice."

Alma turned quickly from her preparations to look at her son. "Leo, you must take off your clothes, now!"

Leo obediently complied. Modesty had long been abandoned in a one-room cabin. Apologetically he explained, "In the barrack there were 170 of us crowded together. There was no way to escape lice." The ladies began their work and gleaned 45 lice from his head.

Leo was given a 10-day respite, but on the eighth day was commanded to begin preparations to join another group in two days. This time the location was only 18 kilometers away and his assignment was ice fishing.

On February 18 Ella and Aino were patching their clothes in preparation for a walk to Tshainsk the next day to hopefully find some work when they suddenly saw a woman hurrying toward their cabin. "Look, it's our postal clerk," said Ella. "She must be bearing some news. She's half running." Alma and Ilse quickly joined them at the window. Soon all four of them hurried to the door in anticipation.

As soon as the clerk arrived, she came straight to Ilse and placed a letter in her hand. Ilse looked at the carefully folded envelope and shouted. "A letter from Peko! One hundred joys!" It had been one year, seven months and three days since she had last seen or heard from her husband, and she had often wondered if he were still alive. Was this real or a dream? A letter was something she had so much longed for, but now she felt apprehensive as to its contents.

The women crowded around her excitedly and ushered her to a chair next to the table around which they took their places with their noses pointed toward Ilse eager as children on Christmas morning. One said, "Now Ilse, don't leave something unread. We want to hear every word."

Though her hands were shaking, Ilse tried to gently, carefully open the letter which was folded into the form of an envelope and addressed on the back. She unfolded the page as if it were a sacred artifact and then began to read aloud:

November 8, 1942

Beloved wife,

I am risking to write this in Estonian [because Russians would not be able to censure it]. When the letter carrier announced that I had become part of a great event, I decided I must be getting a letter from you. One after another visitors greeted me like I had some important jubilee. That day was filled with happiness, and I now breathe much more easily and feel like my legs are firmly on the ground again.

My cold logic establishes surely that you are young, healthy and alive, but my feelings are like an obstinate, persistent, whining child calling and waiting for you, searching and crying after you day and night. Now I am more secure in myself. The four letters of your name (ILSE) are the most beloved letters in the world.

I am especially joyful that near you is Endel, a man who will support you like a relative or a friend. I am again together with Volli [Voldemar Pavelson]. . . . Now we are residing in winter. Snow is completely on the ground and it is cold. I hope, as the maker of birch-bark shoes, to remain under a shelter. Until now hunger hasn't squeezed us. Now and then Volli and I have amply put on weight even though we eat only gruel. We have not tasted fat food or foods with salt all year. In spite of it, I have for my consolation tobacco, and my days of confinement stretch sadly forward.

For daydreaming and tormenting my thoughts, I think of how enjoyable it would be to take a ride to visit Oskar, and I think that in the whole world there is nothing sweeter than rye bread.

Today is Sunday, and that is a rest day for me, so I now have some time to answer your letter of July 27, which I received November 2.

My thoughts are constantly of home. It occurs to me that all those at home right now are probably in church praying for us. My playful boy is under the care of grandfather and occupying himself by crawling around the rooms. Don't you see him in the same way?

Are you completely healthy? How are your kidneys? How are you clothed, and how are you covering your feet in the cold? I always hope that life in the *kolhoos* is not so miserable.

Raha's husband is with me, and there are 40 more Estonians as well. He got a letter yesterday, and it did not mention you. I am hoping you are well. . . .

May the Heavenly Father lessen our trials so that the sun will shine again and will give us back our family and our son. Now may He love and keep you watchfully.

Volli sends greetings to Hilda. Also greetings from me to Endel and others. ... Please write again soon.

Peko

While Ilse was reading, additional friends began arriving. Word spread quickly in the village whenever news from beyond their region was received, and soon the cabin was filled with women wishing to hear the letter read to them. Many of them enviously commented that their husbands do not write in such romantic and poetic terms. Ilse chuckled and said, "Why do you think I married him?"

The following day people still came to Ilse's cabin to hear the letter. "I am an important person now," laughed Ilse. Though she had planned to go with Alma and Ella to find work in Tshainsk that day, she decided instead to remain home and write a letter to Peeter.

A few days later Ilse walked to Guslarov to share the letter with her long-time friend Hilda Pavelson and relay the greetings from her husband who was also with Peeter. As Ilse was reading, another Estonian friend came to Hilda's home. When she learned that both Ilse and Hilda had received news from their husbands, her eyes became misty. She explained, "I have recently received word that my husband has died." The joyous occasion quickly turned to consolation.

When Ella and Aino returned from Tomsk two days later, they advised Ilse of the hunger in the city. "There are many thieves in Tomsk. Boys grab food from you and don't even run away. They say, 'I have hunger, you can eat something else.'"

That evening Ella, Aino and Ilse decided to lift one another's morale by making up humorous stories. One such was that Jüri, Aino's brother, and her mother Ella found a man for Aino to marry. The wedding day was planned, but a problem developed for Ella. She had no upper teeth. Ilse joked, "She at least will need wooden teeth to hold onto her gums and purse out her cheeks. Her cheeks must not be permitted to sag when the vows are taken." They continued in this silliness until nine in the evening when they finally went to bed still smiling at the various tales they had spun. Ilse recorded in her diary as she retired, "I laugh and joke like a fool with a hurting heart."

The next day was Sunday, February 28, and Leo came home in the late afternoon, unkempt and cold. He had been ice fishing in felt boots, and his feet had been wet every day. "The ice is one meter thick, and the snow is up to one's knees," said Leo. "We have no nets so we use spears to catch the fish." Leo also reported, "The cold has taken many Russian soldiers. My supervisor told me that 'every hour a guard checks the men to see that they are not freezing. After each hour, the guard must arouse the men so they turn to the other side. If the guard falls asleep, they all die.'" The following Tuesday Leo returned to work at the *kolhoos*.

Early the next week Ilse went to visit Elsa Reim in her cabin and learned that Tiiu, Elsa's youngest daughter, was very sick with a high fever. Four days later Tiiu died, just eight days shy of her seventh birthday. Ilse came quickly to comfort Elsa. Elsa's tears flowed as she poured out her heartache. "Tiiu's last words this morning were, 'Mother, don't cry! I'm going to live!'" Then she buried her face in her hands and sobbed, "How final and painful it is to lose a child."

A paper house, made by Tiiu two days before she died, still hung in the window. Ilse tried to avoid looking at it. Soon Mall, Tiiu's nine-year-old sister, came through the door of the cabin and stopped. She wore a blank expression as she stared around the room and then stood silently looking at her mother. Elsa asked, "Mall, why are you standing there like that?" Mall instantly burst into tears and ran from the house.

Ilse wrote in her diary that day: "Tiiu was torn from the warmth of her mother's arms. Today I am quite stunned by it all. Only despair remains in the end."

One night at 11:30 someone knocked on the door of Ilse's cabin and ordered Ella to go to Makarov immediately. She returned at 2:00 a.m. her face wet with tears. The cabin family eagerly gathered around her. Alma was smoking one of her precious cigarettes to calm her nerves and was the first to speak. "What happened, Ella?"

"I've just been informed that my husband has died."

"When?"

"February 12 of last year," sobbed Ella.

Alma gave a disgusted look toward Ilse and said softly, "Those scoundrels. They wake you in the middle of the night to tell you that your husband died more than a year ago?"

Jüri immediately came to his mother's side and began weeping with her. He and his mother mourned the rest of the night. Aino had fallen asleep waiting for her mother's return and did not receive the news until the next morning.

In the cafeteria on March 31, the radio carried a speech by American President Franklin D. Roosevelt in which he announced, "The Allies are attacking the German Army in Tunisia."

As spring approached, more work became available. Cow manure needed to be spread on the fields, snow needed to be shoveled from the roofs of buildings. On some roofs the snow was up to one's chest. Jüri worked in the forest cutting trees into logs, and Leo hauled hay and wheat to forest workers in surrounding areas. They both reported, "The horses are so weak they don't move unless whipped."

Kaare Põltsam and her three-year-old daughter, Karin, joined Ilse's cabin family the second week in April. Kaare and her two children had been on the same boxcar as Ilse en route to Siberia. It was her son, Allan, who had died on the way. Allan was only six days older than Vello, and Ilse identified intimately with that loss when it occurred.

Ilse found Karin's twitters and trills delightful and appreciated that Karin would speak softly when someone was sleeping during the day. Ilse and Kaare had much in common. Kaare was just four months older than Ilse, and her husband was 17 years her senior. Her husband Karl had been a prominent businessman who owned an ironworks manufacturing company in Pärnu when he was deported. He like Peeter was now in the Sverdlovsk prison camp.

As the weather became warmer and the ground thawed, wading through the mud became almost impossible. The daylight was longer, so the cabin family went to sleep while it was still light. Ilse enjoyed rocking Karin on her knees and singing children's songs with her before bedtime. Karin slept on the floor in a basket beside Ilse's bed. Having this child so near keenly aroused Ilse's motherly instincts. She thought to herself, I now have two children. One is far away in Estonia, but this one is near.

By mid-May every able-bodied man was conscripted into the army. In Maiga only four men remained—those who were absolutely necessary to sustain the *kolhoos*, such as the blacksmith and mechanic. The *kolhoos* had not yet allotted land for planting to Ilse and Kaare since the leadership said it did not want to take the time to measure out the land. So they watched others carefully planting their gardens from the sidelines as Ilse said, "like poor sinners."

On Thursday, May 20, Ilse recorded in her diary: "Today Vello is two years old. Two years ago on a Tuesday he was born at 1:30 in the afternoon." She shared her memories with some of her friends. They encouraged her. To her surprise, she received many congratulations.

That evening it was announced that everyone must work in the *kolhoos* fields. It was stressed that "those who do not work will not be given assigned land for planting their own gardens." Ilse was worried since she had no shovel, but her brigadier found one for her to use.

The following morning she began digging a rye field with other fellow Estonians. The weather became so warm that they stripped to their underwear. The digging continued for several days. Finally, on June 2, Ilse was given a plot of land to use for a garden near her cabin. Her problem now became trying to prepare her own ground for planting in addition to working in the *kolhoos* fields. Her strength was spent when she returned to her home in the evenings, yet she had to force herself to till her own land before retiring.

Five days later the weather turned cold and then rainy. By June 14 she had not yet been able to plant, and she still needed to gather boards to make a fence around her plot to protect it from the livestock that wandered the village. This day was particularly depressing for Ilse since she was keenly aware that this date marked two years since her deportation. The sparse food, the heavy manual labor, the mosquitoes, horseflies and bedbugs along with the constant lack of sleep were rapidly taking their toll on her. She remarked to Alma, who was herself fighting a fever of 102 degrees, "I feel that I have aged this spring. My life force has disappeared and my heart is heavy."

CHAPTER 15

Heart to Heart

Estonia 1943

The German draft of Estonians caused a number of young men to cross the Baltic Sea to Finland. "Over half of these men volunteered for service in the Finnish armed forces against the Soviet Union. . . . In addition to avoiding the German Army, the volunteers' goal was to acquire military training and experience in order to be of future service to their homeland. Given the emergence of Estonian independence in the rapidly changing fortunes of World War I, the restoration of that same independence did not seem beyond the realm of possibility in the upheavals of World War II."[26]

The Kollist family was relieved that Oskar and Ave had safely escaped to Finland, but this put an extra burden on Jaak who had never been comfortable with the sales end of the leather tannery business. His joy had always been the production of quality leather. But life had taught him much, and at 76 he was more amenable to sales than he was at a younger age.

Oskar, of course, was greatly missed. Amalie and Jaak expressed great loss in having two of their children gone from them as a result of the war. However, they were still hopeful that the conclusion of this strife would once again result in the independence of their little country.

For the present things seemed somewhat normal. Meeta continued working for the German Civil Administration. In her free time she served as accompanist for a singer who was also a young German soldier. Music was still an enjoyable part of their family, and often in the evening Meeta, Jaak and Amalie would join together in song with Meeta on the piano, Jaak on violin and Amalie singing.

One evening in early fall Amalie decided to attend a movie that Jaak was not interested in seeing, so he and Meeta remained at home with little Vello. After Vello had been put to sleep, it afforded Meeta a rare opportunity to be alone with her father. She took the occasion to approach him about something that had been troubling her.

"Papsi, you know that I have been studying the Bible recently, and I have learned many things I never knew before. Mamsi feels this sort of study is better left to theologians and thinks I have my head in the clouds. What do you think?"

Jaak was seated in a comfortable easy chair, and Meeta sat on the sofa opposite him. He had been reading a newspaper and now laid it aside to give full attention to his daughter. He spoke in a serious, deliberate tone. "Meeta, as a child I learned whatever I know about the Bible and God from my mother. She was a godly woman and took us regularly to church each Sunday. More than that, she made certain we said our prayers each evening before we slipped into bed. It is her Bible you are reading, and I'm certain you can see that it has been well used.

"Your mother is not religious in the same way as was my mother. That is not to say she is not a believer. She is just not as intimate a believer as my mother was." Jaak paused a moment and then continued. "I wish you could have known your grandmother. But as you know, because of the age difference between your mother and me, my mother was gone before you came into our lives. You would have had a great deal in common with her, and she would have better understood your biblical adventure than Mamsi does. Each person must be what Providence is calling him to be, Meeta, and you must follow what He is telling you.

"For example, Oskar is following what Providence is telling him. His decision was to escape to Finland while there was still time to do so. I, on the other hand, have chosen to remain here and hope that when all the smoke of this war clears, we will once again have our independence.

"What makes one man decide one thing and another man decide the opposite? I have thought much about this. It seems to me we are guided by past decisions made—no matter how small. Small decisions grow to be big decisions, Meeta. They make us what we ultimately become. Oskar is a man of action. He wants to get things done. When Mamsi suspected my partners were cheating me, it was he who took her to Tallinn to see the Minister of Justice who in turn arranged for Peeter to come to us. When our country was invaded by Russia, he joined forces with Finland to fight the Russians and probably will do the same now that he is back in Finland.

"My life has been one of accepting a given situation and working through it, even if it meant starting over. Perhaps I'm an old fool, but I have adapted to building again and again when my businesses have failed. Perhaps I'm now too old to build again, but that's who I am, Meeta. And you must be who you are, regardless of what Mamsi thinks. We must be who Providence calls us to be. That's our responsibility. The results of that call are His responsibility. He has a purpose we may never understand, but we must follow the call."

Meeta always knew her father had a profound side. It was something she could sense, though they had never spoken on such a level as tonight. The "call" he had spoken about touched a chord.

Liina had once said that she felt the selling of religious books to be "a calling." Now Meeta pondered that call in relationship to herself. She had felt a call to study the Bible like never before. She would have expressed it differently than her father. She would have considered the "call" to be coming from the Holy Spirit. Father, however, identified it as Providence. What did it matter, the name. It was still a call, and her father's words encouraged her to continue doing just that.

She sat pensively looking at him as she contemplated and digested all he had said. Her response came softly, as if still walking through the words. "Yes... thank you for your insight and encouragement, Papsi." It was all she could manage to say. She saw the depth of her father's spirituality, yet it was not overt as she so often demonstrated. His gentleness touched her to the core of her being. She now understood better why each Sunday morning since she could remember, her father had always awoken the family by playing the hymn *"Now Thank We All Our God."* It was his response to the "call" to direct his family to the Providence about which he had just spoken.

A few days after this conversation it was reported that the Italian government had signed an armistice with the Allies. The Germans had lost the Battle of Salerno, and the Allies were advancing to Rome. On the Eastern Front, after defeating the German 6th army at Stalingrad, Russia amassed an enormous army. German commanders were perplexed by the huge number of Russian soldiers and by the quantity and superior quality of the new Russian weapons that appeared.

December 1943 saw the German army disorganized and retreating all along the Eastern Front with a massive Soviet army in relentless pursuit. It seemed only a matter of time until Estonia would once again be in jeopardy.

CHAPTER 16

War Work
Siberia 1943

The summer of 1943 found Ilse 30 kilometers away from Maiga working once again in the hayfields with 15 other people, some Estonians and some local Russians. Through the roof of the hut where she slept the sky could be seen which allowed mosquitoes inside. She pulled a blanket completely over her at night but became so hot that her body was bathed in sweat.

A rat was another unwanted night visitor. She complained to Aino, Alma and another Estonian, Maret, who shared the hut. "Confounded rat! It came right to my side. The stupid thing looked straight at me." The next day Ilse told her story to others in the camp, and a teenaged boy relayed how one night a rat took hold of his ear as he slept.

In the hayfields almost everyone became sick sooner or later. Changing weather conditions, insects, rodents, food shortage, and the constant pressure to produce the norm in their weakened condition took its toll on the strongest. As Ilse saw Estonians weakened and near death, she found herself praying, "Oh God, help our people."

In early August Jüri arrived from Maiga bringing food and horses for the workers. He brought news. "Yesterday at midnight four Estonians were called to the administrative office and told to pack all their things. They are being taken to Grishkin and from there by ship to an unknown location." Ilse and her fellow Estonians listened intently. "Who are they?"

"I don't know, but I also heard reports that from Makarov five other Estonians will be taken and from Berjosov two more families. It's rumored these people will be sent away in two trips."

News that some of their friends were to be sent away caused much anxiety. Relationships were all they had to cling to. They speculated as to who would be included and where they would be sent.

A few days later the command came that Ilse was to end work in the hayfield in three days. She was stunned. What did this mean? Was she going to be sent elsewhere? Why had not Alma and Ella also been told to end their work?

Ilse returned to her settlement village on Tuesday, August 17, and arrived at six o'clock in the evening. Her first concern was for her garden—her hope for provisions for the year. As she approached her plot, however, she saw the ground trampled and routed. Her wooden stake fence had not kept the village pigs out. Her eyes filled with tears and she began to sob. Slowly she walked to the hut she called home, but the door was locked. She used her key and stepped inside. Bed clothes were strewn on the floor. Her first thought was, Kaare and Karin have been taken away. My sweet little girl is gone! The thought of yet another loss overwhelmed her, and she cried out, "Oh, God, I'm alone. I've come home, but I don't have a home." She ran to her Jewish neighbor's house yearning for the presence of another human being. When she saw Rosa Gordin, she burst into tears.

Rosa told her that Kaare and little Karin had been moved two days earlier, but she did not know where they were. By nightfall Ilse forced herself to return to the empty cabin. She tried to sleep, but the bedbugs were intolerable. She took some boards from the cabin and placed them on the ground outside. The evening was cold and damp; heavy dew lay on the ground. She fetched bed clothes and covered herself, but bedbugs were in the boards on which she lay. She buried her face in her hands and mumbled through her tears, "God, oh God, is there no end to this suffering?"

Ilse's spirit was encouraged the next day when Alma and Ella came home. They worked together trying to kill the bedbugs by boiling water and scalding the cots and boards. Ilse took another look at her garden. She dug up the few potatoes that remained, but there were so few that they only covered the bottom of a basket. I have come to ruin, she thought. I will have no produce for winter.

Within three days Ilse was told that she along with other Estonians and some Russians were being mobilized for "war work." They would be leaving the following morning at 11 o'clock. Members of her cabin family were not among them. She was commanded to pack everything, since she would not be returning, and to take enough food with her for 10 days. She became melancholy and anxious. Where would she be taken? What would she be doing? What did "war work" mean? Why was she being separated from those to whom she had grown so close?

Sadly she went throughout the village to bid farewell to her fellow Estonians and friends. In preparation for her departure, friends gave her food to take along. She began packing but became nervous and started to sweat. The memory of the day of her departure from Estonia came vividly to mind, and she could not function. "Alma, please help me," she cried. "I can't even think of what or how to pack." Together they managed to pack two suitcases, one bundle and one shopping bag filled with necessities and food.

It was a tearful departure as Ilse headed toward the office where a wagon drawn by two horses awaited. Friends of those leaving gathered around and wept as they said good-bye.

The wagon traveled toward Tshainsk where the horses were given a rest, then on to Vensk where they spent the night sleeping on the floor of an old building. Early the next morning they were awakened by a soldier and were joined by more Estonians from different settlements. That night at 10 o'clock they arrived in Podgornia and were directed to a schoolhouse where they once again slept on the floor.

The following morning Endel Kalbus appeared and quickly approached Ilse. "I came to see if anyone I knew was among this group, and here I find you."

Ilse was surprised to meet Endel. When she was first deported to Siberia, they had also unexpectedly met during a similar rest stop. "Endel, what are you doing here?"

"I have been working in Podgornia at a children's shelter where mainly evacuees from Leningrad are located. But now I am being sent away, as you are, into the unknown. This is unnerving for me, as I'm sure it is for you. I've been fortunate during my stay here. At the shelter we've received European-style food—even candy."

"We've not been so fortunate," said Ilse, "but I realize I've been better off than many others in surrounding villages and cities. It remains to be seen what our new journey will bring."

Ilse informed him that she had received a letter from Peeter and that he had sent greetings. Endel expressed gladness that Peeter was alive and apparently well.

Soon the command was given that all packs were to be moved from the schoolhouse and carried to a barge in the harbor. The harbor was about one kilometer away, and the women struggled with their luggage. Once there it was determined they would not all fit on the barge, so they were commanded to take their things back to the schoolhouse.

They waited there until dark. Assuming they would remain in the schoolhouse for another night, everyone lay down on their packs to sleep. Then a new order came: "Take your things back to the shore." Once again they trudged to the Ob River where they finally boarded a barge.

The following morning the barge began its journey. Ilse's thoughts were again reminiscent of the barge trip that had brought her to Siberia two years earlier, except this time Endel sat across from her. His presence brought an element of comfort.

A day and a half later they arrived in Kolpashevo. The men were separated from the women and, it was rumored, would be taken to Novosibirsk. Endel promised he would write to her when he could. Ilse and 16 other women were taken to a new but tiny room on Obi Street where they spent the night. The room had bunk beds but was so little that one could barely move about in it.

They awoke early to register at the office by 7:00 a.m. and were sent to a new building. There they waited for nearly two hours until a woman supervisor arrived. She was a large Russian woman quite aware of her position. "Your workday will be from 8:00 a.m. to 5:00 p.m. with an hour for lunch. Your first duty will be to clean lumber and debris from the area surrounding this building."

At 1:00 p.m. the cafeteria opened, and they were given coupons with which they could get food. Unfortunately, the cafeteria was congested and the line so long that they were unable to finish their meal until 3:00 p.m. Ilse was pleased that the food was good—a creamed soup and meat with tomatoes, but because they were late returning to work, they were scolded by their supervisor.

The next day they pulled logs from the Ob River with ropes and fire hooks. Ilse worked with two other women and pulled 11 logs from the river. No one gave them instruction on how to do the work, so the women used their own ingenuity. They waded into the water and grabbed the logs with their fire hooks, floating them to shore. The challenge came later that day when Ilse and nine other women had to drag 12 heavy, water-soaked logs from the shore to a stockpile. The work required enormous amounts of strength and energy. To save the birch-bark shoes they wore, they worked in bare feet. That evening one of the women named Erika became sick with malaria.

The following day was cold and rainy. Once they climbed beside a boat to get shelter. Another time they scrambled up the bank and under the roof of a shed for protection. Erika had another malaria attack; Ilse also had a fever.

The two of them finally went to the shore office where it was warm. Elise Ebber, an Estonian who worked in the office because she was fluent in Russian, listened to their plight and took them to the Russian overseer who allowed Erika to rest. Ilse, however, was sent back to work.

By evening Erika could not walk and had to be taken by horseback to their tiny room. The room was so filled with luggage that there was barely a place to sit. Ilse gave Erika her bunk and then went with four other women to the director and explained their sleeping condition. The director gave the five of them permission to sleep on the office floor.

The next day Erika was taken to the clinic where she waited from 9:00 a.m. until 3:00 p.m. without medical assistance. While there she experienced another malaria attack but was ignored. Finally, she was returned to her living quarters without receiving medical aid.

Later she was told that the best time to come to the clinic was between 3:00 and 6:00 p.m., so Ilse and a fellow worker attempted to take her back that afternoon. They were wet and filthy from rolling logs. Their muddy pant legs were turned up and their feet were bare. Ilse wore her coat inside out because it was so tattered on the outside. Young boys who saw them walking yelled, "Look!" and doubled over with laughter. In the end no help was received at the clinic.

Two days later the women were commanded to pack all their things. They placed them on a horse-drawn wagon and walked seven kilometers to the village of Togor.

At Togor they learned their workday would be 12 hours per day seven days a week and they would have to fulfill a required amount of work each day—the norm. An advance of 30 rubles was given to each of them. They were promised two meals per day using cards that were issued. If they met the norm, they were to receive 9 to 12 rubles per day except Sunday because that day's labor went to support the State. They were told to begin work that evening.

The barrack where they were housed contained about 80 men, women and children all crammed together with no privacy. The large room was lined with two-tiered bunks the full length of the walls on both sides. In the middle of the room was an iron stove used for both heating and cooking. Luggage was stashed under and on the bunks, on the floor and in every nook. The overseer made no apology but pointed to a corner of the room. "That corner has been emptied for you. I will be held responsible for any thievery." Ilse doubted the credibility of that promise. Theft was a way of life in Siberia.

That night Ilse was teamed with five other women and sent to load boards onto a wagon at a lumber factory. After about two hours of this labor they were taken to another location where the wagons were unloaded and the boards placed on a trough that led down to a barge. As they worked it became quite dark. Ilse spoke to Elise Ebber who had been transferred with her to Togor. "I am fearful working in this darkness. I cannot always see another worker, and I fear being hit or hitting someone else with these boards."

"I feel the same, Ilse. Why don't we speak as we work and identify what we are doing so those around us will be aware?" Elise and Ilse suggested this to the other workers. All agreed and each tried to comply.

At three o'clock in the morning the supervisor transferred Ilse to the hold of the barge where the boards arrived down the trough. It was her job to take the boards from the trough and pile them in the cargo compartment preparatory to their being shipped via the Ob River to their intended destination. Each time a worker above threw a board down the trough he or she would shout, "Watch out!" so those below would not get hit on the head. With her in the hold were two Volga German women who said they had worked there for two years. Ilse found them to be congenial and hard working. She also felt fortunate to be in the hold since it had become quite cold outside. Another benefit was that electric light was provided so they could keep a written record of the number of boards that were being loaded.

At 4:00 a.m., however, the electricity was turned off. This provided workers with what was known as the "smoking break" when they could rest or take time for a smoke. The break was intended for 15 minutes but extended until dawn when enough natural light came from the hatch and enabled them to see. Ilse used this break to sleep until work commenced gain. At that time of year it could be a full hour or more.

Shortly before 6:00 a.m. the factory whistle blew its first blast. The whistle blew three times. At the end of the third blast the shift ended, and the next shift had to be immediately ready to begin. Members of the next shift told Ilse they had not been able to sleep in the barrack because of the bed bugs and the noise of the children. Ilse, however, was so tired that when she arrived, she fell into a sound sleep.

Her work schedule was from 6:00 p.m. to 6:00 a.m. Monday through Saturday. On Sundays it began at 12 noon and continued until midnight. The first Sunday, with only six hours to sleep and eat, she worked with Elise, two Russian women and an old Russian man named Saljev who tried to make himself appear important. He cursed the women and made demeaning comments about them being lazy despite the fact that they were working continuously. Occasionally the women would retort, but generally they tried to ignore him.

That week the weather became very cold, and the workers were told that boots would arrive for them in two or three days. Inadequate footwear, long shifts, and lack of sleep caused many to become ill with fevers.

The next Sunday Ilse found herself working with Saljev again. Their job was to pull logs out of the Ob River and up onto the shore. Once more Saljev was commanding the women: "Come here . . . Go there . . . Roll that log . . . Why are you so slow?" At one point Saljev told the women to leave three fire hooks under a log, but Ilse ignored him and retrieved hers. These were necessary instruments required in order to maneuver the logs, and Ilse threatened to complain to the supervisor that he was being irresponsible and wasteful.

Later the members of Ilse's shift struggled long and hard with a log of tremendous size. They finally managed to get one end of it onto the bank of the river, but it was diagonal to the shore. Ilse called out, "Bring it parallel with the bank!" But Saljev immediately shouted, "That's not necessary." Upon his command the others let go of the log. It rolled back into the water and drifted into the river. Ilse was tired, frustrated and furious. She stepped from her normal compliant nature and screamed, "You devil! When are you going to learn to keep your mouth shut?" Two Russian women on the team also began chastising him.

Ret, another man working with them, was already back in the water. "Complaining isn't going to get this log back to shore." Saljev joined Ret, and soon they were all once again struggling with the behemoth. They wrestled the log for nearly an hour before getting it to the shore and finally up on the bank. The rest of the day Saljev worked without a murmur. Once in a while Ilse caught him shyly looking at her and she thought, Ah, Saljev has finally gained some respect for this stupid woman. She received additional satisfaction when Saljev confessed to the supervisor that they had not met their norm because he had caused a delay in their work.

The following day six more Estonians were added to their already crowded barrack. The latrine for the barrack consisted of only a hole. Feces and urine covered the floor and walls. Their only relief from filth was a sauna that was open every other day. Entrance cost each of them 1 ruble, but it was their only luxury. Unfortunately, when the line was long, their tight work schedule did not allow them time to enjoy this pleasure.

Because the weary workers were unable to produce the norm, their work day was increased to 14 hours instead of 12. Ilse became so tired she could not remember things told to her.

By mid-September the promised boots had not yet arrived, and Ilse's birch-bark shoes were disintegrating. She requested and received from the director some birch bark and made five pairs. She kept one for herself and gave the other four to those with whom she worked.

More people were becoming ill, and food and conditions in the cafeteria had waned. Sometimes for a meal they only received one-half liter of soup and cranberries without any bread. There were no spoons and only a few chairs and benches. Each person was required to bring his or her own spoon, and many had to eat standing. Young boys routinely pulled seats for themselves from beneath people who were eating.

Many accidents occurred at the lumber factory, but there was no first aid. One night a doctor, leaving the hospital for the day, became angry and refused to help a man whose hand had gotten caught in a machine because he appeared shortly after 8:00 p.m. when the facility closed. As Ilse witnessed the man searching for help, resentful thoughts surged through her mind. She looked at a faded picture of Lenin that hung on the factory wall and thought: This is where his philosophy has led. How is his philosophy helping the workers? Where is the equality he expounded?

In the distance a ravaged church tower could be seen from the factory window. Ilse had never been openly spiritual, but suddenly she thought, Things will not get better until the cross in that steeple shines again.

One night Ilse, Elise and three others were loading logs onto trains. It was a very cold, windy night, and it began to rain. The next train had not yet arrived, but the logs were in a row ready to be loaded. Ilse sat on the logs and within a second fell asleep. The train did not come for half an hour. However, as it approached, Elise discovered Ilse and shook her. "Ilse, Ilse, wake up! You're freezing to death!" Ilse jumped up immediately realizing the truthfulness of Elise's words.

The following day five pairs of boots arrived. Ilse received hers that evening and was ecstatic. They were made from leather and very large, like slippers without lining. But they were boots, and she was grateful to have them.

Finding their own food became a necessity since the cafeteria was now only providing watery soup and sometimes nothing. Occasionally Ilse and her roommates were able to purchase horse meat, a cow's head or stomach and tripe. These they cooked on the stove in the barrack.

By October 1 the entire day shift refused to go to work since there was no food. When the director heard of the refusal to work, he came to the barrack and shouted, "This is insubordination. It's rebellion!" They responded, "We don't have food. We cannot work without food." The workers held their ground, and finally the director relented and gave permission for them to go to Kolpashevo to buy bread and other food. The entire group went, made their purchases and returned to Togor that evening. But Ilse and Elise stayed in Kolpashevo overnight, though it would mean the loss of a day's wage. The commandant knew these women as good workers and allowed them to sleep in his office. They bought 11 cows' feet, two-and-one-half cows' heads, cabbage and pumpkins. The commandant gave them permission to use a horse to carry their items back to Togor the next day. However, he stipulated that they would have to return the horse that same day and then walk the seven kilometers back to Togor.

Five days later Elise and Ilse returned to Kolpashevo and asked the commandant if they might be released from Togor. He promised to give them an answer by that night. That evening, after checking the records, the commandant determined that those who had been transferred to Togor had worked an appropriate amount of time and could return to Kolpashevo. They received his signed permission papers and rejoiced. "We are finally released out of hell."

By mid-October Ilse and Elise were given an apartment with another Estonian, Jefimia, and two Lithuanians, Lilleht and Simanovits. Later two others were added: Lisa, a Romanian woman, and another Lithuanian who quickly acquired the nickname of Pikk[27] because she was so tall.

Their apartment was located beside a room that housed men. Next to that were the shoe repair shop and another room for men. Across the hall were the seamstress' workroom and the commandant's office. The seamstress generally repaired the workers' worn out clothes with patches.

Their apartment door did not have a lock, so they agreed to always have one person remain in the room as a guard. Fortunately, the room had a stove on which they could cook. Mattresses and sheets had been promised them, but after several days they still had not arrived. Ilse voiced her frustration to Lisa. "This nation is built on promises." Ten more days passed before each received only one sheet, one pillowcase and one towel. In lieu of mattresses they bunched their clothes and slept on them.

Ilse, Jefimia and Pikk were given the job of storing food in preparation for winter. They cleaned turnips, beets, carrots and cabbage. Then they bagged potatoes and brought them and containers of pickled mushrooms, onions and beets into a cellar they had previously dug. Their supervisor, Boris, warned them not to eat any of the food. They, however, could not resist. Once, just as they were popping a divided carrot into their mouths, Boris returned and caught them. He soundly scolded them all. His surprise arrival so startled Ilse that she misplaced the knife she had used to cut the carrot. It was her personal knife, and the loss was deeply felt. She voiced her frustration to her fellow workers. "There is nowhere that I can get another one." Though she searched diligently, the knife was gone.

By the end of October ice began forming on the Ob River, and snow was on the ground. Ilse was given the job of sawing and chopping wood to feed the main heating system in the boiler plant. It contained an oven that would accommodate trees as large as three meters in length. She worked outside with another partner, often a Russian man, using a two-man saw, but the saws were dull which made the work strenuous. All of the axes were loose, and ax heads would often fly off. So, if a log needed splitting, they normally used a wedge and a sledge hammer.

Having jobs provided Ilse and her roommates the right to purchase cards for obtaining bread, but lines were long. Sometimes, after standing in line for an hour, the bread supply would be gone. One day when Pikk returned home from work she told Ilse that the bread line was short and it would be a good time to go.

Ilse took the cards of Lisa and Pikk hoping to get all three of them their allotted bread before going to work. However, when she arrived the store was crowded with people. She appealed to the other women by saying she had to get to work and asked if they would allow her to get to the front of the line. Her request inflamed the women, and they tore at the collar and sleeves of her already tattered coat. She was forced to wait for two hours before getting the bread. The woman handing it out had observed her trying to get nearer the front when she arrived and angrily tossed the bread across the counter at her. Ilse did not have a shopping bag. In the process of trying to quickly gather the bread she dropped one of her gloves—a cherished commodity in the cold climate. The store was so packed with people that she could not bend down to get it. Fortunately, a young boy picked it up and handed it to her. She was so traumatized by the whole encounter that her entire body shook as she left the store. She was late to work but gladly took the scolding since they would at least have bread to eat that day.

Lice were a continual problem since Pikk did not wash her clothes or go to the sauna. Soon all those sharing the room had acquired her lice. To make matters worse, rats were in the room. Lisa had some bread in a cloth bag but came home to find the bag eaten through and the bread devoured. Ilse hid some flour under her pillow but a rat found that, too.

The second week of November, Ilse was delighted to purchase 700 grams of salt, five boxes of matches, 500 grams of sugar, a bar of soap and one kilogram of salt fish from one store. Rejoicing, she came home and told Elise, "I am in seventh heaven tonight." All of those items were scarce commodities, and to find them in one location at one time was tantamount to a miracle. Normally the administrative staff took the best of the products and doled out what remained to the workers under them. Pikk found a way to tap into their wealth, however. She practiced and believed in fortune telling with cards and found that the Russians were willing to give products and even money in return for card reading, so Pikk always seemed to have rubles.

Ilse made only 70 rubles during the month of October. Since she had to pay for her meals in the cafeteria and purchase bread cards in order to get bread, the money did not go far. Except for Pikk, her roommates were all nearly bankrupt by mid-November, so Ilse turned to Pikk. It bothered Ilse terribly to have to borrow money, but she explained her need to Pikk. "I fear I'll not be able to saw enough square meters to reach the norm if I don't get sufficient food. I become so weak I can't do the heavy labor. I'll repay you when I get paid for November."

Ilse wondered if she would be able to repay Pikk. Though she didn't formally pray about it, she thought to herself, With God's help, I will get through this financial emergency. The next day at the local bazaar she was able to sell some items that she still had from Estonia for 100 rubles. Pikk was repaid, and Ilse's concern was relieved.

On November 20 Ilse wrote in her diary: "Today Vello is two-and-one-half years old. It has been nearly that long since I have held him. When will he ever learn to know his parents?"

That night Ilse dreamed of her girlhood home on the bank of the Sauga

River. She walked along its shore and saw fishermen hanging their nets to dry on the opposite side of the river. How peaceful and beautiful was the scene. Then she heard a familiar voice and turned to see her brother Oskar and Mamsi by the corner of the fence in front of their home. She wanted to run to them and embrace them, but the dream ended and they were again lost to her.

Early in December Ilse and her work partner received a new two-man saw. "It cuts like we're sawing into soap," said Ilse. The two of them found much joy in their work that day.

That evening, when Ilse returned to her room, she found that the rat had taken her only bar of soap. Next she discovered her hoard of turnips had completely disappeared. Since her supervisor had loaned her a lock for the room, she knew that a thief was living among them.

The second week of December the administrative office brought them wool socks, quilted soft slippers and gloves, but no food was given at the cafeteria. Ilse, Pikk, Lisa and Lilleht went to the people in charge of the cafeteria and asked if they could be given some food. They were given 12 servings of a thick cabbage porridge that they divided between them. The next day, however, the cafeteria had no food to give. Two days later Ilse and Jefimia walked through all the stores in town and found no bread. The following day Jefimia's face began to swell, and Ilse's stomach was hurting so badly she told Jefimia, "I would eat my hat if it were digestible."

Ilse and her work partner were too weak to saw enough wood. The saws were dull again and in their weakened condition they could not reach the norm. Their supervisor was not sympathetic and told them they must work an extra shift to make up for the lack. The only good news for Ilse was the arrival of a letter from her husband. She joyously announced it to her roommates. "This means Peko is still alive!" The letter was dated August 9, 1943, and was received December 15.

Peko's letter bemoaned that he had not received a letter from her since December 1942. "I worry about you too much. . . . Please make every effort so I can soon receive some news from you." He continued by reassuring her that he is alive and healthy and receives 800 grams of bread per day. His letter appealed for Ilse to "at least send a letter once a month," and closed with "I send you a kiss, Peko."

By the third week of December Ilse's eyesight became blurred and her hands and feet were shaking. It was very cold; when she went to work she had to wear three sweaters, four pairs of pants and two coats—a thin autumn coat and her ragged leather coat over that. Into her tattered socks she put lambs' wool. Because the saws were dull they had to cut wood with the loose axes, but this lessened the quantity of logs they could provide. Due to the lack of wood, the cafeteria was unheated and people waited for food fully clothed with their gloves on.

Three days before Christmas Ilse was able to purchase potatoes, ginger cookies, bread, salt, matches and seven *pirukad*. She ate three *pirukad*, saved one for Christmas, and gave one each to Lilleht, Lisa and Jefimia.

For Christmas Eve dinner Ilse ate some bread, the last of her *pirukad*, six ginger cookies and a cherished jar of pears she had saved from the settlement at Maiga. To Ilse it was a feast. There was no Christmas feeling in the surroundings, but she hummed *"Silent Night"* and went to sleep.

Christmas Day dawned like any other, and she was back at work. That night before leaving her shift she found Pikk weeping in the boiler room. "Pikk, whatever is the matter?" Pikk's tall frame was bent, and her hands covered her face as Ilse approached. "This is such a miserable existence, Ilse. There is nothing to look forward to. Even Christmas is just another day of labor. We're caught in the middle of a crazy quest for power. What is our purpose but to be slaves?" Ilse could only listen. She had thought some of these very things. Her presence was the only solace she had to give her friend.

CHAPTER 17

"We Must Escape"
Estonia/Germany 1944

The war front began approaching the Estonian borders by January 1944. Narva, Estonia's most northeastern city, was almost entirely evacuated.

"On February 1 Hjalmar Mäe, head of the Estonian administration . . . called up all men born between 1904 and 1923 for military service . . . this mobilization succeeded beyond all expectations and totaled about 38,000 men. The decisive factor seems to have been a desire to stave off Soviet occupation of Estonia until the capitulation of Nazi Germany to the allies, thus keeping open Estonia's options for the future."[28] This brought the total number of Estonian military men within their country to between 50,000 to 60,000. Though poorly equipped, they were able to hold the Soviet advance "roughly along the Narva River in the north and near Pskov in the south."[29]

Jaak remained hopeful that Estonia would have its independence returned to it as the war progressed. He was encouraged by the success the Estonians had in repulsing the Soviet advance in Narva, and things continued with guarded normalcy as spring began to awaken new life in the city of Pärnu. Ladies paid by the city administration were once more sweeping the streets each morning, followed by water trucks that wet down the streets. This was customary from spring until fall.

The air was sweet as Jaak entered his beloved factory with Amalie. She was not in a good mood that morning because Jaak had misplaced some receipts from the previous day, and Amalie needed them to balance her accounting books.

"Jaak, try to retrace your steps from yesterday."

"Amalie, I retraced my steps yesterday before I came home. I cannot find those receipts."

"Well, let's retrace your steps together."

Jaak obediently walked with Amalie from the entrance to his office. He showed her where he had laid his attaché case the previous day after returning from a business trip in Tallinn and demonstrated how he had taken out his files and where he had set them. Together they sorted through his desk as he had done the night before, but the receipts were not found. "We will just have to use approximations, Amalie. I don't know where else to look."

"How can we use approximations?" retorted Amalie. My books will not be accurate. Why can't you be more careful with accounting items like Oskar was? You must be more alert to the business end of this factory. You are only interested in production. That's how we got into trouble in the past. You always let your partners handle the finances. Now, when I am trying to be accurate, you are not cooperating."

"I will telephone each supplier and buyer I dealt with yesterday and ask them for the amounts. Then I'll have them mail me duplicate copies."

"That's a lot of wasted time and effort, not to mention the cost of all those long distance phone calls. Why can't you just be more careful and put receipts immediately into a file? Peeter always did that."

Normally a reserved and controlled man, Jaak finally pounded his fist on the desk and shouted, "Keep quiet!" Amalie stared at him in complete silence as Jaak's face returned from a glare to his usual tranquil composure. His voice softened, but his eyes were firmly riveted to hers as he continued. "I told you, I will call each buyer and supplier with whom I dealt yesterday and will get duplicate copies so your records will be accurate." Jaak paused as he studied Amalie's stunned expression. "Now let us get to the work at hand today, Amalie."

That evening found Meeta at home alone with Vello as her parents worked late into the night. She enjoyed these quiet times with Vello playing with his toy crocodile and horse and the two-stringed violin that Jaak had made for his grandson. Sergeant Bublitz had put a cigar box under it so it would have some resonance. Vello enjoyed playing it just like his "Apa."

After Vello had been put to sleep, Meeta seated herself at her beloved piano and began playing. It was a lovely spring evening, and the living room window was open. As she played *"Wien, mein Sinn"*[30] waltz by Johann Strauss II, she became aware of the clicking footsteps of soldiers walking. German soldiers had cleats on the heels of their boots that tapped sharply as they walked. She heard the sound pause for a moment and then resume again. The clicking became louder until she heard the gate of the fence surrounding their apartment home open. She stopped playing and walked to the window. Beneath it stood two German soldiers. One of them spoke. *"Sind Sie ein Wiener?"*[31]

"No, I just have a love for Strauss waltzes," she responded in German.

"I am Heinrich Felthagen; I am from Vienna. Your music makes me quite homesick. I hadn't realized how very much until I heard you playing as we walked by the high school across the street. The music compelled me to see who was playing. You play beautifully. You must have had formal training."

"Yes, private lessons as a child and completed my studies at the Tallinn Conservatory."

"If you don't mind, would you please play a bit more while we listen outside your window?"

While they were in conversation, Jaak and Amalie came home. When they learned of what had drawn the two soldiers to their home, they invited them in. Jaak got his violin and he and Meeta played a number of pieces for the soldiers. After that occasion Heinrich often came to their home in the evening to enjoy the feel of a family and the music which both Jaak and Meeta loved to share together. It was a joyous reminder to them of the many informal concerts their friends and family had indulged in at their home by the Sauga River when their country was free.

As the summer progressed, it became increasingly apparent that the Russians would return. The Soviets took control of the city of Narva on July 26 and were in Võru in the south by August 13. Tartu fell in late August, and the Russians were on the move toward Tallinn. Uncertainty was everywhere. People agonized over whether to remain or to flee the country.

About this time news arrived from Oskar that things were not going well in Finland where they had fled. A son named Heikki Ivar had been born to Oskar and Ave in January of that year, and Oskar expressed concern for his little family and his desire to go to the neutral country of Sweden.

Meeta sat on the Pärnu beach in early September contemplating her country's future and could feel the vibrations from the Russian military beneath her body. Scanning the Baltic Sea which looked so placid, her mind was anything but that. The nearness of the Russian army brought thoughts of the deportation of her sister and Peeter. If we remain here, she thought, we will be next. We must prepare for escape.

It was difficult for Meeta and Amalie to convince Jaak that they must escape. It would mean leaving behind all that he had ever labored to accomplish. His longing was to die in his homeland, but eventually the reality of what would lie ahead if they remained won the day. The family began making serious decisions. Meeta first made arrangements for passage to Germany on a German ship located in the Pärnu harbor. Next they began the arduous task of packing, which took them a week. Heinrich offered to provide a military truck and take their belongings to the harbor.

On Sunday, September 14, Heinrich arrived and, accompanied by Meeta, took two large trunks and some suitcases and put them into the bottom of the designated ship preparatory to its departure early the following day. That evening Meeta bought a pail of salted pork from a neighbor to take with them for food. Heinrich stayed with the family that night in order to take them to the harbor the next morning.

That night Meeta slept on the large couch that the family had retrieved from Ilse's apartment after she and Peeter had been deported. Here I lie, she thought, on the very couch on which Ilse sat the day of her deportation. Tonight I know where I am sleeping, but tomorrow is unknown. Where will life take us? Will we ever see our homeland again? And my beloved piano . . . will I ever have another? She shuddered at the thought of leaving everything behind that was familiar, everything that had meaning, possibly forever.

Arriving at the port early the next morning, they connected with nine other friends who were planning to leave on the same ship. However, as they approached the entrance an official greeted them saying, "No one is permitted on this ship. Nobody!" One of their number, Helga Paimre, linked hands with her three little girls and pushed right past the official and onto the ship. Immediately another police prefect arrived and said in a stern voice, "Did you hear the command? No one can come aboard this ship!" No attempt was made to retrieve Helga, but the nine remaining were stopped.

They soon discovered they were not permitted to board the ship because Russian defectors who had fought for the German army were given first preference for passage to Germany. What's more, they were not allowed to regain possession of their things because their luggage was in the bottom of the ship underneath the soldiers' baggage.

The little band watched as the ship pulled away from shore with most of their earthly goods. They were uncertain as to what to do next. Only one German merchant ship remained in the harbor, so Meeta went to the captain and asked if he would consider taking people aboard.

"How many of you are there?" he asked in a courteous manner that encouraged Meeta.

"There are four of us in my family—three adults and one three-year-old boy. But there are five more that were also prevented from leaving on the last ship. We all had placed our luggage aboard and have only what we are holding in our hands."

"We can accommodate you folk," he said warmly. "The ship will leave at one o'clock this afternoon."

The little group returned to their respective homes and waited until noon. Heinrich waited with the Kollist family, and Tasja also came to accompany them to the harbor. At noon they left the apartment and locked the door behind them. The finality of the sound of the key locking that door remained indelibly in Meeta's mind.

Heinrich and Tasja bade the little family farewell at the harbor, and Tasja handed Meeta a paper bag containing soil from their homeland as a souvenir.

Once aboard the ship, however, Meeta focused attention on her father. As the bow of the ship pulled out of the harbor, it faced the Sauga River beside which her father's factory stood. He appeared statuesque as he looked down that river in the direction of his life's work. In one hand was his cherished violin and in the other his cane. Leaning his cane against the side of the deck, he reached into his pocket and pulled from it the keys to the factory. Without a word or show of animosity he gently tossed them into the water. Meeta could not take her eyes from his face. A passage from the Bible came clearly to her mind:

> The Lord gave and the Lord has taken away;
> Blessed be the name of the Lord."[32]

As the ship continued toward the sea, it passed the beach where she, friends and family members had spent so many enjoyable days. Usually at this time of year the beach would have been crowded, but today not one person was to be seen.

The ship passed between the stone jetties and out into the Baltic Sea. The day was idyllic and the sea calm. How, thought Meeta, could war be raging on such a beautiful day? Why can't men be content with what they have?

She once again looked at her father. Today, in the light of the afternoon sun he looked so old. Life had been so busy, so frantic some days that she had not truly realized how he had aged. Now she looked at him with new eyes and a sad heart. He was leaving all he had ever known. All he had labored and fought to save, gone in one day. Ah, yes, she thought, it's difficult for Mamsi also, but she is 20 years younger and in good health. Papsi has recently developed a problem with frequent urination, and there has not been time enough to get a diagnosis. Where will we find medical help now that we have been launched into the unknown?

The day progressed uneventfully on a calm sea. The warmth of the sun and the gentle sea breeze made this seem a pleasurable excursion, yet Meeta knew back in her homeland men were dying and others were being maimed for life at that very moment. How senseless it all seemed.

As evening drew near all those aboard ship were given oil cloths to wrap beneath and over them to protect against the chill and dampness of night as they slept on deck. The next day their ship arrived at Liepaja, Latvia, where it anchored for a few hours until an announcement was made. "All passengers must leave this ship immediately. A pilot ship will take you to a steamship from which you will continue your journey."

Tugboats carried the passengers to a large German transport ship. Rope ladders hung from its sides, and Meeta and her family saw passengers climbing the ladders as they left the tugboats. Amalie, Meeta and Jaak looked at each other dubiously. There was no time to dialog how they were to manage a swaying rope ladder. As soon as the tugboat approached, German sailors helped each passenger onto the ladder without questioning whether they felt they could handle the climb. One of the sailors grabbed Vello and carried him up to the ship.

Once aboard, the Kollist family realized that the ship had four levels below the main deck. Each served a different national group. The Ukranians and Poles were placed on the lowest level, while Estonians were privileged to be on the first. This made Meeta realize how deeply Adolph Hitler's philosophy of the superiority of the Aryan race had impacted the German people.

The German transport ship traveled for two days and on the morning of the third day arrived at Gotenhafen (Gdynia) Germany. The Kollist family and their friends stood at the railing as the ship entered the harbor. For the first time they observed the destructive results of war. Huge storehouses by the wharves had been bombed, and gaping holes stared at them from the sides of buildings. Deep depressions were also seen in the streets about them.

As the Estonians mingled together at the harbor, they were delighted to see Helga Paimre and her three daughters, who had gone before them on another merchant ship. Meeta was the first to greet her. "Helga, it is good to see that you have made it safely here and can continue the journey with us."

Helga rolled her eyes as she spoke. "I have never been so frightened in all of my life, Meeta."

"Whatever do you mean, Helga?"

"Our ship was fired upon by Russian planes! I thought for certain we would all be killed. My three little girls were terrified." Helga watched Meeta's eyes grow wide as she listened to the story. After giving additional details regarding their adventure, Helga asked, "How was your trip, Meeta?"

"Thankfully peaceful. I feel fortunate now that we did not get on the ship with you. It's frightening enough to see the destruction all about us here in Gotenhafen."

They chatted together until Mr. Orgussar, the police prefect of Pärnu and the leader of their group of 13, led them to the railroad station where they left their baggage. Mr. Orgussar's plan was to continue on to Dingolfing, Bavaria, by train the next morning. A German friend of his had invited him to Dingolfing where the entire group would remain at his home until they could be permanently relocated.

The entourage spent the evening in a quaint but friendly inn but arose early, anxious to travel with the utmost speed toward southwestern Germany. Their desire was to withdraw from the Eastern Front as far as possible and to get as close as they could to the Swiss border.

The train journeyed toward Munich, but in the Friedrichstrasse Station in Berlin they had to change trains. The station was large and was connected by an internal subway system. Refugees filled the station and subway.

Because Jaak was older than the other travelers and Vello was only three, it was hard for the Kollists to keep pace with the rest of their group, and they usually trailed behind. Amalie tried to be the intermediary between her family and the others. Their walking order was Amalie followed by Meeta then Jaak and Vello. Amalie and Meeta both carried suitcases; Jaak carried his violin and cane. No one had a free hand to grasp little Vello so he trailed behind on his own, his little legs moving twice the speed of his adult leaders to keep pace.

In this fashion they proceeded to the underground subway that would take them to the platform from which they would catch the next train to Munich. Amalie was the first to step aboard the car, but after a few moments' wait she exited to motion for the rest of her little brood to hurry. Unfortunately, just as they arrived, the doors of the subway car closed. Amalie had been carrying a briefcase containing German money which had been given to her three years before by Peeter in anticipation of one day escaping. She had left the briefcase on the floor inside the subway car when she exited, and now their only money was aboard the departing train. Meeta heard her mother wail, "My briefcase is aboard the train!" Fortunately, a passenger had apparently witnessed Amalie's predicament and pushed the doors open just enough to enable him to throw it out in their direction. The briefcase whirled across the platform skidding along the cement floor where Amalie was able to retrieve it. Amalie held her hand to her chest and took a deep breath as she looked toward Meeta. No word was spoken, but Meeta felt that God had intervened in their dilemma and mentally gave thanks.

They took the next subway train and were able to reunite with the rest of their group who waited until their arrival. But their wait caused them to miss the train they had planned to take, and many hours passed before another train traveling toward Munich arrived. Its aisles and even the bathrooms were filled with people. When someone needed to use the restroom, the occupants had to squeeze out for a few minutes into the crowded aisle. That maneuver was more difficult because it was night, and all the lights of the train were turned off for fear of detection by Allied airplanes.

The train clicked and clattered eerily down the tracks as those aboard listened for any unwanted sounds of danger. Periodically Meeta prayed silently for protection. She felt fortunate that some man had taken pity upon her father and had relinquished his seat for him. She and her mother were not as fortunate, however, their feet ached and their legs became swollen as they stood tightly packed together. Some men lifted Vello into the baggage netting overhead where he slept quietly high above the cramped conditions below.

Upon arrival at the small town of Dingolfing, Mr. Orgussar searched for the friend that had invited him and his group to their home, but he could not be found. In fact, no one in the town had ever heard of him. Not knowing what else to do, Mr. Orgussar led them to a *Gasthaus* where everyone transferring from one town to another was required by law to register. They were given permission to occupy the second floor ballroom of an inn. Straw was placed on the floor for sleeping, and there they spent the night wondering what the morrow would bring.

CHAPTER 18

Hunger Rages
Siberia 1944

The food situation in Kolpashevo reached a critical point in January of 1944. Only heavily salted, watery soup was being served in the cafeteria. Ilse forced herself to eat it but finally could not help but release her frustration.

"I cannot eat this soup, Jefimia. It is so salty. There is no substance to it—just salted tomatoes. I cannot drink enough water to neutralize it. I eat it as I would take a doctor's medicine, but my stomach is hurting and the salt affects my heart." She stopped eating and took a long look at her friend. "Jefimia, your face is swollen."

Jefimia ran her hands over her face. "I could sense that my eyes were swollen but thought it was due to lack of sleep. Now I can feel that my cheeks are also swollen."

"This food is poisoning us, Jefimia. We simply must get some decent food."

Jefimia pushed herself away from the table and said, "Let's try the stores again."

"We are so weak, and the lines are so long," Ilse sighed. "And by the time we reach the front, so often there is nothing left to buy."

Jefimia's eyes rolled as she said, "That's true. The administrators and local Russians get all their food outside the line. We receive only what's left over." She paused and then changed to a more positive tone. "But maybe today we'll be lucky. Let's try."

The two of them waited in line through sheer determination for two hours but were only able to buy some large fish. "More salt," sighed Ilse. "I don't mean to be unthankful, Jefimia. At least we've found some solid food, but this salt content is killing us."

By the second week of January Jefimia's legs and lower body were swollen. Ilse's legs also were swelling, and her shins were red and sore. Ilse took note as she went to the cafeteria that the children who were attending school had soup with barley and *pirukad* fried in butter, well-seasoned meat and vegetables cooked in a thick sauce. But what she received in line was the same soup—salted tomatoes in water. Her sense of justice was stirred. She rallied Jefimia, Lisa and Pikk to go with her to speak with Galdilini, the cafeteria supervisor, about their lack of food.

Galdilini was a large and rather imposing man, which made him unapproachable. The foursome elected Pikk, who was not easily intimidated, to be the spokesperson for the group. Pikk wasted no time in getting to the point as they met him in the cafeteria. "We are in despair. Unless we get some solid food, we will simply collapse. If you cannot give us food in the cafeteria, could you please give us some meat and vegetables? We will cook for ourselves."

Galdilini's brow creased, and his eyes narrowed as he took a long look at each one of them. His size and look diminished the stature of each of the complainers with the exception of Pikk. Her tall frame stood like a ramrod looking him straight in the eye. His response was firm. "The cafeteria receives orders as to what they can distribute and to whom they can distribute it. What you receive is what we can give." Without another word he turned his back toward them and walked away.

Disheartened and discouraged, the little group retreated to the boiler room where they cried and complained among themselves about such injustice. Mehaanik, Ilse's work supervisor, was in the boiler room and appeared embarrassed as he heard their story. Ilse noticed this and addressed him. "Back home in Estonia the workers have the same rights as the capitalists and can purchase the same items if they have the money. But here workers are treated like dogs."

Mehaanik rose from his seat and left without saying a word. But they later learned he had gone to talk with the superiors. At 4:00 p.m. that afternoon Galdilini came to tell them that they would be given the ears and lower legs of animals such as cows and lambs that they could cook for themselves. The legs consisted of the shank attached to the hoof. Mehaanik also arranged for each of them to receive a five ruble per month raise in pay. That night they cleaned the hair from lamb legs and ears and cooked them with some beets that Pikk had in store.

Another problem they faced as a group was who to trust. Lisa was able to purchase 35 *pirukad* which they put in tins so the rats could not eat them. The tins were placed in a bag and put on a shelf in their apartment. The next morning when Lisa and Ilse went to get some to eat, only seven remained. The bag had been opened and retied.

A week later they once again had to beg the cafeteria for more legs and ears. They were told "maybe tomorrow." As they left, Lisa retorted privately to Ilse. "One very common word in Russian is 'tomorrow.' Using that word one can quickly get rid of the questioner."

Fortunately, Ilse sold a finely made nightgown, which still remained of the clothes brought with her from Estonia, to a local Russian woman whom she had solicited in town. In payment she was to receive bread and hulled barley totaling 250 rubles. The woman agreed to provide the products in installments so the rats would not eat the supply. Ilse was quite pleased with this arrangement and gave her the name White Dame because she was a woman of some prominence and had appeared unexpectedly like an angel sent from heaven.

Early in February their eight-hour work day was increased to 10. They were told they would have to work these hours until the war ended. They would no longer have Sundays off, and there would be no increase in pay despite the longer hours. Mehaanik was considerate of them, however, and told them he would only require them to work one-half hour longer than their normal shift but forbade them to tell anyone that he was permitting them to leave early.

One evening Ilse came to her apartment eager to eat her last cow's hoof. She went to the cellar where she had hidden it and found that it was missing. When she came to her room, Lilleht had exactly the same kind of hoof and a section of leg ready to prepare. Ilse asked her, "Isn't that hoof mine?"

Lilleht responded with an abrupt, "No."

Ilse struggled to keep her voice even. "Amazing, it looks exactly like mine."

Lilleht did not acknowledge the comment but said she needed to relieve herself and left the room.

Jefimia had observed the interaction. When Lilleht left the room, she suggested they examine the hoof and the leg bone to see if they matched, since they were each given the entire lower leg intact. When they tried to match the joint with the hoof, it did not fit together. When Lilleht returned to the room, Ilse suggested in as polite a tone as she could muster, "Perhaps you somehow mixed my hoof with yours because it doesn't look like your hoof matches the leg joint."

Lilleht threw a disgusted look toward Ilse and said sharply, "If you think the hoof is yours, then take it." Ilse did take it and prepared it for herself, but there was a chill in the atmosphere of the room as she did.

On Sunday, February 6, news reached Kolpashevo that "the Russians were now approaching Narva," the northeastern most city of Estonia. Ilse shuddered to think that the Russians were nearing her homeland once again. She had no idea what had happened or what might happen to her family. Many questions arose in her mind. Were they still living in Estonia? Were they still alive? Would the Russians once again deport Estonians? Her diary entry that day ended with a prayer: "God save our land and our people who yet may be alive."

The cold Siberian weather peaked during February, and there was not enough wood to keep the cafeteria or their apartment heated. Bread was lacking throughout the whole city of Kolpashevo, and stores were only selling flour. The sauna was also closed because of the lack of wood. Elise and Ilse went to the home of the White Dame to try to get another installment of the bread and hulled barley promised to Ilse, but there was no answer when they knocked on her door.

Lilleht and Lisa became ill with influenza, and Jefimia's back was hurting. They assumed her back pain was from her kidneys responding to the high salt diet. Lisa obtained some garlic and cooked it in water. She and her roommates drank it hoping it would strengthen their immune systems.

By mid-February they waited in bread lines, as Ilse said, "like hungry dogs." Their cafeteria lunch consisted of water and two tomatoes. Ilse had become a skeleton. Her arms were so thin the veins were popping out. Despite the hunger, Ilse and Jefimia tried to keep a sense of humor—their only hope of survival. They made fun of each other's bony frame. "If we went to the beach," Ilse chuckled impishly, "the birds would pick at us thinking we were cadavers." Privately Ilse thought to herself, I have been fortunate to not become ill, but I will not last much longer.

Their hunger that night was satisfied by cooking flour in water. They made it watery to save as much flour as they could. Later that evening, when Ilse went to the outside toilet, she found a piece of bread in the mud and ate it. That act amazed her as she pondered the degree to which she would now stoop to satisfy her belly. Fortunately, the next day they received some lamb shanks and cows' ears from the cafeteria.

On March 2 Ilse learned that the Russians had crossed the Estonian border. Her immediate response was, "May God preserve Estonia." A week later Mehaanik, with a tone of triumph, told her that 200 planes had attacked Tallinn. Then he added, "Estonians don't understand that a great future is ahead for them." The comment made Ilse cringe. She said nothing, but her thoughts told her Estonia would have nothing left—neither its land nor its people.

The White Dame began coming sporadically to give Ilse the bread and barley installments they had agreed upon. But her visits were not always dependable.

As the scarcity of food continued, it motivated Lisa to ask the commandant if he would give her permission to return to the *kolhoos* from which she had been mobilized. Surprisingly, he gave her permission. Encouraged by this, Lilleht also went to ask the same from the commandant, but his response to her was, "No, I need you here."

Easter was approaching, and one day Pikk saw her boss Mehaanik with his superior's wife and some other public figures. Pikk thought this the perfect occasion to confront him. Her pants were being held up by a string tied around her waist, and her jacket was so patched that the original cloth could not be determined. Her attire was highlighted by a black bag slung over her shoulder onto her back.

She approached the illustrious group and opened the bag to show Mehaanik its contents. It contained nettles and bark. Holding the bag open she said quite loudly, "Look what your workers eat for holidays. "Mehaanik's face turned quite red and he quickly replied, "I will be bringing some bread."

That evening Jefimia wanted to throw away some tripe, but Ilse stopped her. "Give it to me, Jefimia. I will eat it." Unfortunately, she developed diarrhea and was sick for a week. Pikk also ate some undesirable food and became extremely ill with a temperature of 104 degrees. Ilse took her to the clinic. As Pikk entered, she fell on her stomach in the doorway. The attendant came and began to yell: "Out, get out of here! We can't have an infestation of lice in here." A doctor walked toward them. When he saw Pikk's filth and lice on her coat, he, too, said, "We can't have lice in here."

Ilse turned and tried to leave, hoping they would finally serve Pikk, but they were both told to get out. Ilse helped Pikk up from the floor and slowly returned home with Pikk leaning heavily on her. Later Pikk threw up several times and, though weak, felt better.

By mid-April Ilse was able to sell a colorful dress she had brought with her from Estonia. She sold it to the White Dame for 1,300 rubles and was able to buy various products at the market. On Friday, April 14, she wrote in her diary: "Today for the first time this year my stomach is full."

It was hoped that the worst of the hunger was now over. However, one afternoon Ilse came home to her apartment and found a Latvian, Sikstens by name, lying crosswise in front of the door of her room unconscious. He was a former officer in the Latvian army and had been assigned work in construction for which he received 700 grams of bread each day. But with the heavy work they were doing it was not sufficient. His body became weaker and weaker and finally ill.

Because he could not work, he was released from his job and no longer entitled to bread or to an apartment. He began coming at night to their hallway to sleep and a few times had been thrown out.

Not wanting to awaken him, Ilse stepped quietly over him and entered her room. In the evening when Jefimia came from work, Sikstens was in the same position in front of the door. Being a trained medic, Jefimia realized the man was dying of starvation. She took hold of his feet and moved him away from the door and against the wall so they would not have to step over him.

Entering their apartment, Jefimia told Ilse she felt the man was dying. "I have some coffee," said Jefimia. "I will make some and see if he can drink it." But after the coffee was ready and she took it to him, she returned and said, "Too late. He is not responding. He is still alive, but he will die soon." That is all that was said. Inside their room, Ilse and Jefimia talked about the happenings of the day and even laughed together. Ilse was amazed at how unaffected she was about a man dying of hunger just outside her door.

At 10:00 p.m. Ilse went out into the corridor to see Sikstens. His eyes were slightly opened, and his mouth gaped as he gasped for breath. It was a fearful, sickening sight. Ilse quickly turned and ran back inside her room as tears filled her eyes. This has been the fate of some of *my* people, she thought. She fell into a deep depression and would not go near the corridor anymore that night. In the morning he was dead, and Jefimia closed his eyes. "The poor man was living like a dog," said Ilse. "God was gracious to take his life."

The following evening when Ilse and Jefimia returned from work, Sikstens' body was still lying in the corridor. Lice had climbed on his face and swarmed out of his clothes. Five apartments were along the corridor. Ilse and her roommates lived in one, and Russians lived in the others. People were pouring water around Sikstens to discourage the lice from entering their rooms. Ilse contacted a Latvian Jew who knew the man and asked what could be done about him.

Finally, at 7:00 p.m. two Russians came with a horse-drawn wagon. They threw his body onto it and carried him away. He was buried in the ground without a coffin. All his remaining possessions consisted of one boot, one pair of socks and two bags that were found outside under the entry stairs.

By late May vegetation was growing, and Ilse gathered *kalbad*,[33] blue corn flowers and nettles for food. She was told to be careful of some of the grasses since 30 women had been poisoned and died from grass they had gathered by the Ob River. Fortunately, by June each worker had been allotted land for a garden. Food became more accessible, so much so that by mid-June Ilse commented to her roommates, "I am getting fat."

There were periods in June when the work was a bit lighter. One day they were told to move 100 mattresses from one building to another along with pillows, sheets and blankets. A horse and wagon would carry them to the new location, so until the horse came back for a new load they slept on the mattresses. On another day, during their lunch break, they visited a museum filled to the brim with stuffed birds, fish and animals of various kinds. It also contained artifacts of animal and human bones and a display of folk dresses.

The warmth of June also produced some slothfulness. Sometimes Pikk and Jefimia would find a place to sun themselves or leave to go to the store but were careful to return to work just before quitting time, leaving Ilse to cover for them in their absence. This caused Ilse to think to herself, I am the only stupid one who is always working.

In July, for the first time since leaving Estonia, they received cards that allowed them to purchase butter. This was a big event in their lives. It was such a treat that Lilleht was in line by 4:00 a.m. Pikk had to work that day and became upset that none of her roommates took her card along when getting her own allotment.

Most of the roommates did not like Pikk and did not want her near their beds and belongings because of the lice she carried. She had gone only twice to the sauna and had only washed her clothes two times since the previous fall. So they were not anxious to do her any special favors.

When July 4 arrived, Ilse's thoughts were of her husband. She recorded in her diary: "Today is Peko's birthday, if he is still living. We used to so much enjoy strolling in the park by the beach in Pärnu and stopping for lunch or dinner at the Ranna Hotel on his birthday. Those were wonderful times. I felt so sheltered and secure with him walking beside me. It seemed everyone knew him, and it was such fun watching him exchange greetings. I was even pleased when women jealously eyed him. It made me proud that he had chosen me."

Three days later thoughts of her homeland returned as she wrote: "It is Meeta's birthday today. I wonder what the mood is now in Estonia. Probably many are fleeing. My heart is pained when I think of what will happen to the people of small Estonia. What will remain of my homeland?"

CHAPTER 19

Workers' Camp
Germany 1944

The Kollist family and their fellow Estonian friends continued living in the second floor ballroom of the inn they had been directed to for about 10 days. One day, however, a middle-aged Nazi party man arrived with orders for them to go to Neumarkt Oberpfalz, Bavaria, where a foreign workers' camp was located. Many such camps had been set up throughout the country at this time, and he informed them that he would accompany them on their trip.

Their luggage was placed atop a wagon, and at 5:00 p.m. they were taken to the train station. While waiting for the train, a policeman approached their group. "Is there anyone here by the name of Kollist?" he bellowed. Meeta looked quizzically at the man and replied, "Yes, we are the Kollists." As he stepped to her side, she noticed that he held in his hand a very familiar briefcase. The man handed it to her saying, "I believe this belongs to you." Meeta's heart leaped within her. It was the briefcase containing all of their German money.

The policeman explained, "I saw this luggage slip off the wagon and I retrieved it. Fortunately, your name was on it so I began searching for the owner." Meeta thanked the man profusely. When he left, she addressed her parents. "God must be watching over us. This is the second time this briefcase has been returned to us." Jaak responded to his daughter, "We are most thankful, but we must be more mindful of this luggage and keep it with us at all times in the future. We must not be presumptuous of Providence."

The 113-kilometer train ride was not easy for Jaak since he frequently had to urinate and was finding it more and more difficult to fully empty his bladder. They arrived in Neumarkt Oberpfalz shortly before 10:00 p.m. It was a cold, moonless night in late September. The Nazi agent that had accompanied them telephoned the camp where they had been assigned. He informed them that a truck would arrive in about an hour to take them to their destination. Then he left.

The group waited patiently outside. Periodically some of them would go into the station to warm themselves, but the station was not much warmer than the night air. Helga Paimre sat on an outside bench huddled with her three little girls trying to keep them warm. Vello sat between his grandmother and aunt who struggled to do the same. The hours passed slowly. The cold was bone chilling as midnight approached. The children's eyes grew heavy, and they began asking how long before the truck would come. The only response anyone could give was, "Soon."

Meeta watched her father closely and noted how frequently he had to go into the station to relieve himself. She was amazed at his serenity and thought to herself, As uncomfortable as this situation is for Papsi, he never says a complaining word.

Finally, at about one o'clock in the morning the truck arrived. It was an open truck, and the cold night wind drew them close together. The road wound around many hills and through valleys and forests.

After about an hour they reached a camp situated in the middle of young fir trees. They disembarked at the gate and were directed to one of several long wooden barracks. When the door was opened, hot, sweaty air repulsed them. The large room was filled with men, women and children all crowded together. Helga Paimre stepped inside and quickly ran out. "We cannot stay in there, it's overcrowded and unhealthy!" Her voice was frenzied as she pled with the overseer for another place to stay. The man appeared sympathetic and directed them to another barrack similar to the first. It was cold, but only their group was housed in it.

The building was about 33 meters long and 17 meters wide with double bunks on both sides, separated by an aisle. The bunks were covered with straw mattresses. Two small iron stoves were at either end of the barrack.

The German overseer got some wood and started a fire in each of the stoves. While the group shivered around the stoves, the man left and soon returned with some wool blankets. He gave one to each of them. The two small stoves were inadequate to keep them warm, but at least they were sharing a room with people they knew. That luxury did not last long, however, for every day new refugees were added. They were mostly Romanian peasants of German descent, and soon their belongings almost eliminated walking space.

The Estonian group did not receive all their belongings until a week later. One bag was ripped from top to bottom exposing all its contents, yet nothing was missing. "I must admit," said Meeta, "the Germans are truly an orderly and disciplined people even now in the midst of the confusion that is all about us."

Soon the barrack became filled to capacity with about 100 people. After a few days, the straw mattresses became lumpy and hard and made sleeping difficult. Jaak was suffering terribly from what the camp doctor had told them was a prostate condition, which made it necessary for him to use the restroom more and more frequently. During the night, when rising quickly he often hit his head on the bunk above him. Since the restroom was outdoors, washing and dressing was done inside; all privacy was lacking. But they considered themselves fortunate that their barrack was free of vermin.

From camps such as this one people were assigned work in the various defense industries of the Third Reich. Each morning at six o'clock everyone was ordered to wait before the camp employment office where they were given work assignments. All, including children and the elderly, were ordered to meet there. However, Meeta and Amalie disregarded this regulation and left Vello with Jaak in the barrack since they often remained standing in line until the breakfast bell rang at 8:00 a.m. Then everyone ran to the food line forming between the barracks.

The main food consisted of a watered down vegetable soup that Meeta felt had a sickening smell. This soup was presented at every meal as long as they remained in the camp. Only children were provided with an additional pint of milk. Soon Vello developed a temperature and diarrhea. Then rumors began circulating that all those unable to work were to be transferred to Auschwitz, an extermination camp. Meeta feared that her sickly father, who was now nearly 78 years old, and her 60-year-old mother might be considered candidates for that move.

Permission to leave the camp was granted once a week, and one day Helga Paimre returned from town with a radiant smile on her face. "Meeta, I went to the local police prefect and explained my living conditions to him. He made arrangements for my three children and me to get an apartment."

This gave Meeta the idea that she could do the same. In preparation for such an attempt, Meeta began earnestly praying that her family might somehow escape their predicament. For several nights she slipped away from the crowded, noisy barrack into the quietness of the night and tearfully prayed for guidance. "Heavenly Father, You know how incapable I feel of fulfilling the responsibility for the guidance and protection of the three people that have been placed under my care. Both Vello and Papsi are ill, and I have no way of meeting their needs. What's more, rumors are spreading that the elderly and infirm may be sent away to Auschwitz. I have been told that is an extermination camp. Please, Father, show me a way out of this dilemma."

Following a few nights of prayer, Meeta went to the police prefect in town. Since she spoke excellent German, she was able to thoroughly explain her family's living conditions to him. Then she pleaded, "In addition to a place to live I would be thankful for any work you could help me find. I have bookkeeping experience."

The man listened very carefully and seemed genuinely concerned. "I think I can promise you a job if you can give me some time and return next week." Meeta left his presence in a hopeful state of mind. On her way back to the camp she stopped at a beautiful wooded area to thank God for this encouragement and to ask for continued guidance.

The next week she returned to the police prefect. As soon as the man saw her, his expression showed chagrin. "I must apologize to you, Madam. I have completely forgotten about your case. Please come back tomorrow; I will have work for you." He sounded so certain that Meeta found herself promising to return the next day. As she left his presence, however, doubts began to cloud her hopefulness. How would she get permission to leave camp two days in a row? The orders had been very definite that no one was to be allowed outside of camp more than once a week.

She had brought her grandmother's Bible with her from Estonia and read it daily during their flight and while in the camp. As she returned to camp, she turned again to its pages and claimed promises that told of God's ability to help those who trust in Him. She particularly chose Psalm 46:1 and repeated it often that day to strengthen herself.

That night once again she stepped out of the barrack into the darkness for her private prayer. With tears wetting her face, she repeated her chosen text, reminding God of His promise. "God is our refuge and strength, a very present help in trouble." Then, to chase away her doubts she added the beginning of the second verse, "Therefore we will not fear." As she spoke those words, a peace came over her. She knew that God would somehow answer her request.

At 9:00 a.m. the next morning Meeta walked toward the camp leader's office to get permission to leave. Outside her barrack was a road leading between the kitchen and a storage building. At the end of the road was a gate through which deliveries were made. As she passed, she noticed the gate was open. No one was to be seen. The temptation to leave through that gate was intense. She walked back and forth for several long minutes contemplating what to do. Was this God's way of letting her out without getting permission? But how could she return if she left in this manner? What would be the result of her leaving without permission? She finally concluded that if it was God's will that she leave, He would make a legitimate way for her to get permission.

Reaching the camp leader's office she discovered he was absent, but his assistant was there. Meeta asked him if he could give her permission to leave that day to go to town. He was friendly but said permission was not his to grant if the leader was available. "He is somewhere in the camp. I'll go with you to find him," he said. They left the office together and stepped out into the large square in front of the building.

Two paths intersected each other at the square, and they saw the camp leader approaching opposite them. The doctor from the dispensary walked toward him from the side and intercepted him where the paths crossed. The doctor appeared very upset as he addressed the camp leader.

"My patients are waiting for assistance in a cold waiting room. This is especially hard on the children. We must have more fuel to keep the room warm," he exclaimed.

The camp leader became furious at this request. "Under no circumstances can you have any more wood or coal. What you have is enough." Then he abruptly turned back in the direction from which he had just come and disappeared.

The assistant and Meeta looked at each other with astonishment. The assistant was first to speak. "Well, it doesn't appear that he is in any mood to be asked a favor." He paused and then gestured with his hand. "Come on in the office; I'll give you permission."

When Meeta entered the police prefect's office this time, he was prepared for her arrival. He directed a policeman to take her to the Eberhard Faber pencil factory. Mr. Eberhard himself was an American citizen. The policeman introduced her to the factory director who told her he had a job for her.

While Meeta watched, he telephoned a friend. "You have furniture in your attic that is very much needed by a new worker." His tone was charming and confident as he spelled out the needs. After the conversation was ended, he escorted Meeta to a room that had recently been painted. It was located on the second floor of a building that was used for social gatherings of soldiers and workers. He next took her to an outbuilding and pointed to an iron wagon. "You can shovel coal into that wagon." Then handing her a bucket, he said, "Use this to carry the coal up to your room. Waste wood from the factory can also be used for heating and cooking." He smiled as he said, "You may begin work as soon as you move into this apartment."

Meeta's feet barely touched the ground as she laughed and cried her way back to camp. At each step she thanked God for His goodness. It all seemed so unreal—like a dream come true.

It was early evening when she arrived back at the barrack. To keep the news from spreading, she whispered the good tidings to her mother and then called her father outside. He did not hear well, and she needed to take him where she could speak loud enough to be heard. At the news his entire countenance brightened, and his face broke into a large smile. It was the first time in weeks that she had seen him display any joy.

The next day they bade their friends good-bye, placed their few belongings aboard a camp wagon with wooden wheels and pulled it to their new home. They considered themselves extremely fortunate to have spent only three weeks at the camp. Other members of their group remained for months after their departure.

The room was ready and furnished when they arrived. It was quite spacious and contained four iron beds with straw mattresses and straw pillows, an oval table with four chairs, a dresser and a wardrobe. In one corner was a stove and shelves with kitchen items placed in an orderly fashion.

As the family surveyed their new dwelling, each face radiated delight. "Finally, a place of our own," said Amalie with a sigh. It was a humble abode, but after the long absence of privacy it was a haven where they could truly rest.

One of the first families of workers they met lived across the hall from them and consisted of a Polish mother and three daughters. That evening they invited the Kollists for a meal because they saw the family had no food. The Kollists gladly and thankfully accepted. The following day they received German ration cards that were their sole source of food.

Meeta worked in the packing and mailing department where she packed pencils, erasers and ink pens and daily handled packages weighing up to 30 pounds. It wasn't bookkeeping, but she appreciated the physical labor because it gave her time to process all that had happened. Vello was still feverish and weak and remained in bed for the first week in their new home—only arising at meal times. After one week, however, he had recovered his strength and took renewed interest in his surroundings.

The family soon became acquainted with their neighbors and others who worked in the pencil factory. It was a satisfying time. Jaak was able to walk outside on beautiful fall days and even carved a mash potato stomper for his wife out of wood.

During this respite they tried to reconnect with Oskar. The one relative who remained a constant throughout the war years was Anna, who lived in Sweden. She was the daughter of Jaak's younger brother Peeter. Amalie wrote to Anna asking if she had any information regarding Oskar and telling her where they were now located. Fortunately, Anna had received correspondence from Oskar who had fled to Sweden with his little family and provided Amalie with their address.

When communication was once again established, Oskar relayed the sad story of how their little Heikki Ivar had become ill in Finland with a viral respiratory infection. On the boat trip to Sweden his condition worsened, and on October 28, he died. He was only nine months old. Subsequently Oskar and Ave were placed in a refugee camp in Ankarsrum, Sweden.

A few days before Christmas Jaak's prostate condition became worse, and he had to be taken to the hospital. As he left their apartment, he paused at the door and faced his wife and daughter. He had only his walking stick and violin in his hands. Tears filled his eyes as he gestured to the items he held. "This was the way I began my life as a young man, and this is the way I will …" His words abruptly ended as his emotions overpowered his speech.

CHAPTER 20

News from Home
Siberia 1944

Ilse and Pikk worked alongside other local Russians weeding and hoeing a field of potato plants during July of 1944. The field was located about 50 kilometers from Kolpashevo and was so overgrown they could barely find the potato plants.

They worked nearly naked in their underwear in the blazing hot Siberian sun drinking the only available water filled with debris. To get enough to eat they stole cabbage from other fields around them. The overseer's office was their sleeping quarters, where Ilse's bed was a table. They were thankful when occasionally soup with barley and meat and less frequently cheese, milk and fish were brought to the office for their meals.

On July 23 Ilse received word from one of the Russian workers that Hitler had capitulated. This apparently was wishful thinking on the part of the Russian. The invasion of Normandy on June 6 and the breakout from the beachhead had resulted in massive losses to the German and Allied troops in the weeks that followed. The march was on for the liberation of France, but Hitler was not yet ready to concede defeat.

During August Ilse and her roommates were back in Kolpashevo hauling and sawing wood. Once again they fought with dull saws, loose axes and bent wedges. Because they were employed as free agents rather than as members of the *kolhoos*, they needed to obtain permission from their superior to get food products from the collective farm. The letter requesting permission had to be taken to the procurator for approval. Pikk was very aggressive and managed to get to the front of the waiting line. She obtained approval and also received permission for them to eat in the cafeteria for which her roommates were most thankful.

One day in late August while Ilse was seeking to purchase some products at one of the stores in town, she noticed a Moldavian beggar with a black kerchief on her head. The woman looked like the shadow of death. Her face and exposed arms and legs were covered with brown spots. Her soiled dress was severely patched. She was surrounded by a crowd of children joking and laughing at her emaciated frame. The woman stared blankly back at the children without the slightest reaction. Ilse had come pitifully close to a similar fate and understood what the woman was feeling. One in such a condition becomes apathetic and numb to the world. She longed to help the poor soul, but her own resources were so meager that there was nothing she could do but offer a compassionate look.

Even during the most difficult and discouraging times, beauty could be found in the midst of their suffering. One idyllic fall day, as Ilse and Jefimia performed their back-breaking labor of hauling and sawing logs, Ilse noted Jefimia's hair shining in the sunlight as they worked. "The summer sun has made your hair as blond as a young boy's." Jefimia's beaming smile encouraged Ilse to reveal more of what she was feeling. "My mood today is mellow like the fall season. Look at those lovely asters blooming. It's amazing how richly flowers grow here in Siberia." Then, pointing to a beautiful white flower with shades of pink surrounded by large green leaves, she said, "I've never before seen those flowers." Jefimia stopped to admire the beauty, too, and then commented, "It's the tobacco flower."

That day a glimmer of hope that the war might end came with the news that the Allies had liberated Paris. But what would the end of war mean for Estonia? How badly devastated was her homeland? Who of her friends had survived the deportations and war machine? Where were her son and family? Would they ever find each other?

In the evening, she attended a movie starring Sonja Henie.[34] As she watched the film, she reminisced of her homeland. Sonja Henie seemed like an old friend since she had seen her in a film in her own country years before. Look, she thought, how respectable and orderly the clothing is. People are living, eating and socializing as if there is no war going on—as if there is no struggle to exist. Here I am dressed in rags with my pants about to fall down for lack of a belt and struggling to find enough food to fill my belly. Yet in this film everything is normal—the way it used to be. She keenly felt the loss but could not take her eyes from the film. It was a strange sensation. She found two emotions clashing: resentment for the loss, yet contentment to mentally relive better days.

In early September Mehaanik promised his workers that some better clothing would soon be arriving for them. Spirits rose in anticipation. However, no shipment arrived and the workers were sent to harvest oats in fields several kilometers away still dressed in their rags. Ilse had heard empty promises too often to expect their immediate fulfillment. She was much more content if she did not anticipate any change.

During off times and rest periods she did not join the complaining but enjoyed the warmth of the September sun as she sat high on a shore where a tributary flowed from the Ob River. She found serenity as she watched the iridescent glimmer of the stream in the afternoon sunlight and the brilliance of the golden birch and flame-red aspen breaking through the dark evergreens.

Sitting alone, her mind wandered to her girlhood home by the Sauga River. How peaceful her childhood had been with never a want for food or clothing. She missed her mother. Within her heart she knew her mother favored her, though she would never verbalize it. Mamsi would soundly punish Meeta—sometimes with a broom. But even a large offense would not result in a heavy penalty for her. And dear Papsi, such a quiet man yet so accommodating. She thought of the night he was leaving for a movie and she stood at the door and placed her hand in his. He looked at her and asked, "What is on your mind, young lady?"

"I'm going with you, Papsi," Ilse responded.

Jaak never said a word, but his face broke into a broad smile as they walked hand in hand to the movie together. Now those days seemed so far away and long ago. Would she ever see them again? Would there ever be normalcy again? Or was this the new normal? No, I must not think. I must not reminisce, she thought. It's far too painful.

One consolation for working in the oat fields was that they were fed very well. Volodin, their foreman, was very generous with food. One day he arrived too late to eat and complained that the food was at an end. "I will have to go home to get something to eat," he said. "I'm already getting weak." Ilse struggled to keep from laughing as she thought, He's already weak from one day without food. Just one day!

The second week of September Ilse was returned to Kolpashevo and was told that the shipment of clothes had arrived. She was able to buy a skirt and blouse for 60 rubles and was excited to find a dark blue coat and pants. Accenting the front of the coat were metal buttons with USA imprinted on them. What fortune, she thought. I again have working clothes! Another surprise awaited her. The walls of their apartment room had been painted a pleasant pink, a delightful change from the customary stark whitewash that was used.

Ilse worked in Kolpashevo digging potatoes from the garden of the home of one of the administrators for which he and his wife paid her with potatoes, a little meat, rye flour, fried sausage and strained sour milk. She cut logs, stacked them and piled dirt up against the house. Houses were built without foundations and rested on sawed logs. In mild weather the wind blew under the house so the wooden logs would not rot. But in winter dirt had to be piled against the house to stop the cold wind from blowing underneath.

Ilse next had to dig some potatoes from her own garden in preparation for winter. But because thievery was so prevalent, she feared leaving the potatoes in her apartment. Pikk already complained that someone had gone to the cellar and stolen fish she had hidden there. But what was one to do? The choices were putting the potatoes in the apartment or trying to hide them in the cellar. Ilse chose the cellar.

On September 25 the first snow fell, and the weather became quite cold. Pikk told Ilse she had just learned that Viljandi, a town about 70 kilometers east of Pärnu, had fallen to the Russians. On October 7 they received word that the Soviet Union was now in complete control of Estonia except for the island of Saaremaa. This caused Pikk to turn to her cards to see what the future held, and she encouraged Ilse. "The cards say that you will see your son and husband again."

During October Ilse and Pikk were assigned to work helping the *kolhoos* thresh grain, tie sheaves and put potatoes into bags to store for winter. Some evenings guitar playing would commence, and Russian folk dancing would follow. Ilse joined in the merriment, dancing along with the Russian locals. One evening she sang *"Katje Katerina"* to the delight of the Russians. Every evening following they requested her to sing it, and she happily complied.

During the dancing one night Tanja, an 18-year-old, told everyone to follow her lead as the music played. The other youth immediately began to follow; Ilse joined with them, though she was now 30 years old. When Tanja went on her hands and knees, so did Ilse. This produced delightful laughter and endeared the teens to her.

Though Ilse enjoyed the local youth, she found morality there quite "strange." She noted in her diary, "a girl goes to a boy, and without registering in marriage they say the girl has joined with a man." She also noted a young man of 18 named Ljonka who was quite promiscuous, even bringing a girl into their communal sleeping quarters. Ilse's shock was recorded as she wrote: "They don't care at all that others are sleeping in the same room. Ljonka sleeps with another girl every night. He is even infatuated with a 30-year-old married woman."

When Ilse and Pikk returned to their Kolpashevo apartment in late October, they discovered that Lilleht had returned to her former *kolhoos* and Jefimia was now scheduled to be assigned as a hospital orderly. As the days became colder, Ilse and Pikk resumed their work cutting trees and logs for the boiler house. The work required their sawing trees that had been floated to the shore of the Ob River and carrying the logs on their backs up the steep bank to the boiler room. Stairs had been dug into the bank, but the tree sections were quite heavy and demanded much strength and dexterity.

Sometimes in the evening, after working their normal shift, Jefimia, Pikk and Ilse were asked to cut wood for the administrators' homes. One evening Jefimia worked with Ilse for an administrator named Feofanova. After sawing the wood, Jefimia refused to stack it and Ilse complained. "The job isn't done until the wood is piled." Jefimia retorted curtly. "It's cold, I'm tired, and Feofanova should be glad we cut all these logs to size for him. He didn't ask us to pile the wood, too. He can do something for himself." Jefimia then abruptly turned and walked toward home. Duty bound, Ilse piled the wood alone. Feofanova's wife later called Ilse inside and treated her richly with a hearty meal and food to take with her. She asked Ilse why Jefimia had left. Ilse could not bring herself to tell her the truth so just said, "Jefimia was not feeling well and had to leave." Feofanova had a high regard for Ilse's work ethic and was generous with her. He would have his wife prepare her fried potatoes, a rare treat, and would give her additional bread to take with her.

One night in late November Elise returned to their apartment after attending a movie. The apartment door was locked, and Elise knocked on the door for entrance. Inside, Ilse, Jefimia and Pikk were asleep. Jefimia heard the knock and arose to open the door but collapsed in the entrance way as she did. Elise immediately called out, "Ilse, come here! Jefimia has fallen down!" Ilse awoke with a start and realized the room was full of smoke. She hurried to help Elise.

They lifted Jefimia on her feet and half dragged her outside. Once outdoors Ilse remembered Pikk was still inside and was sleeping near the stove. She rushed back and awoke Pikk. Together they hastened outside. Later it was determined that the vent pipe of the stove had somehow been dislodged and was allowing smoke into the room. Ilse noted in her diary that day, "If Elise had not been at the movies and awoken us, we could have all died from smoke inhalation."

Three letters arrived from Estonia in early December. Jefimia learned that her father had died soon after her deportation. Pikk received a letter from her husband. And Elise got a letter from her brother's wife saying that Elise's son was now in the seventh grade. The letters brought news that the university town of Tartu had suffered greatly from the war but that Tallinn was still whole. But for Ilse there was no letter. Two days later Pikk received another letter, but still no letter for Ilse had arrived. That day Ilse recorded in her diary, "I am sad that I get no news from home."

The deep cold had now settled in and ranged from minus 45 to minus 50 degrees. Chopping and sawing wood became an absolute necessity for survival. Ilse's job became increasingly demanding. The requirement was for larger amounts of wood, but it was much more difficult to chop and saw in such severe weather. She no longer could take wood home to her own apartment because of the high demand. Her diary entry at this time read:

> Why do I live like a dog? I have a feeling we are not human beings. I am holding my soul together with great effort. We don't have the most primitive things. We don't dare bring wood into the apartment from the boiler house. The window in our room is a single pane, and it is covered with such thick ice that it is dark during the day. When one comes into the room, it is like coming into a cellar. In the evening only one small bulb lights the room, and the room is so cold that we must wear and sleep in all our outside clothes. Each wall has a bed made of boards. I have a bag filled with hay on mine. Pikk sleeps on a bag that she opens up and wears like a skirt in the daytime and keeps it up with a rope. Because of the darkness one is not in the mood to clean up the room. The floor is filled with trash. Since we have no cupboard or shelves, all our dishes and utensils are either on the windowsill or on the table in the middle of the room. The cookware is sooty, and the walls and floor are black from the smoke of the cook stove. In one word, it is a pigpen.

On December 12 Ilse entered her apartment and began searching for her boots in preparation for work. Jefimia and Elise were in the apartment when she arrived and suggested that she check by her bed. Ilse began looking beneath the bed. Finally, Elise, unable to hold her enthusiasm any longer, said, "Why don't you look on your bed?" Ilse looked skeptically at Elise and then at her bed. "There are no boots on my b..." Ilse's sentence ended abruptly as she noticed that a letter had been neatly placed in the middle of her pillow. Her eyes grew wide and her mouth even wider as she exclaimed, "A letter! A letter from home!" When Ilse looked at the address, she immediately recognized her best friend's handwriting. It was a letter from Tutti. Now that Russia had taken firm control of Estonia and considered it another of its republics, mail was freely passing between Estonia and Siberia which had not been previously possible.

The letter informed her, "Your parents, Meeta and little Vello are not here but have fled. They are all probably alive, although I do not know where they are. Oskar is married and they have a boy named Heikki Ivar already eight months. He was born in Finland. Your small boy has grown tremendously and looks like you. He doesn't like it when he is told he is a small boy. He wants to be a big man." When Ilse reached that portion of the letter, she could not continue reading but began to weep. "My boy! My boy! When will I ever see you and hold you?"

***

The heavy work of carrying logs from the Ob River had taken a mighty toll on their footwear. The entire sole of Pikk's boot had come off. To prevent their feet from freezing, the women wrapped them with rags and tied them to the ankles. Their efforts to avoid tripping over this makeshift footwear caused them to walk with an unnatural gait. One day several school children approached them asking, "Are you drunk?"

Finally, on December 19 felt boots arrived. For 70 rubles each could purchase real footwear to replace their "rag shoes." Ilse was excited and exclaimed, "In my lifetime, I have not gotten a more valuable gift."

On Christmas Eve Ilse and Pikk were able to buy a blood sausage from the administrative store. To add to this Christmas joy, Ilse learned a letter awaited her in the office. It was from Peko who had answered her letter dated July 7, 1944. It was just what she needed to lift her spirit on this holiday eve.

For the Estonian laborers Christmas Day was just another workday. When work ended at 7:00 p.m., Ilse forced herself to fry some blood sausage and cook potato soup before dropping into bed. With no strength left for even humming a Christmas carol, she fell into a deep sleep.

The end of the year, December 31, was no different. Ilse recorded in her diary: "When we had eaten, we started with witchcraft." Pikk put out her cards, and Ilse asked her three questions:

1. "Will I get home in the spring?" The answer came. "No! But sometime you will get home."
2. "Will I get together with my husband before summer?" Answer: "Yes."
3. "Will I get together with my son in Estonia?" Answer: "There will be a disappointment with your son."

CHAPTER 21

City on Fire
Germany 1945

Jaak underwent an operation for prostate cancer in early January 1945, and a catheter was inserted for his comfort in urinating. During the days that followed he began gaining strength and even played his violin. The frequent visits by Meeta, Amalie and Vello were happy times as they all felt relieved that their beloved Papsi would be back home with them soon.

On Sunday, January 14, however, when the three of them walked into Jaak's room, they were shocked at the change that had come upon him. Amalie later confessed he looked to her "like a dead person." They had come that day joyously expecting to receive word that Jaak would be released soon. Instead the attending nurse, a nun, as it was a Catholic hospital, had a serious demeanor. Little Vello stood between his aunt and grandmother holding Amalie's hand as the nurse spoke. "Mr. Kollist was to be released from the hospital, but first the catheter had to be disinfected and replaced. Unfortunately, he has an infection." Then she added sympathetically, "To complicate the matter, Mr. Kollist's heart is weak."

After the nurse left the room, Jaak told his wife and daughter what he experienced when the doctor removed the catheter. "I felt as if someone had pulled at my heart." In obvious pain Jaak asked, "Why didn't you come yesterday?"

Feeling very guilty now, Meeta explained, "We started walking to the hospital, but the snowstorm was pelting us so badly we had to turn back."

Jaak grimaced as he said, "I was in such pain last evening, I cried like a baby." Amalie took hold of her husband's hand. Her shoulders sagged as she said, "I'm so sorry we weren't here for you, Jaak."

Vello's forehead creased as he looked up at his grandfather and said, "The doctor needs to help Apa!"

"We're hoping he will, Vello," said Meeta, but she herself was very concerned with this turn of events.

Throughout the day Jaak suffered much pain and seemed to grow weaker. That afternoon Dr. Krauss approached Amalie, Meeta and Vello in the hallway outside Jaak's room. His eyes reflected sadness. "I am so sorry to tell you this, but there is no hope for Mr. Kollist's recovery. His heart is very weak. We will try our best to keep him comfortable, but that is the most we can do."

Amalie began to weep quietly. Vello looked at his grandmother with bewilderment and then turned to his aunt. "Can the doctor help Apa?"

Meeta was having a difficult time processing this sudden change. She felt anger thinking the doctor must have done something wrong. Just two days before her father appeared vibrant and strong. She bent down to answer Vello's question. "The doctor says he has done all he can to help Apa."

Still appearing bewildered the little boy asked, "Isn't Apa coming home soon?"

Meeta picked up Vello in her arms and held him close. "We thought so, but the doctor says he is sick again."

Trying to make sense of what he heard, the little fellow asked, "When will he get better?"

To Meeta this seemed like a bad dream. She could not fathom being without the father whose kind ways had been such a source of strength to her. How could she tell a child who adored his grandfather that his Apa would never be returning home? She squeezed Vello tightly as tears began making rivulets down her cheeks.

Seeing her tears, Vello asked, "Won't he get better?"

Meeta could not find her voice but shook her head no.

Throughout the day Jaak was tormented by frequent nausea. Two young men who shared Jaak's room suggested to Meeta and her mother that one of them should remain with him through the night. That evening Meeta asked her father who he wanted to stay with him. He looked directly at Meeta and said, "You." Then he turned to Amalie and said, "I have white bread and rolls in my drawer. Take them for Vello. I will not be eating anymore."

Amalie kissed her husband goodnight and held his hand. "I will be here again tomorrow, Jaak." He nodded his head weakly and squeezed her hand. She took Vello by the hand and walked toward the door. Meeta saw the anguish on her mother's face and noted the tears that were beginning to form as she left the room.

The catheter was reinserted for Jaak's supposed comfort, and he was given a sedative. Then the nurse brought Meeta a cloth-cushioned armchair with a high back and placed it at his bedside. Meeta positioned herself at the head of the bed. In a short while Jaak fell into a deep sleep.

Meeta was comforted that her dear Papsi was finally resting. She offered a prayer that God would give him a gentle passing. As she stared at his wax-like face, she noticed two single hairs peeping up from the top of his globe-like head. She smiled as she thought of the times Jaak asked her to cut off those determined twins "to give the flies a clear field for landing." Oh, how precious that silly memory appeared now.

As darkness pervaded the room, light from the hallway effused from behind a partially closed door. It illuminated the ugly plastic tube in which bloody urine dripped slowly in a bubbly stream to a bag hanging from the bed rail. Each drop reminded Meeta of the life before her ebbing away.

Suddenly an air raid siren sounded, and everyone in the hospital, including the two young men in Jaak's room, began rushing toward the basement air raid shelter. Meeta stood by the side of her father's bed realizing there would be no hope of moving him to the shelter. A nurse darted in waving her hand and saying, "*Fraulein*, you must come with me to the shelter."

"*Nein*," Meeta responded firmly, "I will remain here with my father."

"This is no time to argue, *Fraulein*. Come with me!" The nurse tugged at Meeta's arm. But she was small and wiry and no match for the large-boned five-foot-seven-inch woman. Experiencing Meeta's determined resistance, the nurse finally relented and scurried off to the shelter shaking her head and muttering.

Meeta reseated herself close to the bed, her knees touching the mattress as she listened to the rumble of airplanes passing overhead. Fortunately, Papsi did not awaken and snored lightly as he slept. She stared at him, amazed that she felt no fear. Her concern for her beloved father and his imminent passing somehow overshadowed everything else around her—even her own safety. She did not want him to be alone when the inevitable happened, no matter if it came now from a bomb or later from natural processes.

The next morning, realizing the end was near, Meeta called the factory and asked them to inform her mother that she should come as quickly as possible to the hospital. In the meantime, two nuns propped Jaak up with pillows into a sitting position and placed lighted candles around his bed. One of the nurses remained in the room and began praying softly.

Back at home Amalie left Vello in the care of their Polish neighbor and rushed to her husband's side arriving sometime after nine o'clock. As Amalie entered the room, she took Jaak's hand. He looked directly at her and she asked, "Do you know me, Jaak?" He faintly nodded his head. About 45 minutes later they heard a strange sound coming from his throat. He stared off into the distance, took a deep breath and was gone.

Meeta felt her legs weaken, and she folded into the chair behind her. Amalie stood frozen beside Jaak's bed caressing his hand and weeping. The clock in the hall struck 10:00 as the nun who had been praying walked to Jaak and gently closed his eyes. Meeta rose from her chair and kissed her father on his forehead. As she raised her head, she saw the religious calendar on the wall next to his bed. The Scripture reading for that day, January 15, 1945, was from the gospel of John, chapter 10, verse three . . ."he calls his own sheep by name and leads them out."

Jaak's burial was paid for with welfare funds and was quite different from what they had experienced in their homeland. In Estonia the deceased would have been brought to the family's church for a service. Attendees would have followed the bier to the cemetery where there would have been a graveside committal. Then they would have thrown handfuls of dirt onto the lowered cloth-covered casket. Finally, cemetery workers would have filled the grave in the presence of the attendees, and family members and friends would have placed their flowers on top of the new grave as they left.

Here in Germany, however, Jaak lay in state in a large, enclosed room alongside two other unknown deceased men. Mourners viewed them from outside the building through large glass windows extending from the floor to the ceiling of the facility.

Jaak looked as if he were dressed for church in his dark blue suit as Meeta,

Amalie and Vello passed by to view and grieve their beloved Papsi. Vello was solemn but quiet. His three-year-old mentality had somehow come to grips with the fact that his Apa would not be coming home again. Meeta had told him, "One day we will be together again when God wakes him. And when God wakes him he will be well again and will be able to play his violin for you."

The day of the internment dawned cold but sunny. Jaak's coffin glided over the snowy trail to the gravesite on a sledge pulled by two men. A Lutheran pastor headed the procession. Amalie, Meeta and Vello were at the rear accompanied by Helga Paimre and a few friends from the factory where Meeta worked.

Freshly shoveled dirt marked Jaak's gravesite, just one more in a long row of graves in a section of the cemetery reserved for foreigners. The little procession halted near the mound of earth as the pastor presented the eulogy and quoted from the Psalms. On the wooden cross marking her father's grave, Meeta's eyes lingered on the words from John 10:3 that she had read on the wall calendar the day of her father's death. She wished that her father's final resting place could have been in the family plot of his beloved Estonia. Even more depressing, they were not allowed to cover the coffin with earth and flowers as a final tribute and good-bye, for another coffin holding a child was scheduled to be placed beside Jaak's coffin the next day. None of those in attendance had ever witnessed an uncovered grave and sadly turned away to trudge homeward.

The Kollist family was now without a masculine head. Meeta keenly felt the loss of the only man she deemed had ever truly loved her. He had provided the quiet strength to depend on at times when their family had been shaken. Her mother was an independent, strong-minded woman but lacked the compassionate soul of her father. It was an ingredient Meeta desperately needed. Without it she felt vulnerable.

She knew that Vello was also deeply affected by this loss. Apa wasn't there any longer to do the *kratzfuss* with him, nor was there the wonderful mimicking of his grandfather's gestures the family often laughed about. Occasionally when Vello would hear someone play the violin, he would call out, "Apa, Apa."

Amalie dealt with the passing of her husband resolutely. She did not dialog about it but seemed to grieve privately. Sometimes she would sit quietly staring out a window for a long time as if reliving a past event. Sometimes she would be cranky over the slightest thing. But mostly she just surrendered herself to the daily duties as they came along.

Following Jaak's death the air raids became more frequent. Just two weeks later the family was on alert day and night. Meeta's basket, filled with the most necessary items and a little food, was always ready and sat waiting in a corner of the room. On top lay her grandmother's German Lutheran Bible from which she read while sitting for tedious hours hidden under bushes and trees. Often they would have to find a place to hide amidst snow and water. Then Meeta would sit upon a log or rock with Vello on her lap.

Otherwise ordinary activities became frustrating experiences. During one evening meal the fire in their stove had to be rekindled three times before the food was cooked. Three air raids interrupted them, and each time they returned the fire had burned out.

The most difficult air raids occurred at night when Amalie and Meeta had to awaken Vello, dress hurriedly, run downstairs and outside to the woods. All this had to be done in complete darkness since no lights were permitted at such times. On one occasion Vello lagged behind, and Meeta wondered why he was not keeping up with them as usual. She retraced her steps and discovered that in the darkness she had inadvertently put both of his legs into one pant leg.

One night during an air raid Meeta carried Vello gingerly down the dark, stony staircase that led outside. Suddenly she felt herself losing balance. Surely, she thought, I will fall forward onto the child in my arms and down the remaining stairs. Then, just as suddenly, she felt an unexplainable force push her upright and stabilize her. This was the protective hand of God, she reasoned. I would have certainly crushed Vello or seriously injured one or both of us.

As spring approached, the times spent in the woods during air raids became oddly enjoyable. The fragrance of fir and pine trees combined to give a clean fresh aroma to the air in the warm sunshine. Here they viewed nature awaken from its winter slumber for hours while the air raid was in progress.

On one such day Amalie settled into a comfortable place beneath a large fir tree while Meeta and Vello walked in the woods searching for spring flowers. "Vello, look at the butterflies gliding in the warm sunbeams," said Meeta. This was Vello's first introduction to these little, colorful creatures. Laughing at their illusiveness, he darted here and there trying to catch one. As Meeta gazed skyward at a butterfly, she saw two Allied airplanes flying in their direction. Then she noticed cigar-like objects being released. Intense fear gripped her as she scooped Vello up in her arms and ran for the fir tree where Amalie sat. They huddled together beneath the dense branches as the objects passed overhead with a loud, expansive swooshing sound and then exploded in the town just a 30-minute walk from their hiding place.

That evening Meeta walked to the site of the explosion. She discovered that one of the bombs had gone through the roof of a three-story medieval building and into the basement crowded with people seeking safety. All of them were killed. Three coffins on the sidewalk outside the neighboring house told the story of its occupants. As Meeta viewed the scene, she offered a prayer of thankfulness to God that Papsi had been laid to rest before the destruction began. How could he in his feeble condition have endured?

Located just around the corner from the bombed medieval building and house stood a small dairy store where Amalie purchased groceries for the family. A few days after the bombing, when she returned from her grocery shopping, Amalie discovered that her billfold containing the last of the money they had brought with them from their homeland was missing. Fearing the worst, she hurried back to the store. Only when Mr. Schraeder, the store owner, reached beneath the counter and presented her with the billfold did she begin to breath easily again.

Amalie thanked him heartily. "*Herr* Schraeder, this is now the third time this billfold was lost and ultimately returned to us." She explained to him how she had left it on the train at the Berlin station, how it had fallen off a cart at the Dingolfing railroad station and now left behind at his store.

Mr. Schraeder gave Amalie a sympathetic look over the spectacles resting low on his nose. "*Frau* Kollist, I would suggest that you have been very fortunate. May I say that you will need that kind of luck living where you are. Now that the *Heimwehr*[35] have been housed on the first floor, that social hall could become a very real target for the Allies."

Amalie had also thought of that. When Meeta arrived home from work that evening, they entered into conversation about it. "Meeta, it is now common knowledge that reserve troops are living beneath us. I am extremely uncomfortable. Surely the Allies are, or will be, aware of that, which puts us in a very dangerous position."

"Mamsi, I, too, am troubled about this. But there is nothing we can do about it."

"Perhaps, but I would feel safer some distance away from the living quarters of the *Heimwehr*."

"Mamsi, even if we lived in another apartment, would we be any safer? Remember the three coffins outside the bombed house just a few days ago? And there was no hiding place for the people in that medieval building either. We can only heed the air-raid warnings and pray for God's protection."

"God's protection didn't help the people you just mentioned," retorted Amalie sarcastically.

Meeta's voice now rose to a higher pitch. "I can't answer for those people, I just must trust what I read in Grandmother's Bible, and claim Psalm 32:7 that God is our 'hiding place.'"

Amalie mumbled something beneath her breath about Meeta spending too much time reading the Bible and ended the conversation.

During an air-raid on a beautiful spring morning, Meeta, Vello and Amalie walked further into the woods than usual. As they walked, they heard the fearful sounds of attacking airplanes breaking the stillness around them. The whining noise of the planes was terrifying, coupled with sirens of warning, then followed the clicking sound of machine gunners who aimed at anything moving. The three of them were near a mill which lay a few meters from a road. The Allies were aiming to disperse a German transport moving on a highway further away behind an embankment. Circling for new attacks these planes passed over the mill. Nearby was a ditch wide enough for them to fit in, and they hastily threw themselves into it. They could not see out of the ditch but lay there without moving. After a time, they heard what sounded like machine gun bullets hitting the walls of the mill. Then the planes flew on. They rose from the ditch wiping the dirt and dust from their clothes, much relieved that they had escaped the attack. Surely, thought Meeta, God was our hiding place.

One evening as Meeta was reading from the Bible before retiring, the words of Jeremiah 21:10 spoke vividly to her: "'I have set My face against this city for adversity and not for good,' says the Lord. 'It shall be given into the hand of the king of Babylon, and he shall burn it with fire.'"

Those words etched themselves in her mind as if God spoke to her in a personal way. The next day she told her mother about the text and even mentioned it to her co-workers, telling them how it had greatly impressed her.

Interruptions from air raids became more and more frequent, with reconnaissance planes flying very low over the factory area while Meeta worked. Death stalks us, thought Meeta. It is impossible to escape it. It's like an advancing cancer penetrating into the most obscure places. What difference would it make, she thought, if one was in an air-raid shelter or somewhere else? Without God's protective power, the result would be the same—death.

By April the northern part of Germany was controlled by the Allies. Each morning a map of Germany hanging on a wall of the factory showed the markings of new areas controlled by the Allied forces where merchandise could no longer be sent.

A few days later Regensburg and Nürnberg, both only an hour's ride from Newmarkt Oberpfalz, were the target of bombings. The ground trembled beneath their feet and their windows and doors shook and clattered as bombs dropped from planes flying in close formation carpeted Nürnberg. Meeta, Amalie and Vello huddled in the forest as the air-raid sirens sounded. The sky glowed red for a number of days as the city burned. One night as they hid in the forest, Amalie pointed to the trees. "Look, Meeta, how bizarre the trees look backed against the blood-red sky. It gives me such an eerie, fearful sensation."

Little Vello, not quite four years of age, looked wide-eyed at the sight and clung to his grandmother as the ground shook beneath them. The child quietly endured these fearful nights, but his eyes showed the terror he felt. He would stare transfixed as if blanking out what he was seeing and sensing.

Apprehension in their town grew day by day. The Nazi party liquidated all their papers and files in Eberhard Faber's huge furnace. The entire area was scattered with tiny bits of burned paper flying from the high chimney—some of which could still be read.

As the Americans began driving toward Neumarkt Oberpfalz, the mayor and the police prefect decided to defend the town with a small contingent of remaining soldiers. The *Heimwehr* were ordered to report to the front, but it was not long before the ominous sounds of diving airplanes alerted them that the small company had been attacked.

That night Meeta and Amalie decided it would be best to leave their apartment on the second floor and took refuge in a woodshed on the factory premises. The three of them dressed in heavy winter coats, taking Jaak's winter coat with them also. As usual Meeta's air-raid basket accompanied them. Fearing possible loss Amalie packed two suitcases with some cherished photos and their clothing. Entering the woodshed, they lay down on the floor to try to rest, but Meeta could not sleep. Near midnight, she stepped outside and listened. From the distant highway she heard the muted but ceaseless rumble of heavy armored tanks moving through the blackness. Meeta knew that a battle would erupt in the town because of planned defensive operations, and she found herself trembling. Suddenly the words of Jeremiah 21, which had impressed her some weeks before, came forcefully to her mind. Quickly returning to the shed, she awakened her mother.

"Mamsi, I don't feel safe here any longer. We must go into the forest. I can hear heavy artillery in the distance." Amalie woke Vello from a sound sleep. The little fellow's eyes opened with a bewildered stare. Only the most essential items were taken with them in the accustomed basket. Meeta left her suitcase in the shed, but Amalie found a sandy ditch in which she hid the two suitcases she had packed. Quickly the threesome hurried into the chill night air. Meeta placed Vello atop her shoulders and held onto his feet as they walked. Amalie carried the precious basket.

They followed the bank of a small stream that led to a highway and wound up a hillside past the camp where they had stayed before coming to the Eberhard Faber factory. As they began descending the hill on the opposite side, Meeta felt the need for rest. Vello's weight had seemed to increase at every kilometer, and her shoulders ached. They laid Jaak's wool coat on the ground and sat for several minutes.

As the first shades of dawn appeared, Amalie pointed toward two farmhouses that were nestled in a valley ahead of them. "I see a large barn near the farmhouses, Meeta. Why don't we try to make it there. We will at least have some shelter from the chill." Meeta agreed and tried to encourage her sleepy nephew to walk with them for a short distance, promising him rest in the barn. The weary little man stumbled along until they finally entered the large structure. Other foreigners from their former refugee camp were already in the barn. They had also fled there for safety. Meeta and Amalie made a bed of soft straw for Vello and themselves and finally fell asleep.

Meeta had brought along some potatoes, salt, a little milk and a few eggs for Vello. When the sun arose, she cooked some of this food in a tin can outside over a fire built between some large stones. As she prepared the food, she noticed that high on a steep hill above the farmhouses German artillery was entrenched. During the first two days, sounds of battle could be heard in the distance.

After sunset on the second day, Meeta was surprised to see a red glow in the sky toward Neumarkt Oberpfalz. As the night advanced, the redness grew brighter and spread further. All the refugees stood outside to view the horrible yet brilliant scene. One man commented, "Neumarkt is burning." Another said, "There must be a lot of street fighting." Still another said, "The Americans will soon be in control of the town." And so the conversation of speculation continued.

The following day across the valley and off in the distance opposite the German defensive, they detected approaching Allied artillery. Later that day and into the night the fearsome whining sound of shells passed over the barn where the refugees were hidden. The explosions came closer and closer to their hiding place. Straw began falling from the loft above, and dust filled the barn. As the bombing increased in intensity, women began falling to their knees in prayer. Finally one of the men called out, "Let's get out of here!" The refugees began grabbing their belongings and ran out of the barn hoping to make it across a large meadow and into the forest beyond.

Meeta, Amalie and Vello could not run as fast, so after the others had made it to the safety of the forest, they were left alone in the meadow. Each time Meeta heard the whining sound of an approaching shell she would shout, "Down!" As soon as she heard a bomb explode and saw dust spray into the air, she would say, "Let's go!" and they would begin running again. With these sporadic movements they eventually crossed the meadow safely to the woods beyond.

As night approached, Meeta and Amalie gathered leaves together and spread Jaak's old winter coat on top of them. There they spent the night. The events of the day had taxed their emotional and physical strength, and Amalie and Vello were soon huddled together sleeping.

Meeta sat looking up through the tree branches into the velvet night sky sprinkled with silver stars. She sensed an Omnipresent Power and thought, how strange that I can be so peaceful in the midst of such a chaotic time. Soon she, too, fell into a deep and restful sleep.

Early the next morning Meeta and Amalie were awakened by the sound of hysterical screaming and yelling. Looking around them they saw no one, and there was no movement. "You and Vello wait here, Mamsi." I'll go and try to see what is happening."

Amalie held Vello close as the sleepy-eyed little boy clung to her. "Be careful, Meeta," warned her mother. "Try to stay hidden."

Meeta walked reticently in the direction of the voices she heard until she reached the edge of the woods. In the middle of the meadow she saw a company of American soldiers knelt on one knee in line formation with rifles aimed at the foreign refugees who were running from the woods waving their handkerchiefs as emblems of peace. The screaming and yelling was their sound of joy as they approached the soldiers. Many of the refugees embraced them while others shook their hands robustly. Meeta approached them cautiously and addressed an officer. Fortunately, she had studied English in high school and was able to speak to him. "Officer, my mother and a small child are still in the forest hiding. May I go back to them?" The officer gave his permission, and Meeta returned to the woods where her mother anxiously waited.

"Mamsi, American soldiers are in the meadow we crossed yesterday and appear to be in control. The noise we heard was the refugees screaming for joy at their arrival."

Amalie's tense face relaxed as she responded. "Ah, perhaps all this madness will now be over."

Meeta, still uncomfortable with the unknown future lying before them, could only say, "We will have to wait and see, Mamsi."

The little family returned along with other refugees to the barn from which they had fled. In Bavaria at that time bread was often baked outside in a baking house made of field stones. It contained a huge stove and usually enough space for a wooden bench on each side of the oven. That afternoon Meeta was in such a baking house boiling potatoes in a tin can when she suddenly heard the familiar clicking sound of bullets spraying against the tile roof and plaster walls of the nearby farmhouse. Meeta carefully peered out the entrance and saw people hurriedly run inside the house. One man had been shot in the thigh and was being pulled inside. Then the door was closed. Meeta sat quietly on one of the benches and waited.

When the gunfire abated, she walked into the barn. Everyone inside was in a state of nervousness. One of the women approached Meeta excitedly. "A bullet went right through the wall where your nephew was sitting. Look! It went through just a few centimeters above his head!" The woman walked over to the spot and pointed at the hole. Before Meeta could respond, the sound of footsteps was heard outside the barn. They turned to see German soldiers in uniform but without their guns passing in front of the door. Meeta instinctively knew that the war in this part of the country was over.

In the days following Meeta, Amalie and Vello, along with some of the other refugees, remained in the barn until some normalcy could be sensed. During this time Amalie went to one of the farmhouses nearby and begged for some eggs, milk and bread, explaining that they had a little boy with them for whom they were concerned. She offered her golden wedding band in payment. But the farmer's wife responded, "I will give you the items you request for him, but the ring will do me no good. What we need now in order to trade is coffee, bolts of cloth, tobacco and cigarettes. A gold wedding band is useless to me." Both Meeta and Amalie lost weight during those few days because they ate sparingly in order to provide enough food for Vello.

Slowly, however, people began to venture back to their former homes, and so did Meeta, Amalie and Vello. As they walked up the hill from the valley, for the first time they saw an American armored tank with a white star on the front. An American soldier leaned against it smoking a cigarette. Strangely, the sight of the white star on the tank instantly sent a shock of fear through Meeta. It brought back memories of other tanks from which Meeta had fled only a few months before—only their star had been bright red.

As they passed the foreign workers' camp, they saw members of the camp returning from town bent low under heavy loads of goods robbed from German houses. They carried downy bags, pillows, dishes and food which they had looted from the city. The sight was so disgusting to Meeta and Amalie that they decided to take another road to avoid these people.

At the crest of a hill they reached a Lutheran church. From that vantage point they had their first look at the town of Neumarkt Oberpfalz. Meeta and her mother both gasped at the sight. Here little more than a week before had stood neat medieval houses with red tile roofs. Now only walls stood with gaping holes where windows once had been. Lonely chimneys stood like rigid soldiers silhouetted against a beautiful, mocking sunset. As far as the eye could see, nothing but desolation existed. Fire had destroyed 65 percent of the city. Once again the words of Jeremiah came to Meeta's mind, "he shall burn it with fire."

CHAPTER 22

Peace Is Declared
Siberia 1945

Hoping to give Peko good news to begin the new year, Ilse sent him a telegram on New Year's Day 1945 stating: "Received letter. Vello is healthy. They have all fled." She could only hope that he was still alive to receive the news she had gotten from Tutti about their son and her family.

As the bitter winter cold deepened, the wood cutters gained new respect at the camp. Without them, no one would have heat or hot food. In the administrative store, the wood cutters were served bread first so they could begin their work as soon as possible. Office workers, cleaning crew members and the cleaning staff accommodated their needs first, hoping not to be required to join them if supplies ran low.

Their supervisors, on the other hand, hounded them continually, demanding that they cut more and more wood. Ilse complained to Pikk one day. "That supervisor came to the boiler building and just sat there all day. He did absolutely nothing. And he gets paid 400 rubles for the month." The more she thought about the injustice of it, the more irate she became. "Those men make me so mad. They are such lazy dogs . . . sluggards."

"Yeah." Pikk agreed. "Have you noticed that when office workers are sent to help us, they only send the women? The men do the easy jobs."

But Ilse and Pikk had little energy for complaining, and their outburst only put them in a miserable mood. Nothing provided any hope for change.

With the temperature at minus 50 degrees by the second week in January, Ilse suffered continually from frostbite. Her nose and cheeks often turned white, then red and then peeled. It was very painful. Because of the lack of proper clothing the skin on her hips and legs began to crack and break open. Pikk went to the polyclinic because her hands were hurting terribly. Then she went to the office and requested lighter work. She was told she could be released for a month to do easier work, but the next day she was sent again to cut wood. She was told that someone would replace her soon, but the replacement never came and she continued working as usual thereafter. Despite all the wood they cut, they were not allowed to bring any logs home for themselves and were only paid with pails of potatoes. To survive, they resorted to stealing wood.

Even with the inequities Ilse was a dependable worker. On January 22, a day that was supposed to be a holiday commemorating Lenin's death, friends told Ilse not to go to work. But Ilse said, "I know there is a lack of wood at the boiler house. Without sufficient fuel it will mean no warm food and many will suffer from the cold. I must go."

In late January Ilse was surprised to receive a letter from her family's former housekeeper, Miila. She had been employed by the Kollist family for many years prior to the arrival of the Russians and became a friend as well as a servant. Memories of happier days warmed Ilse's heart as she opened the letter.

Her mouth watered for Miila's wonderful cucumber pickles. She had helped Miila gather leaves and branches in late summer and watched in anticipation as she layered sliced cucumbers, black currant leaves, dill branches, oak leaves, finely cut horseradish and salt in a wooden barrel in the basement. After pouring boiling water over it all, Miila would cover the barrel tightly. Ilse would wait impatiently for days until the contents began to sour and Miila would give her the first sample from the barrel. Would she ever taste anything so good again?

When Miila had to be terminated because of Jaak's reduced income after the Russian takeover of Estonia, she had remained a close friend. To commemorate Vello's birth, she planted a lilac bush in her own yard.

"Estonia has changed," Miila reported. "The Russians have cleared the island of Saaremaa of all Germans, and 30 cafeterias have been established in Tallinn." She explained that these cafeterias serve cheaper food and have replaced the quality restaurants previously enjoyed by Tallinn's residents. "The Estonia Theater in Tallinn has been damaged, but the theater group is still playing," she added.

Miila was anxious to know how Ilse was doing and if she could send anything to help her. Strange, thought Ilse, how this war has changed things. My family was always seeking to help her, and now the situation is completely reversed.

On January 31 the temperature plummeted to minus 55 degrees. "It has been 14 years since the temperature has reached such a low," declared one of the local Russians. Ilse and her roommates stayed awake through that night adding logs to their iron stove, but despite their efforts the room felt as cold as if there was no heat. During cold winter nights they slept in their outdoor clothes with their boots on and went for days without removing them. Their clothes became so tattered and patched they often joked that they looked like clowns. One day Pikk chuckled as she told Ilse, "My *fufaika* is so decayed that an old lady in town felt sorry for me and handed me 9 rubles."

In mid-February an Estonian friend came from Grishkin to visit her daughter being held in the Togor prison. While in town she visited Ilse and shared news she had received that in Pärnu a German church, the Endla Theater, and many houses on Janssen Street had been badly damaged. She paused before continuing but finally lowered her voice and said, "Volli Pavelson has died . . . but his wife Hilda does not know this yet."

The news stunned Ilse. No response came for several seconds as her mind processed what she had heard. Her first dazed words were, "Poor Hilda." Then her face became somber as she said, "You know Peko is with Volli in that prison camp. How devastating the loss of such a close friend must be for him. I fear how this might affect him."

When she had regained some degree of composure, her voice dropped to almost a whisper as she said, "Dear Volli . . . I saw him last in February 1941 on Hilda's birthday." As she spoke her eyes focused past her friend, as though recalling the occasion. Then, from the depth of her soul came an agonized cry. "Providence, Providence, what are You doing with us? Is it possible we will never see our men again?… Will they *all* die?"

* * *

At the beginning of March Ilse and Pikk were sent to the forest where once again they slept in a large, dark barrack made of improperly pitched logs that let in the cold. Six-foot-wide shelves lined the length of the room on either side of a center aisle. On these shelves a total of 120 men and women slept side by side in full dress like Baltic herrings in a can.

One night after Pikk left for her shift additional men came to sleep, but there was no room for one of them. He pulled Ilse from between the other sleepers and lay down in her place. This forced Ilse to sleep on the floor sitting up beneath the window located at the end of the barrack. The wall behind her was cold, so she did not rest well. The great advantage of sleeping side by side was the warmth that was generated by the surrounding bodies.

Later that month Ilse received a letter from her parents' last maid, Tasja. Enclosed with the letter was a picture of Vello taken four months before he turned three. At first glance she turned away and thought, I will try to look at him with impartiality. She tried to control her eagerness yet urgently anticipated the first glimpse of the son she had not seen for three years and nine months. Slowly she lifted the photo and stared at the little boy who was standing against the arm of a bench. His blond hair was cut short. A cute, round face smiled at her with eyes reminiscent of someone she remembered. He looks healthy and well fed, she noted thankfully.

She stared at the picture for a long while, her mind struggling with a range of emotions. Oh, how I long to hold him, she thought. How I long for him to know his father and for his father to know him. Peko wanted so much to have his own child. He is such an extraordinary man. I want Vello to be just like him. Her heart ached as she recalled the fatherly pride Peko exhibited each time he held his son—but for only three short weeks. She felt anxiety rising within her as she thought of the lost years…the years that would never be. How could one replace all the joys of watching a child grow and develop? How could she ever replicate holding her own little one close to her bosom? How could she ever establish a mother-son relationship with a child who had never known her?

At last, however, her practical, disciplined nature took control. It was good that I left him behind, she thought. He would never have survived what I have lived through. But the maternal longing was very strong, and she asked herself a hopeful question. Is it possible we could yet be a family?

Her heart cried out for the dream she desperately wished could become reality, and her mind eagerly entertained possibilities. If the war ends soon, if Peko and I were released to return to Estonia, if we could find where my family has fled there might still be time. Then, contemplating the magnitude of the events she had just envisioned, her spirit fell. I fear it's too far out of reach.

* * *

Work in the forest included burning the branches of the trees they felled. It was upsetting to Ilse that they were paid for the number of square meters they cut but not for the time spent burning branches. Everything about the work they did benefited the State at their expense. Because an ax was missing, the director deducted 33.30 rubles from her 49.60 pay to apply it toward the cost of the missing ax. The price of an ax was 100 rubles, so the three people who were on duty when the ax was lost were each charged. Another time the cost of potatoes that had been originally given to them was deducted from their pay. The deduction was so great that they did not receive any money.

Now that the worst of the winter was passed, they even found themselves being cheated by the kitchen staff that had been accommodating to the wood cutters during the colder weather. One day when they went to the cafeteria window to redeem the coupons they were issued for fat and barley, the coupons were returned to them minus 500 grams of fat and 800 grams of barley which had been cut off. This meant the kitchen staff would be benefiting from their allotment.

Pikk noticed that a number of potatoes had been thrown out by the cafeteria and were behind the barracks. They were frozen and therefore discarded. She cleaned them and brought them into their barrack. When they thawed they became blue, but Pikk cooked them and Ilse and Pikk ate them. "They're not so bad," said Ilse. Pikk smiled as she gave the response she received when she had asked about them. "One of the cooks said, 'We have no pigs to feed them to, so when they became frozen we threw them out.' I guess that makes us pig replacers," said Pikk. They both enjoyed a hearty laugh.

By the third week in April Pikk and Ilse were so weak from hunger that on the way back to the barrack they had to rest three times. During one of these rest periods Ilse had a stern talk with Pikk. "Pikk, you simply must do something about your lice. You are infesting the people sleeping next to you, and even I do not want to be near you." Pikk accepted Ilse's comment and promised her she would go to the sauna that day to rid herself of them. In actuality it took two trips on two different days to finally kill them all. But following her delousing Pikk proudly announced, "I am now free from lice!"

Pikk had begun broadening her "sorceress artistry" and was finding more customers among the Russians to make up for the money she was not getting from her regular work. To celebrate Pikk went to the city and bought some potatoes which Ilse and she cooked in the forest.

At the end of April they finally were released to return to their apartment in Kolpashevo. One of their first stops was to see the White Dame. She gave them a bucket of potatoes and one kilogram of bread for a simple silk handkerchief they presented her.

Ilse and Pikk were put to work carrying heavy boards from the barge up the high, steep bank of the Ob River. They tried to carry them by twos, but decided, even with the excess weight, it was easier done alone.

Ivanovits, the *pretsedatel*,[36] was present and noticed that some planks had been cut in firewood lengths and piled behind a large salt hill. Salt was brought by ship to the bank of the river and from there gathered for distribution. A lady stood guard by the salt. Ivanovits realized someone had stolen and hidden the planks behind the salt. He sent Ilse to gather them. As she approached, the woman guard cried out in protest. Ivanovits shouted to her, "Whose wood is stacked there?"

The woman called back, "The administrator of the pharmacy asked me to guard it."

Ivanovits firmly retorted, "By whose authority did he cut *our* planks into firewood?"

The woman was silent, and Ilse obediently gathered and carried the wood to a waiting horse-pulled wagon destined for the Communist headquarters.

Pikk did not work on May 9 but remained in the apartment because of a malaria attack. Ilse was at work when the telephone rang; her supervisor took the call. His usual stern face was transformed before her eyes as he announced loudly, "Peace has been declared! Today we celebrate! Consider this a holiday." Then he added, "There will be a meeting at 11:00 a.m." Ilse immediately ran home to share the news with Pikk, but Pikk had already heard the good tidings and was weeping for joy. Jefimia and Elise had also been released from work for the day. "Oh, Ilse," said Jefimia excitedly, "what do you think this means for us?"

"I don't know. We will have to see what happens when the dust settles," said Ilse. "The Russians are still in our homeland. I would like more information."

Ilse put on a winter coat, the best of what she had, and walked outside. Here and there flags were raised. People were grouped together excitedly discussing this latest news. Ilse was told a meeting would be held at the stadium, and everyone began flocking to the meeting. A heavy rain began, however, and Ilse turned back to her apartment fearing the ruin of the only decent coat she had.

Two ladies from Grishkin who had come to see Elise were in the apartment when she returned. They brought sad news that many Estonians who were in the Makarov settlement had died in the last year and that eight of the nine in another settlement had also died.

One of the visitors expressed her feelings about the peace agreement. "I have doubts about what will happen to our dear Estonia. The Russians are not likely to want to give it up now that they are so deeply entrenched in a land they have long coveted. Much will depend on what the other Allies can negotiate. Our own fate, too, hangs on the negotiations." All agreed it was too soon to know what the outcome would be. The two guests spent the night in the apartment and left the next day.

Life did not change in the days that followed. The work continued as normal. However, on May 14 Ilse received 300 rubles from Tutti, sent to her by means of a money card.[37] Suddenly the world seemed brighter. She was able to buy some potatoes, beets and fish and was thankful that she was now in contact with a friend who knew where she was and was able to help her. This, plus the fact that warmer weather was now approaching, greatly lifted her spirit. Hope arose that life might become more bearable.

The following day Ilse was assigned work at Galdilini's home, the cafeteria supervisor. She dug away the dirt from under the house so warm air could circulate beneath. It was a seasonal task. She would have to replace the dirt in the fall in preparation for winter, but it was a job for which she received two good meals. She also dug a garden for Galdilini over the next few days and planted cucumbers and potatoes. Mrs. Galdilini tried to help a bit but said her back could not take the strain. Ilse asked her if she might be able to get some land for a garden of her own this year. Mrs. Galdilini replied, "I promise this year will be better than last." Ilse said nothing further but thought to herself, I am fed up with these empty promises. I will believe it when I see the land.

On Sunday, May 20, Ilse wrote in her diary: "Vello is four years old today. How I wonder where he is and what he is doing."

Early that morning she was told by a supervisor that she was to go immediately to plant a field with other workers who would meet her there. It was raining so Ilse questioned the command. "In the rain? There will be no one else there." The supervisor responded firmly, "An order is an order. Tomorrow you will get a free day."

Ilse walked the six kilometers to the field in the rain. When she arrived, as she had thought, no one else was there. She waited until noon for an overseer to appear, but none came. Ilse mentally complained as she walked back to Kolpashevo, I am upset that on a Sunday and in the rain I cannot have a day of peace. These Russian supervisors are just controlling, power-hungry egotists.

Though the supervisor had promised Ilse a free day, the following day she was sent to Togor with a truck driver to pick up some boards. When they arrived, however, they found no boards at the designated place. When they asked the guard on the premises who had taken them, his reply was, "I don't know." Ilse and the truck driver looked at each other, and the driver shrugged his shoulders saying, "Strange things happen in this land." Then they turned the truck around and returned to Kolpashevo.

The next two days Ilse planted potatoes in the gardens of administrative personnel and then was sent to work in a garden near the boiler house where she had spent so many days cutting wood in winter. The sun was very hot as she worked. But then the sky darkened, and a powerful storm arose. She quickly ran to the boiler house for shelter. The storm was so mighty she feared the boiler house might be swept away. Three windows were blown out—including the frames of the windows. The rain and pea-sized hail whirled into the building. Soon another worker joined Ilse. As the worker entered, she wrung out her rain-soaked skirt. Then a truck driver joined them. As they peered outside, it was hard to tell where the sky and earth separated. It seemed to be united in blackness.

The rain lasted for about half an hour. When they finally ventured outside, they saw wires and fences down and windows and broken glass scattered everywhere. A small, round-roofed building in the children's play area now looked like a giant mushroom growing out of the ground. It had collapsed in the storm. All the boats on the river were overturned, and one man was reported to have been swallowed by the river.

By the end of May Ilse and Pikk had been given some land of their own for a garden. Eagerly and quickly they planted it, fearful they might be sent to other administrators' homes before they could complete their own planting. While they worked, Pikk told Ilse of a Polish man who had recently come to Kolpashevo. "He said he was in a camp just north of us where 200 men had been shot to death."

This information gave a chilling thought to Ilse. "Oh, Pikk, this makes me wonder what will become of my Peko now that the war has ended."

Pikk looked sympathetically at Ilse and said, "I was not wise in telling you this, Ilse. Unfortunately, this is a time of transition. Only God knows the outcome."

Much of June Ilse worked at Galdilini's home cutting, sawing and piling wood. The food given to her was poor. Since the war had ended the Galdilinis were receiving many visitors. Ilse was given only the leftovers from the meals they provided their guests, usually consisting of a chunk of bread, some potatoes and a little soup. She thought to herself, I would never know the war has ended if I had not been told.

CHAPTER 23

Instability Reigns
Germany 1945

When Meeta, Amalie and Vello returned to the Eberhard Faber factory premises where they had been living, they found it had been subjected to heavy machine gunfire. The upper corner of their resident building had been blown out, but their room had not been damaged.

They next examined the shed where they stayed until midnight before fleeing into the countryside. Everything in the shed had been riddled with machine gun bullets from diving airplanes. Meeta examined her suitcase, which still remained in the shed. Bullet holes studded it every few centimeters. "It looks like a sieve," said Meeta to her mother. "Not one piece of clothing is wearable." Then she paused and looked into her mother's eyes. "This could have been us, Mamsi. God has spared us this fate."

Amalie was also moved by what she saw. "I am thankful we did not remain in this city. The devastation is remarkable." Amalie stepped outside and looked for the sandy pit where she had placed the family's two other suitcases when leaving the shed that fateful night. They had contained clothes for her and Vello along with cherished pictures they had not wanted to leave behind in their room. As they approached the pit, they discovered that the contents of the suitcases had been stolen and their coveted pictures were soiled and strewn in the sand. Their only remaining belongings were the clothes they were wearing, and they were without food as well.

Meeta and her little family went back to their apartment and met the Polish lady who lived across the hall from them. She, too, had returned to her apartment. After sharing their plights together the Polish woman said, "Meeta, why don't you go with my 12-year-old daughter. Damaged homes are everywhere in the city. You can go into the basements of these ruined houses and find just about everything you will need." As Meeta stood in the woman's doorway, she could see china and bundles of goods and clothing in every corner of her room. Meeta privately suspected that the contents of their suitcases were probably among the goods but made no accusation because of insufficient proof.

The next day Meeta walked into the city proper and was shocked by the terrible destruction that surrounded her. The streets had gaping holes. Walls of buildings stood menacingly alone without the support of their former three sides. Ash residue was everywhere, and the smell of burnt debris floated disagreeably to her nostrils. She found the city in complete chaos, and food products were not available to buy. The area was now a conquered territory, and the citizenry had no rights or protection. In town some unscrupulous American soldiers went from house to house demanding gold items such as rings, watches and jewelry. Later she learned that one of her friends had to relinquish her own and her husband's gold wrist watches to them. Her husband had been killed at the Russian front, and the watch was her cherished memento. Later American commanders had signs erected saying "Off Limits," but immediately after conquest no laws protected the people.

Witnessing the looting, Meeta thought, This is revolting. How can people take advantage of those who have already lost so much?

She continued walking up the main street of the city and suddenly became aware that she was approaching the house of Miss Baumann, a dear fellow worker in the factory. Meeta's stomach tightened as she stood before the house. It was in total ruins. Fear gripped her as she thought of the possible scenarios: Had Miss Baumann been in the house when it was attacked? Had she left the city as Meeta and her family had done before the devastation began? Had she survived in a bomb shelter somewhere in the city?

Gingerly she entered the house, not knowing how stable the remaining walls might be but wondering if anything had been spared the looting. As she stepped into what had once been the living room, she found a stock of dishes in a niche of the great stone stove. Incredibly, some of them had withstood the intense heat. What shall I do with them? she thought. They will surely be stolen if left here. She looked across the street and noticed a house still completely intact. She walked over to the house and knocked on the door. Someone peeked out the window from behind a drape. Soon the door opened just a crack and a woman's voice asked, "What is it you want?"

"I am a co-worker with Miss Baumann. Do you know her?"

"Yes, I know her." The woman answered in a hesitating manner.

"Is she okay? Where is she?" Meeta asked eagerly.

The door opened, and Meeta stood face to face with a middle-aged woman who eyed her suspiciously. "Why do you want to know?"

"I'm concerned about her things. Much looting is going on in the city, and I fear what remains of her belongings will soon be gone."

The woman seemed to relax as Meeta spoke and responded congenially. "Miss Baumann has fled to the country and is with relatives."

Meeta also relaxed as she learned the good news. "Would it be too much to ask that I bring some of her things to your house to hold for her until she returns?"

The neighbor now smiled at Meeta. "There probably isn't much that is of use. Her house is almost totally demolished."

"I did find some dishes that can be salvaged."

"You're welcome to bring them here," the woman said politely.

Meeta carried the dishes to the neighbor's house and then returned into Miss Baumann's basement where she found a large bag of potatoes. Strangers peered at Meeta through the basement window, and she knew it would only be a matter of time before they would be stealing these for themselves. She took the bag of potatoes across the street to the neighbor and explained to her the plight in which she and her family found themselves.

"I will either pay Miss Baumann for these potatoes or return the same amount to her when she returns," explained Meeta. "I will leave you my name. I live above the social hall on the Eberhard Faber factory premises." The neighbor was kind and provided a wagon, which Meeta later returned, to transport the potatoes back to her apartment.

When Meeta arrived home, she discovered that a kind soul had left them some additional vegetables outside the door of their room. But the potatoes provided the mainstay of their diet for the next several days.

The pencil factory, too, had been looted—by both American soldiers and civilians. Fountain pens, pencils and erasers were taken and strewn all over the floors of the halls so that when walking the pencils crunched underfoot.

While walking in town one day Meeta met two Estonian soldiers who had fought for the German army. Hearing them speak Estonian, she engaged them in conversation and learned they had no place to stay for the night. She offered them lodging with her family. Since they had four beds in their apartment, the two soldiers slept in two of the beds, Amalie in one and Meeta and Vello in the other. The arrangement turned out to be mutually beneficial. Townspeople had broken into the former army storage rooms and had scattered yards of cloth that had been used for army uniforms. The two young soldiers had retrieved some of the material, and out of gratitude for their lodging gave some to the Kollists. The material was of two colors—khaki and yellow.

A Polish neighbor who was a seamstress sewed Meeta a yellow blouse and a khaki skirt. She also made pants for Vello from the khaki material. Amalie sewed herself and Vello yellow shirts.

It consumed most of the day to shop because everything was rationed. Many items such as salt were not available. At the bakeshops people stood for hours in long lines to receive bread. At other stores they stood in equally long lines to receive vegetables, milk, butter or lard. For meat one had to go to the slaughterhouse where animals were killed right where people stood waiting.

The first time Meeta witnessed the slaying of a cow it left an indelible impression upon her. The cow was hit with a heavy mallet between the horns and fell to the ground with a loud thump that caused the ground to quiver beneath her feet. The throat was quickly cut and the hide stripped off. Then the meat was cut and distributed. She received her portion, but that night she could not bear to eat it.

One day Amalie and Meeta heard a commotion in the yard below their apartment. Amalie stuck her head out the window and saw people running toward the factory. "What's happening?" she called to one man who had just begun to join the others. He excitedly replied, "The factory is on fire!"

Amalie remained in their apartment with Vello and watched from afar while Meeta went to see the severity of the blaze. As she approached, she saw the director of the factory and other lady clerks from his office attempting to extinguish the blaze with water hoses. She learned the fire had begun in the storage and packing area where she had previously worked; arson was suspected. Unfortunately, the front portion of the factory completely burned down. Meeta resented American soldiers whom she saw standing nearby who made no attempt to help extinguish the fire.

Within a few days an order was received from the American command that all civilians living in apartments surrounding the factory were required to leave. Since the Kollists had no place to go, they moved into a glass-partitioned foreman's office in the factory where they slept on the floor. Their few belongings remained on work tables outside the office.

One morning as they were returning from receiving their rations, they saw a teenaged girl carrying a big armload of things out of the factory. They hurried into the building and found that their meager things were also missing.

"Mamsi, I know the girl we saw taking things," said Meeta. "She is the daughter of a Polish woman who lives in another section of the factory."

Amalie was livid. "Take me to her. I'll teach that girl a thing or two."

Meeta knew her mother's confrontational skills and readily complied.

Arriving where the girl was quartered, Amalie walked straight to her and looked directly into her face. "We saw you taking things from our part of the factory. You ought to be ashamed of yourself, young lady. Hasn't your mother taught you any respect and decency? We lost everything when we left our homeland, our business, our home, and our furniture. My daughter and son-in-law have been deported to Siberia, and I have no idea if they are still alive. I have also lost my husband. We have only the clothes on our backs and the few paltry things that you have now robbed us of. I demand them back!"

The girl looked terrified and seemed to wither as Amalie spewed forth all that had apparently been bottled up for so long. When she responded, her voice was weak and wavering. "I'm sorry. I'll show you where they are." The girl's body literally trembled as she walked down a hallway.

Amalie followed almost on the girl's heels with Meeta and Vello trailing until they reached a closet. The girl opened it exposing a content of stolen items. Amalie gave the girl a disgusted look and then turned to the closet throwing all the items into the hall as she searched for their things. After retrieving what belonged to them, Amalie once again turned to the thief.

"I would suggest that you take the remainder of these items back to whom they belong. If anyone complains to me about any losses, I will direct them right to you, young lady."

Amalie and Meeta picked up their items, and the Kollist entourage left the trembling girl standing red-faced by her pile of stolen goods.

The second week after the American invasion of their city the director of the factory organized a cleanup of the premises. The Kollist family was moved to one of the small washhouses located beside the factory. These were formerly used by the employees to freshen themselves before going home for the day, but now they were vacant.

The social hall where they had previously lived on the second floor was now operating as the American mess hall. After each meal served there, hungry children and civilians from the community came to get leftovers. Meeta also went. One time she received a large bowlful of leftover pancake batter. On another occasion she got a large can filled with orange marmalade which she shared with her long-time friend Helga Paimre and her three little girls. Potatoes, however, were their mainstay. As their potato supply grew scanty, Amalie became concerned.

"You must go into the countryside and see if you can get some potatoes from a farmer, Meeta."

"Mamsi, I have nothing to exchange for food. Besides, without a wagon, even if I was able to get food, I have no way of carting it back to the city. We will have to depend on God to provide for us."

Amalie's voice rose. "Do you expect God to drop potatoes through the ceiling?"

Meeta creased her brow and responded, "If He has to, He will."

Amalie shook her head in disgust and threw up her hands.

The following day they heard a knock on the door of the washhouse. It was Meeta's former supervisor in the packing department.

"Meeta, I have been wondering how you and your little family are getting along in these living conditions."

Meeta invited him in, and during their conversation Amalie mentioned their lack of potatoes. Without hesitation he said, "Oh, I have plenty of potatoes in my basement. Meeta, if you come this evening I will give you a supply. But please come after dark. I don't want the world to know I have these stored in my basement."

When the man left, Meeta asked her mother, "What do you say about that?"

Amalie turned away without a response.

Shortly thereafter, the Kollist family received yet another order to leave the factory premises. They were told a large sawmill, whose owner was Mr. Pfleiderer, was accepting all German and refugee workers from Eberhard Faber as workers in his mill. Meeta took advantage of this offer, and the Kollists were moved into the former gatekeeper's house that was located at the gate of the entrance to the Pfleiderer factory compound on Ingolstädter Strasse.

The interior of the house measured approximately 3 x 4 meters. It also had a small fore room where there was a large iron stove for heating on which they cooked their food. The main room was used as a bedroom. Foreign workers had been living in it previously. It was furnished with a wardrobe and three beds, but they contained countless bedbugs. Every night Meeta picked 70 to 80 from Vello's bed as he slept. She told her work supervisor about the infestation, and he arranged to have the house exterminated. The windows and doors were taped, and a pungent gas was sprayed into their quarters. The Kollist family had to sleep outside that night. Fortunately, it was now summer and the weather was mild.

When the family entered their abode the following morning, the floor was covered with the dead bedbugs. Unfortunately, one treatment did not solve the problem which meant that the extermination had to be repeated a second time before the situation was alleviated.

Shopping was something Meeta did not look forward to doing. In addition to the lines being extremely long everything had to be carried home in shopping bags for three to four kilometers. By the time she reached their home, her arms were so stretched from carrying the load that she was hardly able to bend them at the elbows.

Waiting in line did have some advantages, however. She became acquainted with people she often saw. One such was Mr. Schiffman. He learned that Meeta had studied piano at the conservatory in Estonia and encouraged her to visit a friend of his who owned a farm located on the crest of a hill several kilometers away.

"They own an organ, Meeta. Tell them I sent you to ask if you could practice your music on their organ. They are good people with whom you should become acquainted. They would also likely supply you with some food items for your family."

Meeta followed Mr. Schiffman's advice and walked the distance to the farm one Saturday morning. She discovered that they had a harmonium and that their son had been the organist for their church before the war began. They encouraged her to play the instrument and were pleased to hear its tones again. Before she left that day they provided her with some bread and milk. Meeta became a frequent visitor thereafter.

One evening as she was returning from their farm, she heard someone in a house playing "Traumerei,[38] *Op. 15, No. 7*" by Robert Schumann on a piano. Meeta had often played this piece, many times with her father playing along on his violin. Now she had no piano and no father. Oh, how very much she missed him. Sorrow overwhelmed her as she put her arm on a nearby stone wall, leaned her head on her arm and cried uncontrollably.

For the first months after the Americans had entered Newmarkt Oberpfalz, food had been given in exchange for German ration cards. Later, however, the International Refugee Organization (IRO) took charge of the refugee camp in the woods where the Kollist family initially had been placed. Refugees inside the town were also given provisions through that organization which required weekly trips to the camp. Finally a distribution station was established in town. From the IRO they received powdered and canned milk, powdered eggs, flour, sugar and fat.

One day Helga Paimre visited the Kollist home to relate to them news of an American order requiring all foreign refugees to return to live at the IRO camp. Both Helga and the Kollist family shuddered at the thought of returning to the camp they had been so delighted to leave the year before.

The news was pressing heavily on Meeta's mind as she walked down the hill from the farm where she routinely practiced her music. This day she carried four large loaves of bread and some fresh milk the family had given her. As she walked, she prayed that God might somehow intervene again in their behalf.

Meeta decided to go to the American authorities to request permission to remain in Neumarkt Oberpfalz. She was directed to an office and knocked on the door, but no one came to open it. Finding it to be unlocked, she entered. Before her was an American officer sitting behind a table. Both his feet were on the table with the soles of his shoes facing her. She had been raised to be respectful and mannerly in public, and to her this was a most discourteous and unprofessional behavior.

The officer was conversing with another American soldier and completely ignored her entry. She stood waiting acknowledgement. After some time the officer raised his arms, put them behind his head and yawned broadly. "What is it you want?" he asked.

Meeta was benumbed by what she considered rude decorum and could scarcely speak. Then in a wavering voice she began: "My request, Sir, is that I and mother and four-year-old nephew be allowed to remain in Newmarkt Oberpfalz instead of returning to the IRO camp as ordered." Regaining her voice she added, "I have a job here, and we have a place to live."

The officer remained in his initial position and said, "That order cannot be altered."

Feeling herself in an unfriendly environment and still digesting the man's unfamiliar propriety, she turned hastily and left the office without saying another word.

Meeta explained her discouraging encounter to her friend Helga, and the two of them decided they would go together to the new German mayor of the town who had been appointed by the American commander.

Fortunately, Helga knew him personally and so won an audience quickly. After explaining their plight to him, he showed sympathy but informed them, "This is not something I can do. The Americans have the authority to decide your cases."

Helga looked downcast as she spoke. "Please help us. Do you know what that camp is like? There is no privacy. Meeta has an elderly mother and a little nephew, and I have three little girls." She paused briefly, searching the mayor's face. "We both have jobs and apartments to live in here. Please, can't you just sign this letter of authorization for us?" Helga laid a carefully typed letter on his desk that they had prepared beforehand.

The mayor read the letter slowly and then reached for his pen, poising it to write his signature. But then he put the pen down. He began pacing back and forth across the room. He took the pen in hand again and once again put it down saying, "No, I cannot do it!" He commenced pacing back and forth, back and forth. While he paced, Meeta prayed silently claiming the words of Moses to the children of Israel as they faced the daunting Red Sea before them and the fearful Egyptian army behind them, "The Lord will fight for you, and you shall hold your peace."[39]

The mayor again picked up the pen and began to sign the paper. But once again he put it down and said, "No, I cannot do it!" Once more he began pacing, and Meeta continued her silent prayer. Finally, he grabbed the pen and signed the permission document.

CHAPTER 24

Changing Times
Siberia 1945

Ilse, Pikk and Jefimia were moved into a small house with three rooms, on July 1, 1945. The three of them slept in one of the rooms. A Russian family of four was given another room. All of the occupants shared the front room. They were glad for the additional space, but they had no furniture, and there were many cockroaches in residence. Ilse was able to take along her old bed from the previous apartment, Pikk made herself a makeshift bed from boards, and Jefimia found a wooden box on which to sleep.

After settling into their new quarters, Ilse and Pikk were assigned to cleaning and refurbishing the barge which had been lifted onto logs. Ilse and Pikk stuffed cracks with cotton strips and then built a fire under a large kettle of tar. When the tar melted, they dipped brushes into the pitch and began covering the filled cracks with the substance.

The supervisor had told them to just fill the cracks but not to tar the underside of the barge. Ilse felt this was a mistake but said nothing. Experience had taught her not to question. She did voice her concerns to Pikk, however. "I simply don't understand how we can leave the barge uncovered beneath; it will start to rot." Pikk gave Ilse an understanding look and then said, "We're not supposed to think. We're expected to just follow orders."

After the tarring was finished, all the workers from the Communist headquarters were summoned to help push the barge back into the Ob River. Once it was afloat, Ilse and her two roommates were sent to work with a truck driver to bring wood from Togor to load the barge. Because the summer heat was so intense the truck tires would not hold air, so they had to stop several times on the way to and from Togor to pump more air into them.

One day Pikk received a letter from a Russian woman. As Pikk read the letter, her eyes widened and her mouth gaped. "Ilse, listen to this. This is from someone claiming to be my husband's wife. She says she has lived with him for two years!" Pikk had Ilse's attention as she continued reading. "We get along very well and could send a request to Communist headquarters that you come and live with us. We have put in a vegetable garden and feel the three of us could get along very well."

"Can you believe this letter, Ilse?" said Pikk. "Do they expect me to be a participant in a threesome?" Pikk frowned as she crossed her arms in front of her. "How do I respond to something like this?"

Ilse was as dumbfounded as Pikk. "I have no advice to give you, Pikk. War produces some strange situations." Ilse began thinking of her own husband.

Since she had not received a letter recently, she wondered where he was and how he was handling being without a woman. But she kept these thoughts to herself.

While Pikk was still pondering the letter, orders came from their supervisor, Volkov, that they were to prepare to go to the hayfields. This meant they would have to gather food enough to take with them for the trip. "Well," said Pikk, "I won't have time to deal with this letter now." Then she added in a disgusted tone, "And I don't know if I *ever* want to."

Since they had not been paid for their work since May, Ilse had been buying food with the money Tutti had sent her. The money was now at an end, and she wondered how she would get food enough to take with her. Later that day, however, she received mail from three people: Miila and two Estonian friends. They each sent her 100 rubles. Ilse was overcome with emotion as she addressed Pikk. "When my need has been the greatest, then the help seems to have always come." Tears spilled from her eyes as she said, "These people don't have enough for themselves." Her lips began to quiver, and her tears turned into streams as she continued, "These lovely people are thinking of me! Not just one . . . but three of them!"

The trip to the hayfield was delayed because no bread was available. In the meantime, Roska, one of the horses that they used for the field work got loose, and no one could catch him. Four workers and Ilse began the chase and found the horse in the potato field by the side of the river. As soon as he saw them he turned into a brushwood area. One of the workers, Suvotsilov, entered into the thicket, and both he and the horse disappeared from view. At the top of a hill two other workers and Pikk looked on, ready to be of help. As the horse emerged from the brush, the workers resumed their chase. Another man from the *kolhoos* who was mounted on his own horse saw the predicament and ran after Roska, but Roska headed toward Togor.

The group thought they would break for lunch and give the horse time to calm down. Following lunch the search continued. Roska was found near Togor in the midst of a group of other horses by the shore of the river. As soon as he heard their voices his ears began to twitch. They hoped to catch him with a long rope they had brought along. As they approached him, however, he turned away, went into the water and swam toward the opposite side. The water was up to his chest when he reached the other side, but he remained standing in it and began to leisurely eat grass from the high bank. Ilse turned to Suvotsilov and said, "Look, now he is eating with the greatest serenity. He must be feeling quite safe from us." She chuckled and then added, "His trauma has become suddenly pleasant for him."

Suvotsilov scowled and said, "Not for long!" He then took a boat and paddled over to Roska, chasing him back to their bank. As soon as the horse jumped from the water, he headed for more brushwood. Everyone followed him, but he went deeper and deeper into the thicket. Niina, one of the workers, got within three meters of him and called out, "Give me the rope!"

As soon as Roska heard her speak, he turned around and went once again toward Togor. The chase was on again, and they followed him into a petroleum yard where gasoline was stored. Two openings led to the yard; Ilse stood guard at one of them. But the horse jumped over the gate that closed the second opening and was on the run again. This time, however, he headed toward Kolpashsevo; everyone followed. The whole group was extremely tired by the time they reached their home base. They had walked at least 40 kilometers in the chase, and Roska was once again back where they had initially started—in the potato field.

A day later Volkov and Suvotsilov met together to plan a strategy for getting Roska and set out. That evening Roska was on board when the barge left for the hayfield with the workers and necessary equipment. Ilse never discovered just how the two of them finally roped Roska, given the difficult time a whole group of workers had the day before. It seemed particularly amazing to her since Volkov was a war veteran with only one hand.

The workers had only a few of their own potatoes with them instead of the customary food products. Rather than delay the trip any further Volkov said the food would be brought to them in the field. When they arrived at their destination, they discovered there were no huts for them to sleep in and that they would have to erect hay huts.

The huts looked like large haystacks and slept four to six people. They were assembled with a frame of long thick sticks into which hay was woven, such as one would do on a thatched roof. Hay was also placed on the floor of the hut so workers could sleep on it when they retired. The huts were quite protective and in a primitive way rather pleasant. They provided warmth at night, shielded them from the rain, and smelled of the sweet, fresh hay as they slept.

Pikk was the designated cook during their time in the field, and either she or Volkov brought food products from the headquarters for them to eat. Their diet consisted mainly of bread, butter, cream and potatoes. Once in a while they would be given sturgeon or canned meat.

While working in the field Volkov, a married man with a son, became romantically involved with one of the Russian workers named Natka. She would sometimes accompany him on his trip back to Kolpashevo. At other times he would remain overnight in the hayfield and was observed sleeping with Natka in a haycock.

Time in the hayfields, however, did have some fun moments. In the evenings often someone would play the balalaika. The workers would sing and even sometimes dance.

On August 9 Volkov announced to the workers that Russia and Japan were at war. Two days later Pikk heard that Japan had pleaded for peace with Russia. Rumors circulated freely during this confused, isolated time, and one was never sure of the facts. News they received from their supervisors was a bit more reliable, but even that needed to be weighed against their prejudices.

They finished work in the hayfield on August 14. The next day they returned to Kolpashevo. A letter awaited Ilse from her long-time friend Tutti with another money card for 200 rubles. It was very much welcomed and appreciated since they had not been paid for working in the fields. They had only received food products which were scanty at best.

Back in Kolpashevo Ilse was once again sent to saw and chop wood in preparation for winter. The days became rather boring until the next Sunday. Liida and Mihail Novikov, who shared the three-room house with Ilse and her roommates, provided some excitement that made Ilse desire rather to suffer boredom.

The house did not allow for much privacy. Ilse was seated on her bed with the door open and heard Liida complain to Mihail that he was drinking away their money. Angered at this, Mihail threw a soup bowl at his wife as she stood in the doorway of their room. Next the intoxicated man threw a porcelain tea cup at her which shattered into pieces. Then, seeing Ilse seated on her bed, Mihail threatened to throw another object in her direction. Liida ran into Ilse's room and pulled the door shut. Ilse's eyes opened wide, and her face flamed. In a loud voice she cried out, "Mihail!" Suddenly the room next door became silent. After a few moments Liida left Ilse's room thinking her husband had calmed. But as soon as Liida appeared outside the door, Mihail threw a stool that hit her on the calf of her leg causing a bleeding wound. Ilse moved into the front room and called out, "Mihail, stop this!" But Mihail shouted, "How can my wife complain when I drink at home? It would be another thing if I were drinking with girls!" Then he grabbed a waste pail full of water and threw it at Liida. Fortunately she was able to sidestep it, but water saturated the front room floor.

The warring parties moved outside where Jefimia was cleaning potatoes in a tin basin at the corner of the house. Afraid she would get between the factions she came indoors, leaving her potatoes behind. Mihail grabbed the basin and threw it, potatoes and all, at his wife and then went back into the house.

Ilse gathered some bandages and stepped outside to assist Liida who sat some distance away on a log assessing her leg. As Ilse began to swab her wound, Mihail came out of the house toward them with the stool once again in his hand. Liida ran and Ilse stepped toward Mihail. Just then his four-year-old son, Vitja, who had witnessed the whole event, approached his father crying. Mihail turned away, took his son by the hand and led him back into the house. Fortunately, he spoke kindly to his son and did not vent his anger on him.

Ilse brought Liida into her room where she treated her wound as best she could. After some time Ilse heard Mihail tell his son, "Go and call Mother here. Tell her I will not hit her again." The little fellow did as he was told, but as soon as Liida appeared at the door Mihail stood up in a threatening manner and moved toward her. Ilse intervened between them and ushered Liida back into her room. After shutting the door she said, "Liida, it would be best if you spent the night here in our room. Give your husband time to sleep off his alcohol." Liida agreed. The next morning Mihail left early and was gone for the day.

During the following week Mihail did not drink, and things remained quiet.

The next Sunday, however, Mihail was drunk again, and his disposition was angry. His little boy was fearful and began crying. Fortunately for the entire household, Mihail's brother came and provided a soothing influence which prompted Ilse to say to her roommates, "It appears we will not have another war today."

The following Sunday, however, Mihail and his brother spent the day drinking together. Ilse and her roommates kept the four-year-old son in their room as he was fearful whenever he now saw his father drinking. Late in the day Mihail's brother came into their room in a drunken stupor and sat on Ilse's bed. He spoke incoherently and soon stretched out on the floor and fell asleep. Ilse, Jefimia and Pikk eyed each other as they observed the snoring man on their bedroom floor. Pikk spoke first. "I sure hope he doesn't plan to spend the night in here."

Ilse responded, "Let him sleep a while, then we'll encourage him to leave." More than an hour passed, and the threesome began to be concerned that they would have an overnight guest. Ilse finally attempted to wake him. "Come now, it's time for you to be on your way."

The man half opened his eyes and asked, "Can I sleep with you?"

"No!" Ilse responded firmly. Then she took him by the arm to encourage him to rise.

"But you don't have a man. Why is that?"

"I do have a man," said Ilse.

The man staggered to his feet. "Where is he?"

"Never mind that. It's time for you to leave."

The man stumbled to the door with Ilse still holding his arm. Pikk and Jefimia watched the interaction and stood ready to help oust the man, but he offered no resistance. As soon as he passed the threshold, Ilse shut the door.

When Ilse reported for work on September 3, Volkov met her with good news. "Stalin has announced the war with Japan has ended. This day is a holiday, Ilse." He handed her one-half liter of wine to celebrate. When Ilse returned home with it in hand, Jefimia suggested she give it to Mihail, but thinking that would not be a good idea Ilse and her roommates decided they would drink it themselves.

The following day Ilse was sent to work in the oat fields and took enough food for five days with her. Those accompanying her were Suvotsilov, Dusja and Niina. Volkov was once again their supervisor. During the day they tied oat sheaves, working with two wagons and three horses. Their water source was one kilometer away. The water had to be put into barrels atop one of the wagons and pulled back to the work site. In order to keep the water from spilling out of the barrels they put hay in the water. Then, before drinking it, they would strain the water through someone's head scarf or some other rag. Cleanliness, thought Ilse, is not a priority in this strange world.

One evening following their meager supper of potatoes and bread, the workers sat for a long time by the fire, each lost in his and her own thoughts.

The only sound that could be heard was the distant whistles of ships traveling up the Ob River. In the stillness, Ilse's thoughts became melancholy as she wrote in her diary: "Why is my heart so heavy? Is it because of the cold? Or is it that winter is coming, and I will pass another winter without being able to go home? I don't have a home or loved ones who are awaiting me. No one needs me for me. Rather, I am like a very small cell structure in the world—like a machine that is put into operation when needed, a machine that does not work at its own will, a machine that cannot have its personal desires and wishes met."

Early on September 10 they began their return to Kolpashevo. The two horse-drawn wagons carried oat sheaves and provided a soft ride as they sat on top of them. They arrived in time to take the barge back to Kolpashevo, which saved them some time. The ride cost them each one ruble. Ilse took a seat high on the deck so she could see the water.

From her perch she imagined she was riding on the Sauga River in her family's rowboat, the water sloshing against its sides. On the shore she envisioned her childhood home situated next to her father's factory. How often she and Oskar, just two years her senior, would row together. He made a wonderful, fun playmate—both of them always desiring some new adventure. One time when there was a good wind on the river, they opened their coats to catch the breeze and turned their rowboat into a sailboat. She smiled as she thought of their creativity.

Then she remembered the time Oskar tried to teach her how to fish. They were fishing from the rowboat, and Ilse said, "This is boring. How can you enjoy doing this?" The words had barely come out of her mouth when there was a tug on her rod. She became excited. "Oskar, I think I've got a fish on my line!" Her brother dropped his fishing pole and stood behind her coaching. "Begin reeling it in, Ilse." She began reeling but became so anxious that as the line came closer to the boat, she jerked the rod up so hard the fish flew over the boat and into the water on the other side, escaping his fate. Oskar had some unpleasant words to say that upset her then, but now she cherished them. Strange, she thought, how time turns disappointing moments into endearing ones.

Arriving back in Kolpashevo they were able to purchase five kilograms of cows' feet and ears for 10.50 rubles. It was a welcomed meal after the scanty fare they had endured over the past week.

During the rest of September, Ilse and her roommates worked storing potatoes, carrots, turnips and beets for winter in the cellar of the Communist headquarters. Once again they shoveled dirt under the houses of the administrators, installed double windows to insulate against the winter's cold and whitewashed for the administrators.

Ilse was given a day off on October 1. Ah, she thought, that means I can earn some rubles for myself today. She contacted Tamara, a lady who worked for the Communist headquarters who had five children at home and a husband at the front. She had offered to pay Ilse if she would come to her home and whitewash the interior of the house for her. Tamara's youngest son was almost four years old and caused Ilse to think of her own boy. He must be about Vello's size, she thought. My son is now four years and four months. How big he must be now, and he still does not know his mother.

The rest of October was spent threshing grain, bagging oats and loading and unloading grain to and from the barge. At the end of October the women workers were paid 160 rubles while the men were paid 260 rubles. "We are always undervalued," said Pikk, "We live in an unequal society."

November found Ilse back in the forest felling trees and chopping logs. Once again they lived in a cold barrack.

In mid-December Isle wrote a letter to her friend Tutti describing what life was like in the forest:

> Dear precious Tutti,
>
> I have written to you quite often. Now I am sitting in the barrack in the forest. It is nighttime. The barrack is lighted by two small bulbs with very low light. Today it is quiet since there are few people here. Usually there is such noise and clamor that my ears are tingling with the most crude cursing, which seemingly no Russian can get along without. It makes one think their youth learned Russian cursing first and then the Russian language. I, fortunately, have not fallen into that habit.
>
> I am seated at a table. Next to me is a Latvian man about 45. He is reading a book. On the opposite side of the table two others are playing cards. We only have the one table.
>
> On both walls of the barrack are two-tiers of wall bunks that we sleep on—heads toward the wall, feet toward the aisle. We sleep like herrings in a bowl, one next to the other. Last year when there were so many sleepers there was no room for me, so I lay down simply on top of the people and sunk between them. There was only enough room for each to have one plank of wood, about 25 centimeters wide. When one person wanted to turn to the other side, all of the sleepers had to turn. I always sleep in the same clothing I wear in the forest, even my felt boots, since by morning the barrack is cold.
>
> Once I froze even when I was on the upper tier sleeping with potatoes under my head. Another time I sat until about one in the morning because there was no room on the bunk to lie down. Then I remembered that the sauna was heated, so I went there. The sauna was pitch black. I felt my way and lay down on the floor. In the morning my partner Pikk came looking for me and found me in the sauna.
>
> The walls of the barrack are wet, and the water steadily drips into the bunk. Since we work in the forest about three kilometers away from the barrack, we do not come back for lunch. We take bread with us that is encrusted with ice. The soup we take with us is also frozen. When we burn branches we melt the soup. We don't have the

desire to make a fire every day since it takes much time, and the winter's day is short. Every organization sends its workers into the forest because they all need wood, so I have become accustomed to forest work. Since we got new cotton-filled coats and cotton-filled pants the cold does not penetrate our bodies. ...

In a week you will have Christmas. I wish you and all your friends and the whole homeland happy holidays, and especially a happy New Year. We are thankful that the terrible war is over and life is improving. ...

Many good wishes and much health,

Ilse

On Christmas Eve Ilse was back in her apartment. She wrote in her diary while Jefimia slept. Pikk had earlier taken letters to the post office and did not return. As Ilse pondered her feeling of loneliness, she wrote of "the Christ Child being born in a place forgotten by mankind." She became more personal as she continued: "It is a strange Christmas Eve. We are far away from friends and relatives. I envision us sitting in a large room. Papsi and Oskar are playing their violins, Meeta is seated at the piano, I am on the cello, and Mamsi is singing. On the right side [of the room] in the corner stands the decorated Christmas tree under which are the presents. Each one of us has a bag of sweets. Miila and Peko are listening to our concert. Also, Uncle Peeter and Aunt Ann are with us. And in the midst is a young boy who is called Vello—whom I cannot clearly imagine."

CHAPTER 25

Love At Last
Germany 1946

The Kollist family continued living at Pfleiderer's Sawmill gatekeeper's house undisturbed throughout the winter months of 1945 and 1946, but the living conditions were unhealthy. The walls of the house were stone and very cold. Lack of insulation made it quite damp. Birch branches that were used to heat their home could be found in the woods beyond them, but they burned quickly and Amalie, now 62, lacked the energy to gather enough to continually keep the fire fed.

In April 1946, as Vello approached his fifth birthday, he became sick with a high fever. Meeta and Amalie became very worried about him, and Meeta walked to the medical dispensary located at the IRO camp to ask a doctor about his condition. He sent a Red Cross ambulance and nurse back with her so that Vello could be brought to him for a thorough examination. When the nurse entered the Kollist home and observed the damp, cold conditions in which they were living, she voiced her concern. "The child cannot remain in this house. He must return with me to the dispensary."

Meeta accompanied Vello with the nurse back to the IRO camp where the doctor determined that he had pneumonia. Vello was taken to the women's section of the hospital barracks. He was placed in a long room with several beds lining one wall. All were empty with the exception of one bed occupied by a Ukrainian lady who appeared to be about 30 years old. "What's wrong with your son?" she asked Meeta sympathetically.

"The doctor says he has pneumonia. But he isn't my son. He's my nephew." Meeta, sensing the warmth of the woman, began telling her about the deportation of her sister and how it came to be that Vello was now in her care.

"Ah, yes, we all have our stories from this war." Her brown eyes clouded, and her face became sullen as she spoke. "I escaped Ukraine with my husband. But my mother and father remained. They owned a farm, and the Russians not only took their food supply but also the grain reserved for the next planting season. They literally starved to death along with many of their neighbors."

Meeta stayed with Vello through the night and was allowed to sleep in the unoccupied bed beside him. The nurse rubbed his chest with what Meeta thought was a eucalyptus ointment and put cold compresses on his head. The barrack was warmed by an iron stove. A supply of large logs was stacked next to it. This is wonderful, thought Meeta, warmth without having to gather wood from the forest.

Vello slept soundly through the night though his stuffy nose produced a tiny snore. The next morning the nurse bathed Vello and once again rubbed his chest with the medication. Both he and Meeta received porridge with milk for breakfast.

Later that morning a bald-headed man with a beard visited Ulanda, the Ukrainian lady. Meeta did not regard him with much attention except that she thought it funny that a man without a strand of hair on his head would grow a beard. When he left Ulanda began to tell Meeta about him. "Wasyl is also Ukrainian. I met him in the camp. He came to the dispensary because of a duodenal ulcer." Ulanda hesitated for a moment and searched Meeta's face before continuing. "He is a lawyer by profession, Meeta, and was asking about you as he visited today. He said he would like to get acquainted."

Meeta scowled, "He's an old man!"

Ulanda made no further comment.

That afternoon, seeing that Vello's fever had decreased, Meeta desired to return home to refresh herself. Ulanda was also recovering from pneumonia and told Meeta she would keep a watch on Vello. Meeta addressed Vello who was still quite weak and resting in bed. "Vello, I will go home for a while this afternoon, but I will be back tonight to spend the night with you." Pointing to Ulanda she continued. "This nice lady will be here with you. So if you need anything, she will help you. Okay?" Vello responded with a whispered, "Okay." Then he turned his head and closed his eyes.

That evening Meeta returned to find Vello sitting up in bed and looking bright eyed. "Ati!" he called out and raised his arms to hug her. "My, little man, you look much better." Meeta embraced her nephew and kissed his cheek. "Did you eat anything today?"

Vello smiled and said, "I ate soup and bread."

Ulanda added, "He ate every bit of it, too, Meeta."

"Well, young man, it seems you are getting better." Meeta then looked at Ulanda and asked, "Has he been out of bed today?"

"The nurse did get him up for a little while," Ulanda responded, "but he is still weak. She thought tomorrow after another meal he would have a bit more energy. He is beginning to cough up some nasty phlegm which, of course, is a good sign that his lungs are beginning to clear."

Ulanda and Meeta chatted together throughout the evening before retiring. Ulanda demonstrated some songs that she had sung with Vello during the day to keep him occupied.

"How very blessed we are that you were in this room with him," said Meeta. "It would have been a very lonely time for this little boy without you to brighten his day."

"I love children," said Ulanda. "I hope that my husband and I will yet be able to raise a family once we get settled somewhere in this war-torn world. He is an architect. If we could emigrate to Australia or the United States, perhaps he could go back to his profession. It's a wonderful dream of ours, Meeta."

The next afternoon Wasyl again visited Ulanda. Meeta was very surprised when she saw him. This time his beard had been shaved off revealing a round, ruddy face that easily broke into a broad smile as he walked into the room. He looks much younger, thought Meeta—like a man in his 40s. She noticed that he often looked in her direction as he spoke with Ulanda, but she could not make out their conversation.

Vello had eaten a good breakfast of porridge and a lunch of soup and bread. He was now getting out of bed and becoming eager to move around the barrack. It was a sunny and warm April day, so the nurse suggested that Vello might enjoy the sandbox that was in a play area outside the barrack. Meeta and her nephew went outdoors. Soon Vello was enthralled with a pail and small shovel, moving sand from one location to another in the sandbox and building an army ditch and mound.

Meeta had brought some sewing along with her to pass the time. She sat nearby on a wooden bench tending to her handiwork. Soon she became aware of someone standing beside her.

"It's been a while since we've had such a warm and beautiful day. Do you mind if I join you here in the sunshine?" Wasyl asked with a very disarming smile.

"It's a public bench, Sir," Meeta responded as coyly as she could manage.

Taking a seat beside her and still smiling he continued. "My name is Wasyl Myzak. I've become acquainted with Ulanda and her husband here in the barrack. She told me your story of escape." His smile faded and his voice lowered. "I was sorry to learn that your sister and her husband were not so fortunate. Do you know where they are?"

"If they are still alive they are somewhere in Siberia. We have no way of knowing." Meeta felt a sadness pulse through her as she spoke. It was a deeper sadness than she had experienced when speaking of this subject to others in the past. Why was it so?

Wasyl looked off into the distance. "Uncertainty is a difficult thing to live with, Miss Kollist." His voice was low, and his tone seemed to imply that he was also living with uncertainties.

Meeta felt it so intensely that she found herself asking, "Do you have a family?"

"No one of any consequence," was his nonchalant response. Then he turned his attention to Vello. "Your nephew seems to be enjoying that sandbox," he smiled as he spoke.

"Yes," said Meeta, not yet willing to be light-hearted. "He knows a lot about army ditches and military mounds." She didn't quite understand why but she wanted to have this man sympathize with her and to realize what this child and her family had lived through.

Apparently sensing her need he once again became serious. "I'm certain it's been a very difficult time for you, Miss Kollist. It appears that a lot of responsibility has rested upon your shoulders."

She felt tears beginning to form as she contemplated his words. Over the past year and a half she had made decisions out of necessity, but now to have someone voice compassion caused her to rethink the losses and trauma she had experienced, and her emotions rose. She felt the need to get away and sort out what she was feeling. She stood and called out, "Vello, it's time for you to come in now. You've been ill and you must not overdo."

"Just a little longer, Ati. Please."

"I think not, Vello. We can do this again tomorrow. But now you must rest." Then addressing Wasyl, she said, "Excuse us, Mr. Myzak. It's been a pleasure meeting you."

Wasyl also stood, and Meeta realized he was a bit shorter than she though his body was muscular and stocky. "I hope I didn't say anything that offended you, Miss Kollist." Wasyl spoke in a courteous and apologetic manner.

"No, not at all, Mr. Myzak. It's just that I have to be concerned with Vello's welfare." She took Vello's hand and then turned again to Wasyl. "Good day, Mr. Myzak."

Wasyl slightly nodded his head and replied, "Good day, Miss Kollist."

That evening Meeta engaged in conversation with Ulanda and discovered that Wasyl had visited her later in the day after he had first seen Meeta. "Wasyl asked me if you had commented at all about him," said Ulanda. "I told him you were not interested in an old man." She laughed as she continued. "He sure didn't waste any time shaving off his beard. I think you have an admirer, Meeta."

The following day Ulanda was released to go back to her regular barrack. Meeta remained with Vello until the next day. The weather was warming, and he was doing so much better that he was thought well enough to return home.

The nurse approached Meeta with a bag full of canned goods in her hand. "Take these with you. This is our farewell gift to you and your little family. I will request the ambulance to take you and Vello home."

Meeta and Vello went to say good-bye to Ulanda in the barrack and to thank her for her kindness to them. While there Meeta asked if she had a can opener she could use to open a can of peaches she thought Vello would enjoy. Ulanda handed her the can opener, but just then the ambulance arrived. Meeta had not expected it to arrive so quickly. In the rush to pick up her things and take hold of Vello, Meeta inadvertently put the can opener in the bag with the canned goods. On arrival at home she discovered what she had done and felt quite embarrassed.

The following day she walked back to the camp to return the can opener and apologize to Ulanda for her forgetfulness. Wasyl Myzak happened to be in the barrack, and the three of them conversed for a time. As they spoke together Meeta felt an attraction to Wasyl. When she rose to leave she felt exhilarated when he asked, "May I walk you home, Miss Kollist."

"I live several kilometers away, Mr. Myzak."

Undaunted he responded, "I need the exercise, and I have the time. This will give me a purpose for walking. Do you mind having some company?"

"No, not at all." Meeta felt somehow enlivened as she walked beside Wasyl.

And the length of the walk afforded them much time to become better acquainted.

"How did you escape Ukraine, Mr. Myzak?" Meeta asked as they walked.

"Actually, I didn't escape Ukraine. I escaped from Romania."

"But you are Ukrainian."

"Yes. I was born in Germakivka in the Ternopol region. That's located about 400 kilometers southeast of Kiev. But I grew up in Chernivtsi which is only about 35 kilometers from the Romanian border. An older sister of mine lived in Romania with her husband, and as a young man I went to live with her in order to get an education. Romania was offering an education to those who could pass a test. It was my only hope of escaping a peasant's life. Fortunately, I passed the test and was able to eventually become an attorney."

Wasyl paused a moment and then added, "Just to show you how desperately we young men coveted this opportunity, my sister allowed two other young men from the Ukraine to stay with her and take the test. Both of them failed to pass it. Realizing they had no hope for a better life, one committed suicide by lying down on a railroad track and allowing a train to run over him. The other ran away and was never heard from again. It can only be assumed that he also committed suicide."

Meeta grimaced as she thought of the apparent despair that had motivated these young men to such ends. Her voice became low and contemplative, "How sad."

The two continued walking in silence for a time. Then Meeta rephrased her question, "So how did you escape from Romania?"

"I was working for the Romanian government. In April of '44 the Red army attacked Romania, but the German-Romanian forces were able to withstand them. They made a second attempt later that summer, on August 20, to be exact. This time the German-Romanian front collapsed. I was . . . I believe . . . providentially able to board the last truck allowed across the border to Hungary. From there I continued until I reached Germany, and here I am."

Meeta was impressed by this man. He seemed devoid of pretense, and her spiritual nature took note of what he had said about "providentially" boarding the last truck. That statement encouraged her to share how she, too, had been miraculously led to leave the IRO camp and find a job and living quarters. Finding Wasyl interested in this story, she continued telling him of the night she felt impressed by the Bible passage in Jeremiah to take her little family from their apartment and how they ultimately were spared the destruction of the city of Neumarkt Oberpfalz.

Wasyl listened intently, then responded. "I have only twice in my life felt that God had intervened. One was the boarding of the last truck allowed over the Romanian border of which I have already spoken. The other time was when I was driving a team of horses pulling a wagon. Something spooked the horses, and they took off at a full run. I struggled to regain control, fearing any minute the wagon would topple over and I would be crushed. In my anxiety I called out, 'God help me.' As I pulled with all my might on the reins, to my surprise the horses responded and came to a stop. I felt certain that God had heard my simple prayer."

Meeta internalized what he said. "You might want to consider a third 'providential' leading . . . that being when you passed the Romanian education test."

Wasyl smiled as he looked at her and cocked his head, "I never thought of that, but you might be right."

By the time Meeta and Wasyl ended their walk together, a bond had formed between them. Thereafter, Wasyl became a frequent visitor to the Kollist residence. His presence was always welcomed. Even Vello enjoyed having another "Apa" around, and the feeling seemed to be mutual with Wasyl engaging the little boy in play and conversation. Amalie also appeared to feel comfortable with this man. What each saw and received from Wasyl was personal, but one thing was certain, their household seemed more content and complete when he was present.

Wasyl sought and found employment as overseer of a group of men at the American Workers Legion in Hanau near Frankfort on the Main River where the American Headquarters for Germany was located. At intervals he returned to Neumarkt Oberpfalz. When he did, he brought cigarettes and coffee with him which he gave to Meeta to be used to exchange for things her little family needed. Local Germans would chop wood or farmers would give fresh milk for these items. Wasyl always remembered Vello with a treat of candy which caused the little boy to especially cherish and look forward to his visits. Occasionally Wasyl would even send money to help the struggling family.

The road outside the gatehouse where the Kollist family lived overlooked mountains where Meeta would sometimes go to pray after dark when no one was around. One night when the family had depleted their funds, she went to this quiet place to ask God to provide them with some money. As she prayed she saw a falling star in the very spot where she was looking. To her this was a sign from God that her prayer was answered and immediately said, "Thank You God." When she returned home, she told her mother, "Tomorrow you will see a solution to our money problem." The next morning they received a letter from Wasyl that contained a money order.

Meeta found herself drawn to this man more and more, and it was obvious that he was encouraging a romantic relationship. Amalie took note as well. "You're becoming quite fond of Wasyl, aren't you, Meeta?"

Meeta hesitated before answering, not really willing to make that admission to her mother. "I guess I am. He seems so sympathetic and concerned for us and our needs. It's a good feeling—like I'm not completely on my own trying to make ends meet. Do you see a problem with that?"

Amalie seemed pensive as she spoke. "Well, he isn't Estonian. Would you ever consider marrying someone who was not Estonian?"

"I never thought I would, but now I . . . " Meeta broke off her sentence without completing it. In her heart she knew she was falling in love with Wasyl.

She shared her feelings with her friend Helga Paimre. "Helga, it means so much to finally have someone who cares for me, someone who has chosen to care for me. Wasyl makes me realize how lonely I've been—especially since Papsi died. He listens to me and makes me feel like a woman."

Helga listened but expressed concern. "Meeta, I am happy for you, but I must tell you I have a feeling about this man. I hesitate to tell you this, but truly I fear this man could be married."

Meeta dismissed Helga's fears. She did not want for one moment to entertain such a thought. It was too wonderful thinking that love had finally come to her at nearly 36 years of age. She had thought the day would never come, but now she was living it. It was an exciting experience for her and made the daily struggles of the aftermath of war more bearable.

She found the summer to be especially enchanting. When Wasyl visited, she felt good strolling with him hand in hand among the other lovers in town. It was all so new. She felt a deep sense of belonging and of being a part of something she had never thought she would experience.

Her mother, too, realized her daughter was in a serious relationship and wrote to her son Oskar asking how he felt about Meeta considering marriage with a Ukrainian. He replied in a letter dated July 7, 1946, in which he expressed a lack of concern about the difference in nationality. Instead he reassured his mother by pointing out the commonness of such unions. "The newspapers speak about how people are marrying Englishmen and Americans, even Russians." He went on to say, however, that both he and his wife Ave were "shocked" at hearing that Meeta was already considering marriage with anyone since this was the first they had learned of her having a relationship with a man. Oskar's concern was her proceeding with any marriage too quickly and addressed a separate paragraph in the letter directly to Meeta. "One must be careful in making such decisions and think." He also admonished her to consider how such a union would impact her nephew. "Vello has lost his parents, his grandfather, and his homeland. What will this mean for him?"

At the time of that writing Oskar was holding a managerial position in a leather factory in Tidaholm, Sweden. He had been hoping that his mother and Vello could visit him there. But in the same letter wrote that those plans would not be possible because they were moving to Australia. They were scheduled to depart by ship from Gothenburg, Sweden, on July 27. He also advised that Ave's brother, who was now settled in Sydney, was going to assist them in relocating. He ended his letter by saying, "We are leaving behind a beloved little grave that we will probably leave forever," meaning, of course, that of their infant son Heikki.

In August Meeta read in an area newspaper that the Seventh-day Adventist Church was holding a series of meetings in Augsburg. She knew this was the denomination Liina had been a member of in Pärnu when Meeta and she were studying the Bible together. Meeta had even been invited to play a piano solo for the congregation during a worship service. That was the only time she attended, but she enjoyed the service and the studies she had received from Liina. Warm feelings arose in her as she read the announcement, and she decided to write to the address of the church in Augsburg to request spiritual literature and to ask if there was an Estonian congregation meeting in the area.

On September 7 she received a response from an Estonian church member named Heinrich Tiik. "There is no Estonian congregation in Germany, but V. R. Vinglas is working and corresponding with the Estonian church members that are spread throughout Germany. He is their representative in the German Union, and I have forwarded your request to him. You will receive a reply in the near future."

The summer passed by all too quickly and soon it was fall. Vello had become acquainted with a few playmates that helped broaden his world. Across from the gatehouse was a meadow, beyond which was a stream. The stream provided endless hours of fun for the boys as they waded in the water and watched minnows and sometimes frogs. Vello and his friends often explored the nearby woods and walked along a railroad track where they found shell casings and other debris left behind by soldiers which thrilled the imagination of the young boys.

Meeta would sometimes give Vello onions which she had gotten from her farm friends. American soldiers passing by in trucks or jeeps were happy to exchange chewing gum for the onions. The reward was enjoyed immensely, but just approaching a uniformed soldier and military vehicle was exciting for a boy.

Meeta's world was also exciting as her relationship with Wasyl deepened. Her life, too, was broadening, but she could never have predicted what the coming year would bring.

CHAPTER 26

The Aftermath of War
Siberia 1946

Ilse and her fellow deportees welcomed even small changes in their struggles for survival after the war ended. The availability of bread, flour, milk, sugar and even some fish eased their hunger.

When Ilse learned early in January that Jefimia had been given a vacation of sorts—three weeks off work without pay—she approached Romanov, Volkov's and Mehaanik's superior, to ask if she and her fellow workers would be given time off as well. Romanov was a kindly man, tall and erect, with the perfect stature of a wartime leader, despite his walking with the aid of crutches as a result of being wounded in the war. He gave permission for Pikk, Tonka, and Ilse to take time off beginning January 11. They would not be required to report for regular work again until February 1.

Vacation time afforded Ilse the opportunity to sew herself a much needed jacket and dress. When that was finished she and Pikk searched for work for which they could be paid in either food or rubles.

The Galdilinis hired them to saw wood, clean the cow barn, feed the cow and carry water from a nearby well. On January 21, the day before Russians commemorate Lenin's date of death, the Galdilinis invited 19 people to their home for a party. Ilse and Pikk were outside the home sawing wood and heard the laughter and music. Ilse looked sadly at Pikk, "I cannot stand hearing this. The happy sounds remind me too much of home." With head bowed and shoulders slumped she dropped her saw and walked toward their humble abode.

On February 1, when their time off came to an end, they were able to purchase butter, lamb meat, three boxes of matches and salt. The following day they bought wheat and smoked fish. All this was a tremendous treat after the scanty fare to which they had become accustomed. Unfortunately, wine and liquor were also more readily available to the general populace.

One evening after Mihail, Liida and the two children were already in bed, two men came to visit them. Gregorovits, who was a local Russian, brought a friend named Nikolai from Podgornia. Mihail arose and came to Ilse requesting to borrow several rubles with which to buy more wine for them to drink. A little later Galja, the couples' baby girl, awoke and began to cry, so Liida asked Ilse to care for her while she went to the cow barn to get some milk for the child.

The men sat in the front room drinking. When Liida returned and Ilse brought Galja to her, Gregorovits said to Ilse, "You work in the hospital." Ilse responded in Russian, "Not true, I am a common laborer. It's my roommate Jefimia who is an orderly." She then returned to her room, where Jefimia was already in bed, and shut the door. Soon there was a knock at the door and Ilse opened it. Gregorovits, who was drunk, came into the room saying he was not feeling well and needed some care from Jefimia.

Jefimia, who was not yet asleep but was undressed and under the covers, said, "I have to sleep since tomorrow I must be on duty for 10 hours. What malady do you have? I am mostly familiar with children's diseases."

Gregorovits went to her makeshift bed and put her blanket around him as he sat beside her. Fortunately, Jefimia was securely wrapped in her sheet and was not uncovered. At that point Mihail entered the room and said to Gregorovits, "You had better come now or the liquor will be all gone." This seemed to placate Gregorovits, and he left with Mihail. Jefimia quickly arose and put on her clothes. Soon Gregorovits returned and walked toward Jefimia who was now standing. He was followed by Nikolai, who was also drunk.

Nikolai came directly to Pikk and said, "Let's sleep together in your bed." Liida hurried into the room and shook her fist at Gregorovits. Then she and Pikk took hold of Nikolai and ushered him out of the room. As Liida walked, she said firmly to Nikolai but loud enough so Gregorovits could hear, "You are an out-of-town guest. You can sleep in our room, but Gregorovits must go."

After Nikolai was safely out of the room, Liida returned and she and Ilse joined forces to motivate Gregorovits who was now lying on Jefimia's bed. Liida yanked his arm and Ilse pulled his feet to the floor. The man unsteadily stood up, looked at the women through bloodshot eyes, slightly bowed and said, "Excuse me. That was fun," and left the room. By the time Gregorovits had left and Nikolai was soundly asleep in their neighbors' room, it was 1:30 a.m.

On the morning of February 11 Volkov commanded Ilse and Pikk to dig a grave for the mother of the head administrator of the Communist headquarters who had died. Pikk gave him a bewildered look and said, "You're joking! The temperature is minus 25 degrees; the ground is entirely frozen."

"No," said Volkov, "I'm not joking. The ground will have to be chopped, but the burial will be today."

Soon the administrator's brother came with his young son and Vitka, another young worker, and they all went to the cemetery. The brother chose a spot where the snow was about one meter high. After shoveling the snow away, Ilse and the administrator's brother took turns chopping the ground while Vitka chopped alternately with Pikk. The wind was cold and soon became unbearable. By 2:00 p.m. they had only dug the grave one-half meter deep.

At the edge of the cemetery was a small village of Volga Germans who had been sent by Catherine the Great in the 1760s to settle Siberia. Seeking a brief respite, the grave diggers approached one of the homes in the settlement and knocked on the door. They were allowed entrance to thaw themselves and were able to purchase some bread from the home owners.

After warming themselves and eating some bread, the group returned to the gravesite where they were joined by a friend of the administrator named Aleksei, a strong, middle-aged man who chopped with great vigor. His efforts so warmed him that he threw off his fur coat and chopped only in his shirt. Noticing Pikk and Ilse shivering at the edge of the grave, Aleksei wrapped his fur coat around them and continued working as his sweat turned into ice. Gradually, the earth gave way to the blows from his ax and shovel.

By 6:00 p.m. the casket was brought to the gravesite, but the depth of the grave was only a little over one meter. Suvotsilov and Aleksei's brother finally came to help with the digging and provided additional strength. Soon the administrator, his wife and two ladies arrived thinking the burial would occur. But the grave needed to be dug deeper, and the ladies could not stand the cold. They stood for a moment staring at the coffin and then left.

Ilse and Pikk looked incredulously at Aleksei who tirelessly continued chopping and digging. He was completely wet and his shirt frozen. Ilse trembled with cold as she said to Pikk, "Oh heavens, keep us from a winter death. This digging is impossible!"

When the grave was finally deep enough, no one sang a song or uttered a phrase of commitment. The casket was simply lowered and quickly filled.

Everyone who had helped dig the grave was invited to the administrator's home for the dinner that always followed a committal. Fortunately, his house was comfortably warm, but Ilse struggled to clear her eyes. It seemed the extreme cold had caused her vision to be clouded.

The guests sat at a narrow table—the ladies on one side, the men on the other. Each person in turn stood to remember the deceased; then they passed wine. Since there were only three wine glasses, guests drank their wine and then passed the glass onto the person next to them. Soon guests began toasting in honor of the departed.

The table was set with china. Instead of napkins the hostess had provided beautifully decorated hand towels for each guest. The food was abundant: blintzes with black currant compote, fish stuffed into pan-fried dough, oatmeal porridge with butter, soup with meat, fresh cabbage, and lastly hot tea with some berry filled *pirukad*.

When Ilse drank her second glass of wine, she began to feel lightheaded and very jovial. She had made the statement to Alexei while digging the grave that she "would never drink until she was drunk." Now Alexei watched Ilse's face become more and more flushed and told her, "Don't worry if you get drunk. They have a private apartment. You can sleep it off there."

Soon thereafter guests began rising from the table and leaving for their homes. Ilse pulled away from the table and tried to rise, but her legs were weak and she sank back down into her chair. The other guests said, "Ilse is drunk," and laughed. The hostess assisted her to her feet and helped put on her *fufaika*. Ilse felt quite embarrassed as Pikk and Vitka escorted her back home.

A few days later Liida developed a very high fever and was so ill she was in tears. Mihail asked Ilse to stay with the children and brought a horse-drawn wagon to take her to the polyclinic. Once there she was transferred to the hospital and was placed in the section where Jefimia worked. Mihail began crying. "Will she be all right, Jefimia?" he asked anxiously.

"We will have to wait to see if her fever breaks," said Jefimia in a serious tone. "One thing you can be sure of, she will remain here for a few days so you will have to make arrangements for the care of the children."

Mihail seemed frightened and confused as he looked at Jefimia and then at his wife lying in obvious discomfort. "I have to work, and all of you do, too," he said as if thinking aloud. He paused for a time and then continued, "My mother and sister live in Togor. Perhaps on a run to pick up boards from the factory I could take the children with me and leave them under their care."

Mihail did as he had said. That night Pikk began feeling sorry for him as he sat alone in the front room. "He seems so totally lost without his family."

Ilse agreed. "I'm sure he's realizing how much Liida really means to him. He's very concerned about her condition."

Pikk looked downcast as she spoke. "It seems so strangely quiet without the children. Sometimes I've longed for some peace, but I must admit I miss hearing Vitja's childish voice and even Galja's crying. Can you believe that?" Pikk was so moved with compassion for Mihail that she brought him some bread and offered to feed the family's cow for him.

Within a few days Liida was back home as were the children, but there was a new atmosphere that bordered on respect as Mihail addressed Liida. Unfortunately, Mihail's love of drinking was still a problem because it caused a constant shortage of money. As a truck driver, he earned 350 to 400 rubles each month, but the family was always short financially. In addition, drink made him forgetful, and one night after returning from the sauna he realized he had forgotten his shirt. In that society what one forgot was never seen again. To a family short on money, the loss of a shirt was costly.

The accessibility of drink began affecting others as well. Volkov began imbibing. Sometimes at work his face would be flushed and his words slower and a bit slurred. It did not help when a bar opened in town. The day after its opening Mihail came to work with a hangover. Ilse and Jefimia tried to dissuade other workers from visiting the new attraction.

Fortunately, food was becoming more varied and plentiful. Ilse assessed the result and reported it to Jefimia and Pikk. "I measured myself today. My waist is wider, but my hips and chest are the same. I'm as wide as each of you, but because I'm shorter, I look fatter."

Another sign of a new era arising was that Easter Sunday was celebrated as a holiday, and many people went to church. After church Ilse spent the day with her neighbors while Pikk went to a friend's house for what she said was going to be "a feast." Jefimia spent the day with her friend Elise.

With the arrival of spring, one job Ilse enjoyed was whitewashing the Communist social hall because it housed a piano that she would stop to play. She found it only a slight annoyance when one day the music teacher chastised her for playing with "whitewashed hands."

By May 9, a year after the war had ended, Ilse had still received no letter or word concerning her husband Peeter. She sent another letter requesting information about him.

As the river water began melting, Ilse was commanded to once again catch logs as they floated down stream. This she did alternately with the removal of dirt from under the houses so the summer breezes could freely circulate beneath them. Next came the spring planting of cucumbers, potatoes and other root vegetables.

On May 20 Ilse recorded in her diary: "Today Vello is five years old . . . completely unbelievable. It is a cold spring day just as it was the day he was born. I remember a crease came to his forehead when I did not have enough milk for him to drink. He pushed me away with his hands and began to cry." The thought pained her. She had not been able to satisfy him then, and now she felt helpless to ever be able to meet his needs.

That day she, Tonka, Pikk and another woman named Dusja were sent to a peat bog to cut peat. Two chopped the peat and the other two took it away with a wagon. During a rest period Dusja cried out her sad story to Ilse.

"I thought my husband had been killed in the war, but last night there was a knock at my door; it was my husband. I was shocked but recognized him. He asked me, 'Will you accept me back?' I said, 'Yes.' He then told me to put on the light. When the light came on, I realized he had no hands." She began crying. "This is too much, Ilse. I must do everything for him—even when he goes to the toilet."

Ilse listened with compassion but had no comfort to offer. She had seen many invalids and realized the horrors of war were not pleasant to live with.

On the way home from the peat bog, Volkov saw them and asked if they had finished at the bog. When they acknowledged they had, he ordered them to the Communist administrator's home to plant potatoes. The entire next week they dug, hoed and planted for the administrator during the day. Tired and aching, Ilse returned home each evening to dig and plant her own garden.

At the end of the week the Russian workers received 100 rubles while the Estonians received roughly half the amount. Additionally, Russian workers received two shirts and two pairs of pants while Estonians received one shirt and one pair of pants. Walking home that evening Ilse remarked to Pikk, "Sadly all nationalities are not equal here."

In late June Ilse developed a severe headache and shivered even when she put on her winter coat. Then she collapsed. Her blood was checked at the polyclinic, and it was determined she had malaria. She was put into a hospital room with four other adult women. Ilse received her first injection of quinine but shivered through the night. The next day she was surprised to see lice on her hospital bed. Another patient also found lice in her bed. Ilse requested that her clothing and the blanket she had brought with her be disinfected before leaving the hospital. The staff graciously complied. Six days later she was released. It was another six days before she was well enough, though thinner and weaker, to return to work at the shore sawing logs. Her teammates consisted of Dusja, Niura and Pikk.

Later in the summer the same team was sent to the hayfields together. They were joined by Suvotsilov and later by Merkulov who operated the mowing machine. Merkulov's wife, Merkuliah, would sometimes join him as she was distrustful of her husband and suspected he was philandering with Dusja who had separated from her invalid husband.

One night Merkulov, Dusja and Ilse were sleeping side by side in a hay hut. Merkulov was on the left side with Dusja in the middle. Merkuliah thought either her husband or Dusja was sleeping on the right side where Ilse slept and thrust a scythe through that side of the hut narrowly missing her. Wide-eyed and trembling Ilse awoke and shouted, "What are you doing?" Merkuliah crawled into the hut and realized she had missed her intended mark. The ruckus awoke the other two, and Merkulov grabbed his wife and dragged her out of the hut using a creative array of what Ilse called "vituperative Russian words." Merkuliah was taken back to town the next morning. Fortunately, the rest of the field time was relatively calm.

Returning to Kolpashevo Ilse learned that three acquaintances had been arrested by the NKVD while she was away. One of them was Kalev Kloomeister, a friend of Jefimia's who had visited their home. Jefimia explained what had happened. "It seems Kalev and two of his friends had been overheard talking about the possibility of being recruited to work on Sakhalin Island, north of Hokkaido, Japan." (According to the Yalta Conference agreements of August 1945 the Soviet Union was given control of the island.) "Kalev heard that there was a possibility of being sent there to work the rich oil and gas reserves, and he and his two friends saw it as an opportunity for possible escape from the Soviet Union. Unfortunately, an informer overheard their conversation and reported it to the NKVD." Jefimia was quite tense as she spoke. "What was truly scary for me was that I was interrogated by the NKVD."

Ilse's hand covered her mouth as she exclaimed, "What? Why did they interrogate you?"

"I guess because Kalev was a friend. They were trying to find out if plans had been formalized and if I knew about them. It seems the three of them were planning to somehow get to the United States through Japan. I have no idea how. The NKVD asked me several questions, but I knew nothing. The only thing I knew was that Kalev told me he would let himself be recruited to work on Sakhalin Island. They asked me that question and I said, 'Yes, he said that.' That's all I told them. That's all I knew, Ilse." Jefimia's brow wrinkled as she spoke. "Now I feel like even that might have been too much for me to say. I feel so bad. I wonder if I made things worse for them."

Ilse stared at Jefimia still trying to process what had happened. Fear gripped her as she thought of an informer in their midst. "Jefimia, we must be very cautious about what we say in the presence of others. An informer could be anyone, and he could construe an innocent comment into something of value to the NKVD."

September 1 Ilse received a letter from Kristjan Sillaste who was the clinic nurse in the same gulag where her husband Peeter had been. In the letter Kristjan informed Ilse that her husband had died on January 7, 1945, of pneumonia. Ilse felt a shock wave begin in her chest and radiate to her stomach. Then she began to feel nauseous, and her heart beat erratically for a few seconds. Her thoughts raced wildly. That was over a year and a half ago. Could I have helped him somehow? I would have sold my last rags to send him whatever he needed. She sat silently with the letter resting in her lap, too stunned to cry but too weak to move. My dreams of reuniting are gone. . . . Our child will never know his father. . . . No husband, no child, no family.

When Pikk arrived home Ilse shared the letter with her. Pikk looked sadly at Ilse but said nothing. Instead, she sat silently as if not knowing what to say. After several minutes Pikk rose from her seat and put her shoes neatly beside her bed instead of leaving them in front of the door where she had removed them. Then she folded some clothes that were lying on her box bed and began sweeping the room. Ilse realized it was Pikk's way of trying to make things as pleasant for her as possible. Pikk's untidiness was usually a bone of contention between them. But that night Ilse's mind was not on the tidiness of the room. She really wanted to be alone, but felt she could not ask Pikk to leave her own room. Her diary entry for the day ended with, "I am left behind—alone with God."

Later as Ilse lay trying to sleep, gentle tears began to fall onto her pillow. Her husband's face came to her mind as vividly as if he were alive. She remembered the way he would purse his lips when he took a shot of spirits, the characteristic snicker he would cast when something unexpected happened and the way his eyes sparkled when she told him something humorous. I wanted so much for Vello to be just like him, she thought. Then I would have at least had a reminder of Peko. . . . Why did our fate have to be such? What has all this suffering accomplished? What do I have to live for now?

* * *

In mid-September another incident with alcohol occurred. Providentially all three of the women were returning home from work at the same time. As they approached their house they saw two men fighting in front of their home. One was obviously drunk.

The sober man ran away in the direction of their house. The drunk was not sure in which direction he had gone, so he circled the house looking for him. In the meantime, the women ran into their home, shut the door, and put a wooden stick into the handle of the lockless door on the inside so it could not be pulled open. Then they went into their room. But soon they heard the drunk in their front room and realized he had broken the stick in the handle and had entered. Then he began opening their bedroom door. All three of them pushed against the door so he could not get in. Ilse held the doorknob so tightly her hand began hurting. On the other side of the door the man began crying. Ilse shouted, "What do you want?" but the man did not answer. Pikk grabbed an ax ready for any eventuality. The drunk finally became weary and left.

After some time the women became courageous enough to venture out of their room and looked outside. In front of their house they saw several of the workers surrounding the drunkard. One of the workers took him by the arm, but the drunk hit him in the head with his fist. The worker wrestled him to the ground and then others joined in taking him away.

This situation provided the catalyst for Ilse and her roommates to at last request another apartment. Their request was granted. Soon they moved to an apartment in the large building on Ob Street where the various repair shops were located.

The routine of everyday living returned to normal with work fluctuating between hauling wood and grain to preparing the local houses for winter. But in mid-November Ilse received notice from the NKVD that she was to report to them that very day.

Ilse arrived at the Communist headquarters at 3:00 p.m. and was told to take a seat. As she waited her thoughts were extremely troubled. She rehearsed any statements she might have made that could have been interpreted in an accusatory manner and could think of none. Since learning of what had happened to Kalev Kloomeister and his two friends, she had even been careful not to complain about the inequities that existed in the Russian system—even to her roommates.

What could they possibly want with her? The hours passed torturously slow … 4:00 … 5:00 … 6:00 … 7:00 … Finally, shortly before 8:00 p.m., the door opened and an officer invited her into a room and introduced himself as Officer Petrovitz. He was of medium height and dressed in a uniform with the typical revolver strapped about his waist. His demeanor was serious. Was he being intentionally intimidating? Or was this his normal composure? Ilse tried to accept the latter appraisal in order to calm herself. She felt warm, her hands clammy.

He pointed to a man seated at a table in front of her with an open notebook before him. This is Officer Staupkovitz. He will be taking notes on our discussion today.

Officer Petrovitz stood beside the table; his brow furrowed as he began. "Do you know a woman by the name of Jefimia Maasik?"

Ilse's mouth felt dry as she fought to keep her voice from wavering. "She is my roommate."

"How long have you roomed together?" His eyes seemed to be riveted on Ilse with an intensity that made her feel as if she were a fugitive.

"About a year and a half to two years, Officer," Ilse responded as firmly as she could manage.

"Well, which is it Comrade Kotter, a year and a half or two years?"

"Comrade Kotter" was a term with which Ilse was totally unfamiliar, and it set her aback for a moment. That, coupled with his requirement for such exactness, caused her face to flush, and sweat broke out on her forehead.

Seeing her delayed response the officer spoke again. "Well, Comrade Kotter, which is it, a year and a half or two years?"

"I'd say it's been closer to two years, Officer."

"You don't know for sure, is that what you're saying?"

"Not to the exact month, but I would say closer to two years."

The officer began to pace. "Two years. That's an appreciable time to get acquainted with someone, isn't it, Comrade Kotter?" He stopped pacing and looked directly at Ilse.

"Yes, I guess so."

"I would imagine that you both have shared some personal things together. Is that a correct assumption, Comrade Kotter?"

Ilse had never dreamed she had been called there to discuss Jefimia. She had suspected it was something she had said. Now she considered how to protect her friend. She must not answer in an incriminating way. "We have two different jobs, Officer. We do not see much of each other because of differing work schedules."

Undeterred, the officer continued. "Yes, I realize she works at the hospital and you as a laborer, but two years is a long time to live together. Surely you have shared some free time."

"Jefimia has her own circle of friends, and her free time is generally spent with them."

The officer now stood in front of Ilse causing her to look up at him. "Isn't it true that Kalev Kloomeister often paid a visit to see Jefimia at your shared room?"

Ilse now realized why she had been called. Jefimia was in danger of being tied into the supposed escape plan for which Kalev had been arrested. "He only came two times that I know of, Officer," answered Ilse.

"Only two times? I understand they were good friends." The officer began to pace once again but stopped to look directly at Ilse.

"That's all I know of." Ilse held tightly to her hands as they lay in her lap.

"Were you there when he came those two times, Comrade Kotter?" Once again he stood directly in front of Ilse waiting for her answer.

"Yes." Ilse looked up at him searching for some sign of softness in the man's eyes. There was none.

"What did they discuss?"

"Nothing of any consequence. Their work schedules. The weather." Ilse almost said "mutual friends" but decided that would be better left unspoken.

The officer continued standing in front of Ilse. "Nothing more than that?"

Ilse squeezed her hands until her knuckles turned white. "Not in my presence, Officer. Their conversation, in my presence, was very general. She might ask him if he would like a drink or something to eat, but they discussed nothing of any significance that I can recall."

The officer now sat on the edge of the table with one leg on the floor but still looking straight at Ilse.

"You are aware that Kalev Kloomeister has been arrested?"

"Yes."

"Did Jefimia tell you that?"

"Yes." Ilse wondered if she had said too much by making that admission, but it was the truth.

"Was Jefimia sad over his arrest?"

Ilse's voice grew a bit louder. "How would I know that?" Then she intentionally lowered her tone. "Jefimia does not talk a lot."

"So she showed no outward emotion?"

"No. She merely said she didn't know why he was arrested."

"Did she tell you how she found out he was arrested?"

Ilse looked straight into his eyes and responded as firmly as she could. "No. And I didn't ask. I barely knew the man. Why should I pry?"

Ilse's last comment seemed to satisfy the man, and he told her she could leave. Her legs felt shaky as she walked from the room and made her way quickly to her apartment where she collapsed on her bunk still shaking. Fear gripped Ilse for many days following that interrogation. She spoke of it to no one, not even Jefimia. She was learning that silence was her best defense.

A fellow Estonian, Elsa Reim, arrived from Maiga in early December. She told Ilse that Lisette Silm and Aino Nirk, with whom she had roomed for a time in Maiga, had been brought to the prison in Kolpashevo. Ilse was shocked to hear that they had been imprisoned. "What on earth for, Elsa?"

Elsa told her how they had planned to escape and return to Estonia. "Lisette's husband had sent her money from Estonia, and Lisette sewed it into her underwear to keep it from being stolen. She, Aino and two other ladies planned to escape together. They met one morning outside Lisette's residence and made their way to a ship where they paid the fare. They were on their way to Novosibirsk where they planned to board a train. But as they boarded the ship, they were identified and arrested. Lisette has been given two years, Aino three, and each of the other women, who are over 60 years of age, received one year imprisonment."

Ilse listened with rapt attention. "It doesn't pay to try to escape. Imprisonment is far worse than being a worker in the settlement."

Elsa next told of a married couple who had died suddenly, most likely from taking poison, and of eight men in a labor camp who had all committed suicide. "It seems death is to be preferred above life, Ilse. People are sensing the hopelessness of this existence now that the war has ended and nothing has changed in their status. These are people whose only wrong was being successful, and they see no end to their unjust deportation."

Ilse sensed it, too. As she sat alone in her room later, she thought, My life seems so empty and without meaning. There is no need that I am fulfilling. What do I live for? I am as one dead to the world.

CHAPTER 27

Betrayal Precedes a New Future

Germany 1947-1950

By late January 1947 Meeta realized something needed to be shared with Wasyl during his next visit to Neumarkt Oberpfalz.

The evening was chilly as they walked together in the twilight down Ingolstädter Strasse. The snow-covered mountains in the distance reflected an array of sunset shades in coral and magenta backdropped by a sky of turquoise. It would have been a lovely evening to enjoy the beauty that surrounded them, but Meeta had something more pressing on her mind.

"Wasyl, I need to share something with you."

Wasyl stopped walking and looked directly at her, apparently sensing the serious tone of her voice. "I'm listening, Meeta."

Meeta looked down at the street as she spoke. Then haltingly the words came, "Wasyl, I'm pregnant." She continued staring at the street for what seemed forever as she awaited his response.

"Are you certain?" His tone was tense, almost fearful.

"Yes. It was confirmed by a doctor just last week. I am four months pregnant." Slowly she raised her head and looked at him. His face had drained of its normal color and was void of expression. She waited for his response, but it did not come. Instead he took her by the arm and continued walking beside her in silence. Her mind was in confusion. She had hoped he would comfort her and tell her not to worry—they would soon marry. In the past he had always encouraged her when she had expressed vulnerability. But silence—this she did not understand. She felt anxious to know his thoughts.

As they walked, they came to a destroyed apartment house that still had its front stone steps intact, and Wasyl motioned for her to sit down. He sat next to her as he began to speak. "Meeta, I have not been completely honest with you."

Meeta's heart pounded against her chest and she felt her face flush, yet she remained silent.

Wasyl continued in a serious, halting tone. "I would like to tell you all will be well." He paused, closed his eyes and rested his forehead on his hand. For a moment Meeta thought he was ill, but he continued. "Meeta, I would love to tell you we will be married, but I cannot." He paused again as if struggling internally. "You see, I'm still legally married."

Meeta felt a pain that radiated from her heart to the pit of her stomach. She rose from the step and realized her legs felt like rubber. "You lied to me!" she shouted.

Wasyl quickly stood beside her. "Meeta, please, please! Listen to me! It's true I misled you. When you asked if I had a family, I told you 'no one of any consequence.' That was true in a sense, but it wasn't fully honest."

Meeta's mind was fevered and she felt her temples pulsate as she spoke. "You are no better than the heartless men who deported my sister. You have lied, betrayed and used me for your own selfish purposes." She turned to leave, but Wasyl grabbed her arm.

"Meeta, please listen to me. I never intended to hurt you. I truly did and do care for you. My wife and I are separated. The marriage wasn't working. I filed for divorce and the marriage would have ended, but the war came and we went our separate ways. When I told you I have no family of "any consequence," that was partially true. I do have a daughter who is married and has a two-year-old son. But they live in Romania, and I can't go back there . . . I just fled from Romania. Please realize it's not that I don't want to marry you—I can't!"

Meeta stared at Wasyl like a frenzied animal trying to process all he had said and trying to control the pounding in her head. "Why didn't you tell me this before? . . . Why didn't Ulanda tell me?"

"Ulanda didn't know any more than you did about me, Meeta. What I have done I've done myself." Wasyl took hold of Meeta's shoulders and looked into her eyes. "I deserve all you've said and more. But, please, Meeta, please know that although I cannot marry you, I will help you in every way I possibly can."

The revelation of Wasyl's marital status was extremely difficult for the Kollist family. Amalie was livid when she discovered his deceptive behavior. She called him a "manipulator" and charged him with using his attorney skills to entice her daughter. But she was equally shocked that her daughter, who had such lofty religious convictions, could have allowed this relationship to become so intimate.

For Meeta it was another heart-wrenching loss, another betrayal of love that she had first experienced at the conservatory. She had given herself completely for the first time in her life, thinking Wasyl was truly compassionate and benevolent. Now she saw him as a self-centered egotist. What made matters worse was her sense of guilt and the thought that she had sinned against God.

Little Vello manifested his innocent sense of right and wrong as he put his arm around his Ati as she wept. "It was wrong to lie to you, Ati." Meeta felt Vello's loss, too. She knew how very much he had loved his grandfather and how gratified she had been to see him develop an attachment to Wasyl. He had lost his beloved "Apa," and now his substitute "Apa" had proven untrustworthy.

Wasyl continued to provide assistance to the family in the months that followed as he had told Meeta he would, but it was looked at as a payoff of guilt rather than benevolence. Trust had been replaced with suspicion. The joyful anticipation of his arrival became cold courtesy and his help accepted out of necessity.

To make some extra money during her pregnancy, Meeta found a second job playing the piano in a dance orchestra in the town hall for which she received 30 marks a night. However, when her child was born she relinquished the job in deference to motherhood.

On July 16, 1947, a bright-eyed baby boy was born to Meeta. She named him Hillar Roman. As she held him in her arms in the hospital, her heart was drawn to this new life as she could never have imagined. She had experienced the thrill of life within her during her pregnancy, but to now hold him was an unspeakable sensation. He had come from her body, and for once in her life she had someone who was truly her own, someone who could not be taken from her. As she suckled him, she felt a bonding she never thought possible. Here was someone she could safely love. He was totally dependent upon her and truly needed her. Only she could fulfill his needs. It produced a deep sense of endearment and a desire to protect this child at any cost.

Yet Meeta's spiritual nature was in conflict. She struggled with the dichotomy of how very much she loved this child and the guilt of the circumstances that brought him to her. It was a shadow she would encounter numerous times in the future whenever someone would ask, "What happened to your husband?"

Her search for peace took her once again to her faith. She began studying the spiritual literature that V. R. Vinglas, the German Union representative, had sent her and wrote to him requesting additional information. He informed her of a series of Bible lectures that were scheduled to be held in Nürnberg, and she decided to attend. As she listened from night to night, she discovered that the speaker believed as Liina had taught her about the dead resting in their graves until the resurrection. But something else was presented that she had not considered before.

The speaker spoke of the immutability of the Law of God—the Ten Commandments. Historically, he introduced the Council of Trent which met during a period of 18 years to counter the Protestant Reformation. During that Council, among other things, the Protestant's watch word of *sola Scriptura* (Scripture only) was challenged on the basis of church authority. "The big question addressed," he said, "was whether the Bible and the Bible alone should be followed, as Martin Luther had taught, or was the authority of the church preeminent?"

Suddenly Meeta's interest was keenly aroused. She had been raised and confirmed a Lutheran and had heard much of Martin Luther, but she had never heard what the speaker next presented.

"As the Council of Trent was nearing its final sessions on January 18, 1562, Caspar del Fosso, Archbishop of Reggio di Calabria, gave a speech in which he stated:

> Since the Scripture received its authority not from human will, but from God Himself . . . Likewise the church acquired from the Lord no less authority, so that whoever has heard or rejected her may be said to have heard or rejected God Himself . . . Such is the condition of the heretics [Protestant reformers] of this age that upon nothing

do they rely more than that, under the pretense of the word of God, they overthrow the authority of the church . . . the legal precepts taught by the Lord in the Scriptures have by the same authority become invalid. The sabbath day, the most distinguished day under the law, has passed over into the Lord's day; . . . precepts similar to these have not become invalid by a declaration of Christ (for he says that he came to fulfill the law, not to abolish it), but they have been changed by the authority of the church.[40]

The speaker pointed out that the Council of Trent subscribed to the belief that the church had a right to change the Law of God on the basis of its traditional authority. But he challenged this conclusion and cited Christ's own rebuke to the religious leaders of His day who attempted to change the Fifth Commandment asking them, "Why do you also transgress the commandment of God because of your tradition?"[41]

"Here," said the speaker, "Jesus clearly states that no religious authority has the right to alter God's commandments. The Ten Commandments were written by God Himself.[42] They were *always* intended to be 'written in the heart' of His people in every age," and he cited a number of Bible texts to validate his statement.[43]

"For this reason the Fourth Commandment, regarding the holiness of the Sabbath, is still a reality today. And just as God 'ceased from his works' at creation, the Sabbath is a weekly reminder that we cease looking to our own works as a basis for salvation and instead rest in the finished work of Christ."[44]

Suddenly pieces of the Bible Meeta had not understood began making sense to her. She had respected Liina, with whom she had studied the Bible some years before, but thought it strange that she kept Saturday as her day of worship instead of Sunday. When she asked Liina about it, she simply responded, "I worship Christ as my Creator *and* Redeemer.[45] Jesus left us baptism and communion as memorials of his work as Redeemer. The Sabbath is the only memorial we have of His creative act."[46] But that statement did not register with Meeta until now.

As the speaker expounded biblical passages covering the Sabbath, Meeta became convicted that this was something she needed to accept in her personal life. Some days later she was baptized by immersion and joined the Seventh-day Adventist Church.

***

As fall drew near, Vello entered the first grade at the German school. With winter approaching, Meeta became concerned for the welfare of her two-month-old son. The gatekeeper's house was cold in winter, and often the damp walls would freeze on the inside. Keeping it warm required constant feeding of the stove. Finding enough fuel was a challenge, and they were delighted to see spring approaching.

When the war ended, the Marshall Plan[47] provided funds for Germany to rebuild. However, personal opportunities were minimal in the country because it was overcrowded with refugees, and the economy was at a standstill. Like many others, the Kollists decided to try to relocate to a country that promised a better future.

Meeta thought perhaps her church, with world headquarters in the United States, could be of assistance. She wrote to the Southern European Division headquarters in Berne, Switzerland, telling of her situation and her desire to relocate to the United States. The response she received was disappointing. The letter explained that financial backing would be necessary and that at that time only "established Adventist workers who have been called to America" were being processed. The writer, M. Fridlin, expressed his compassion by saying, "your matter and your tragic misfortune have moved me greatly, and I am sorry that I am not in a position to help you more."

Meeta traveled to Amberg seeking work at the International Refugee Organization headquarters. She felt if she could establish herself there it would be another step closer to her goal of emigrating to the United States.

She continued making her desire known through correspondence with her church, finally making contact with Pastor Eduard Mägi who was also an Estonian. He was living in Washington, D.C., and was a member of the Displaced Persons Committee at the General Conference of Seventh-day Adventists. He personally decided to sponsor the family. On January 9, 1949, he wrote, "Your papers are being processed, but housing is not yet ready. When you arrive we will have work and an apartment for you and yours."

Meeta did not idly wait for her papers to be processed. On February 15, 1949, she secured a position as clerk-typist at the IRO in the Vocational Testing Office in Amberg. After establishing herself with a job and a residence in the Placement Section of the Pounds Barracks, she applied for her family to join her there.

It took two months for approval of the transition. These were difficult days for Amalie who struggled to maintain warmth enough for the little family and also care for two small children. Meeta lived meagerly as she sent the majority of her paychecks to support the rest of her family in Neumarkt Oberpfalz.

In late April 1949, the Kollist family joined Meeta and lived in a large second-floor room in one of five huge stone buildings formerly used as barracks by Hitler's soldiers. One of the buildings in the compound housed an Estonian school for refugee children. In the fall, Vello entered the school but had to repeat second grade because he had to learn to read and write Estonian.

At this time Wasyl entered a sanitarium in Amberg because he was suspected of having tuberculosis. Though he had been faithful in financially helping Meeta whenever possible, their relationship was still politely reserved. Wasyl enjoyed seeing and having more access to Hillar now that the family had moved to Amberg. He also desired to relocate to the United States and applied for processing.

In January 1950, the Assurance for Resettlement of Displaced Persons in the USA was sent to Meeta from Church World Service, Inc. in New York City. It was official. Edward Mägi, a minister of the Seventh-day Adventist Church, would be sponsoring the family to the United States.

CHAPTER 28

Drudgery, Reunion and Another Loss
Siberia 1947

The usual round of forest work began for Ilse on the first day of the new year. Along with some fellow workers, Ilse sawed and hauled wood with a horse and wagon to supply the boiler house with fuel enough to keep the compound buildings warm.

Later that day she and Pikk were able to purchase hamburger and white bread which they enjoyed while Pikk laid out cards for a friend who stopped in to see what the new year held in store for him. Ilse, too, wondered what the year would bring for her. Some Estonians had been allowed to return to their homeland, and Ilse thought perhaps this year would be her year, but she did not ask Pikk to read cards for her. She wanted no more false hopes.

A letter had been received from Mia Treufeldt who had returned to Estonia the previous fall. Mia wrote that she was disappointed with things back home and complained in her letter: "Now I have curls in my hair, my eyebrows have been made narrow and I wear high-heeled shoes, but I do not feel free."

By the second week in January a letter was received from Endel Kalbus who had returned to Estonia in September of the previous year. He, too, expressed disappointment with how his homeland had changed since he had last seen it. No specifics were shared, however. Ilse knew Endel had become a fearful man and understood his reticence in relating details. She well knew that all letters were censored and felt certain he feared any reprisal.

At 1:00 a.m. on January 15 Ilse was awakened and commanded to wake Dusja and Mehaanik and go with the horses to transport logs to the courtyard of the compound. They worked until 4:00 a.m., and then had to report for their regular work in the boiler house at 8:00 a.m. The temperature was minus 43 degrees.

The following day it was minus 46 degrees, but Ilse noted in her diary how very lovely her surroundings appeared: "With the great cold, fog is hovering through the day. It is quiet, and the trees are covered with thick hoarfrost. Nature is then very beautiful. Even the houses and fences are white, and the telephone wires are like white ropes hanging between the poles. The only problem is that the cold nips at your nose and cheeks. Tonka had her cheeks terribly frostbitten today. She had ridden with a horse, and riding is especially cold. Today her hands are swollen and stiff, and she was not able to unhitch the horse."

The following Sunday Ilse began making gloves from grain bags. January and February were largely spent sawing and hauling wood from the forest, sometimes with a horse and wagon and sometimes with a truck. However hard the work, it was a relief for Ilse to now be receiving a regular salary of 258 rubles each month, less 6.23 rubles which were deducted for rent. In the evenings she busied herself sewing gloves and taking a class to improve her Russian.

On March 2 she received 250 rubles from her family's long-time house-keeper Miila. Ilse felt deep warmth for this dedicated woman who had been such an integral part of their family during her formative years. How continuous has been her love and faithfulness, thought Ilse. She is quite elderly now, yet she sends me assistance. How time changes things, she thought. Once employed by us, now she helps support me. Life has many surprising turns, and these turns reveal the hearts of the people involved.

These thoughts caused Ilse to think of the diverse people she had met during this period of her life. She thought back to the morning of their deportation and of the four men who came into their home in the wee hours of the morning. They were not rough or brutal. Under different circumstances she could have offered them a hot drink and invited them to sit down for a chat. One of the Russian soldiers even tried to be helpful by encouraging her to take along her faceless gold watch and a package of cocoa he found in the cupboard.

She had also worked alongside people of different countries—Russians, Ukrainians, Lithuanians, Latvians and Volga Germans. Some were congenial and some were slackers, but circumstances revealed the hearts of each one. Some were moved with compassion and a giving spirit, others were rude and concerned only with what they could get. She had seen men and women at their worst and at their best. Of one thing she was certain, no one ethnic group was superior to another.

Ilse now had some Sundays free and would often go to the local market where she could purchase a wider variety of food. Sunday evenings were sometimes spent at a friend's apartment who owned an accordion. Ilse found joy in playing and singing with others who would join them there. That time was a little oasis for her in an otherwise barren land.

By mid-April Ilse began cleaning the tugboat. On a warm sunny day as she was cleaning the cabin of the boat, she and Ivan, the captain, noticed a piece of ice half the width of the river moving slowly toward the shore. Realizing it was headed directly toward them, Ivan and Ilse jumped off. Mehaanik, too, had seen the situation and shouted, "Carry the paint off the boat!" Ivan ran back to the tugboat and began handing the paint buckets to Ilse and another worker. Ilse accepted one and then feared taking more because she saw the ice moving steadily toward the vessel. Ivan bellowed at her, "Don't be afraid! Take it from me!" Quickly Ilse grabbed another bucket and began running away. Within seconds she heard a huge clatter. When she reached what she thought was a safe distance, she turned to see the boat resting on its side with its nose now into the bank of the river. Ilse wondered what had happened to Ivan, but soon she saw him safely on the shore. He, fortunately, had jumped down just before impact and was able to avoid the collision.

Within minutes workers from the boiler house were on the scene to investigate the possible damage. Fortunately, only the propeller was damaged. A storage cabinet, however, had been tossed into the river, and Ilse and her coworkers had to use barge poles to reclaim it.

Righting the tugboat so that cleaning and repairs could be made was another issue. Ilse and the boiler house crew worked until 10:00 p.m. using manpower and a jackscrew to finally set it upon the blocks where it had formerly rested.

There was more time now for socializing. One such occasion was the homecoming of a Russian worker's husband who had been working for the Russian army as a civil engineer. His arrival on May 1 produced a joyous evening. The balalaika and guitar were played while some in attendance danced. During the merriment some celebrants danced on the couple's cellar door which broke from the weight. The dancers fell into the cellar. Fortunately, the result was only a few scrapes and bruises.

That spring Ilse and Pikk were sent to a field for potato planting. One morning as they worked, Ilse happened to glance toward the drying barn where they and the other workers had slept the previous night lying in a row in the loft. Ilse shouted to Pikk, "There is smoke beginning to rise from beneath the barn!" Both of them ran toward the barn. As they approached they saw flames rising. Dusja, who had also noticed the smoke, began climbing up into the barn to get her belongings from the loft. "Throw our clothes down," shouted Ilse. While Dusja threw everyones' clothes and belongings out the hayloft door to the ground, Ilse, Pikk and the other workers tried to carry out boxes of wheat and as much hay as they could manage. Unfortunately, the potato eyes that were stored there for later planting could not be salvaged. The barn burned quickly and was a total loss. That night the workers slept outside atop what remained of the burned out building.

The following day the band of workers collected wild onions while they waited for a launch to retrieve them. It finally came at 8:00 p.m. They were transferred to a barge that took them near the location of another barge to which they would have to transfer. To get to the second barge, it was necessary for them to walk a distance. Sometimes they sank to their knees in mud. Near their destination they had to wade through water waist high before reaching the barge that took them home.

In mid-June a woman named Elvi Reppo arrived from Estonia. Her husband had been a policeman in Narva, Estonia, who had been deported to Sverdlovsk. All police officers were considered a threat to the Communist government, so he was shot and killed there in 1942. She had been sent to Tomsk where she was jailed in 1943 for stealing a few kilograms of flour to feed herself and her daughter. While she served her sentence, the authorities put her three-year-old daughter into a children's home. When Elvi was released from prison in 1946 and received her personal identification documents again, she immediately returned to Estonia. Her hope was to earn and raise enough money from friends and family so she could return to Siberia and find her daughter. She did not know which children's home housed her daughter but traced her to somewhere in the vicinity of Kolpashevo.

In Kolpashevo Elvi became acquainted with Ilse and told her of her search. Ilse invited Elvi to stay with her, Jefimia and Pikk in their apartment during her visit. She was delighted to accept the offer.

Her search began at the Kolpashevo Children's Home, but her daughter was not there. She next tried the Barabelli's Children's Home some distance away and learned that a Russian woman named Marusa had taken her daughter as her own. The governess at the home told her there was no record of a Milvi Reppo, but she did recall such a child and knew where she was now living. She promised to take the matter to the administrator to see what could be done.

Unfortunately, Milvi, now seven years old, had accepted the Russian woman as her mother. "I don't want to leave my home," cried Milvi to her supposed mother. Marusa, too, was in despair over the situation and did not want to forfeit a daughter whom she had grown to love as her own. The administrator of the children's home, however, explained that legally the child did belong to her biological mother and would have to be returned.

Elvi had to pay the round trip for the governess of the children's home to bring Milvi to Kolpashevo, but getting the child to Kolpashevo was only the beginning. Milvi ignored her mother but took a liking to Jefimia.

The evening following her arrival Ilse placed a sleeping mat on the floor for Elvi and her daughter, but Milvi would not lie down on it with her. Instead, she sat on the edge of Jefimia's bed and said, "Auntie, I will lie next to you and sleep." Then she paused and looked about the room. "You don't have an icon in a corner shelf where I can pray."

Overhearing the conversation Ilse thought a moment and then said, "Why don't you imagine that you see a picture of Jesus? If you close your eyes, you can see Him in your mind." Milvi agreed to that and after a short evening prayer lay down next to Jefimia.

After Milvi fell asleep, Elvi lifted her from Jefimia's bed and put her next to herself on the floor. However, in the morning when Milvi awoke, she immediately separated herself from her mother and returned to Jefimia.

Jefimia made a suggestion, "Why don't we all go to the sauna this morning?" Everyone agreed that was a good idea. While Elvi was preparing to go, Ilse, who had just started a two-week vacation from work, went ahead to the sauna. She was undressing when she saw Elvi at the door of the changing room. Elvi quietly told Ilse, "Milvi won't allow me to take the clothes off of her. You try."

Ilse stooped down so she was at eye level with Milvi and said, "One cannot wash fully dressed. You have to take your clothes off." Milvi did not say a word. The lady in charge of the sauna became aware of what was happening and came over to assist Ilse. In a motherly tone she said to Milvi, "You need to take your clothes off. You don't want them to get all sweaty in the sauna, do you?" Finally, after some additional gentle prodding, Milvi looked at Ilse and said, "All right, but *you* wash me."

Ilse helped Milvi remove and store her clothes in a cabinet and then entered the sauna. After some time in the sauna Ilse forgot that she was to wash Milvi. Elvi took a washing cloth and put soap on it, but hardly had she touched the girl with the cloth when she started to scream. Immediately Ilse remembered that Milvi had wanted her to wash her. She took the cloth from Elvi and slowly touched Milvi with it. She feared that Milvi would scream again, but to her surprise Milvi quieted down. Ilse washed her and then took her to the changing room where she began to dress the child in the same clothes she had taken off. But Elvi rushed into the room carrying some new underclothes and a beautiful red dress.

"Here, Ilse, these are new clothes for Milvi. I brought them with me from Estonia."

Ilse smiled and took the clothes from Elvi. Then she turned to Milvi, "Look Milvi, brand new underwear and a gorgeous new dress."

Milvi glanced at the clothes and then said, "I don't want new clothes. I want to put on my old clothes."

"But Milvi," said Ilse, "your old dress is grey and this one is bright red. Your underclothes need to be washed and these are brand new."

"I don't want new clothes," said Milvi as she turned her back toward them and picked up her old underwear.

Ilse tried to reason with her by saying, "Why not wear the new things until we've had a chance to wash your old clothes? Then you can put your old clothes back on."

"No," said Milvi as she began stepping into her old underclothes.

Elvi looked at Ilse with a look of resignation and took the new clothes back.

That evening as Jefimia readied Milvi for bed, she asked her to put on her new underclothes to sleep in so she could wash the old ones for her. Milvi agreed to do that. While Milvi slept, Elvi hid the old dress and placed the new colorful one in its place. The next morning, however, Milvi began to search for her grey dress.

Ilse picked up the new dress and said, "Put this one on, Milvi. It's so pretty."

Still as determined as ever Milvi replied, "No, I want my own dress—my old dress." Then she began to cry, "Where is my dress?"

Ilse happened to look out the window at that moment and saw a two-year-old boy she knew run out the gate of the compound. She immediately turned to Milvi and said in a very excited voice, "Look, a little boy just ran out of the gate. He must have gotten away from his mother. Let's run and catch him before he gets into trouble!"

Jefimia had left for work, and Elvi watched quietly from a corner.

Milvi quickly looked out the window and saw the small child as Ilse had said. "Oh, we must catch him," said Milvi.

"Yes," said Ilse with excitement mounting in her tone. "But you can't run out there in your underclothes. Hurry, put on your dress . . . we must go quickly!"

In the midst of the great rush to save the little boy, Milvi put on the dress, and she and Ilse hurried out to catch the child and return him to his mother.

Later that day when Jefimia came from work, she, Milvi, and Elvi walked to a store across the street from their apartment. The store sold bread, but it also sold puppets with heads made out of paper mache. Elvi watched as Milvi eyed these puppets and asked her, "Would you like to have one of these?" Milvi said nothing, but after a short pause she turned to Jefimia and said, "Auntie, let us go and buy a puppet."

That evening when they returned home, Ilse asked Milvi, "Who bought you the puppet?" Milvi was quiet as she held fast to the gift. Ilse waited patiently for a response. After a long silence Milvi said, "Stepmother bought it." Ilse said, "Oh, you mean Aunt Jefimia bought it?" Milvi quickly answered, "No," and again became silent.

Another such incident occurred the following Sunday when Jefimia, Elvi and Milvi went to market. Elvi asked, "Milvi, do you want some cedar nuts?" Once again Milvi would not acknowledge her mother's question. Elvi bought her the nuts despite Milvi's silence. When she arrived home, Ilse asked her, "Did your mother buy those for you?" Once again Milvi was silent. This time Ilse let the question die and inwardly pondered whether Milvi would ever be able to accept her mother and willingly return with her to Estonia.

One day Ilse and Milvi took a walk together, and Ilse told her, "I have a small boy almost your age. But he lives far away."

Milvi turned toward Ilse with wide eyes and asked, "Why don't you bring him to you?"

Ilse said, "Your mother came after you, but you don't want to go with her. My boy may not want to come to me either, and that would make me very sad."

Milvi did not respond, but Ilse watched a surprised look appear on her face. Then she became quiet and pensive.

Eventually, Milvi began to warm toward her mother, and two days before Ilse's vacation ended, they departed for Estonia together.

Elvi Reppo was one of many who came trying to locate their children. Many of the children's homes sent children back to their homelands where they were placed in the care of their grandparents or other relatives.

A number of Estonians were escaping back to their homeland. One night a loud knock was heard on Ilse's apartment door with a command to open. When Ilse opened the door, she was greeted by two Russian soldiers who entered with search lights and combed her apartment thoroughly looking for a female escapee. She later learned that the woman had dressed as a Russian and had escaped to Estonia successfully.

Ilse also started laying plans for an escape and began selling items she had accumulated to raise capital for such a venture. However, it was common knowledge that if a person was caught attempting escape, they would be given a prison sentence of two to five years which would further delay any hope of release. Prison was not a desirable place to find oneself. After careful consideration of the possibilities, Ilse decided to remain in Siberia and wait for a release. She even approached her supervisor about that possibility, but no response was given.

One day in late August Ilse received a letter from Estonia. It was from her friend Tutti. She eagerly opened it since Tutti had not written in a long while. The first line of the letter caused her heart to beat faster. It read, "Take a seat somewhere and then read on." Ilse did not take a seat but eagerly read the next line. "Just now I came home from Miila's burial." The words jabbed at Ilse's heart. Dear Miila, she thought, my dear, dear Miila. Miila had been such a faithful friend throughout the years—far more than just a housekeeper for her parents. She was like family. Ilse had known her since she could remember. Miila had encouraged and supported her in Siberia. Quiet tears began to flow as she continued reading: "Miila's passing came so quickly. One week ago I was chatting with her, and she intended to write you. But now her earthly life has ended."

Ilse took a seat with the letter resting in her lap. Life is so brief, she thought. It seems like such a short time since Miila showed me the lilac tree she had planted in her yard to commemorate the birth of Vello. That's who Miila was, she thought—a person who was happy when we were happy and sad when we were sad. She knew us so intimately. How does one ever replace a friend like that?…The truth is you can't. She buried her head in her hands and sobbed, "How many more of my loved ones will die before I ever see them again?"

CHAPTER 29

The New World
Germany/United States 1950-1956

The Kollist family was undergoing complete medical examinations in preparation for emigration by late April 1950. All emigrants had to be assessed "free from infectious diseases and fit for travel."

By early May the family was relocated to Schweinfurt, Germany, and taken to the seventh floor of a large red brick building where they would await their final processing. Their new living quarters was a large room partitioned into family compartments where they slept on army cots in close proximity to other families like them. Though the partitions did provide some modicum of privacy, there was no scheduled time for lights out and no designated quiet time. Thus some people remained awake late into the night playing card games or talking beneath the glaring lights which remained on until the last of them retired.

During the first week in their new location the family received ceaseless rounds of shots and inoculations, it seemed, as Meeta said, "for every conceivable disease known to mankind." These were followed by interviews with a first and second American consul.

The second consul told Meeta, "Your case is a difficult one. You are a lone woman responsible for not only yourself but also for your mother and two small children. I cannot make this decision. I am referring you to a third consul to evaluate."

During Meeta's consultations, Vello and his grandmother sat outside on benches playing checkers together. The open area where they waited with many other refugees was surrounded by loudspeakers erected on poles that announced the time and place of appointments for those waiting. In between announcements and orders, many Viennese waltzes by Johann Strauss were played. Vello, now in his ninth year, enjoyed this time of play with his grandmother and commented to her, "This music makes me feel happy." That statement resonated with Meeta. She wanted so much for both Vello and her son to find real happiness, but their future was tenuous. Would a single woman be allowed to emigrate to the United States? Once again she reached out to God.

While waiting for news of the third consul meeting, Meeta was surprised to see a familiar form approaching her. It was Wasyl. She knew he was interested in emigrating, but did not know he was currently at this same complex. He greeted her with his usual warm smile, "I see you are headed in the same direction as I am, Meeta."

Meeta, still very much keeping her reserve, asked, "Are you also now processing for the United States?"

"Yes, I am hoping for New York City. And you?"

"If we are approved, we will also be sent to New York. A minister of my church has arranged to sponsor our little family.

Wasyl's eyes met hers directly and in an almost pleading tone said, "Meeta, let us please keep in touch."

His warmth disarmed her, and she felt her pulse increase. But she steeled herself and distanced her initial feelings as she said, "Of course. I have your child." They exchanged their current locations, and Wasyl reluctantly turned and walked away.

Finally, the day arrived for a meeting with the third consul. Before arriving at his office, Meeta recited Proverbs 3:26:

> For the Lord will be your confidence,
> And will keep your foot from being caught.

The text gave her the courage she was lacking for this encounter.

The little family waited for a full two hours before gaining admittance. The wait was nerve-racking, but Meeta utilized this time to pray silently and to repeat the Bible text she had read that morning. In between her prayers and recitation, she anticipated the questions that would be asked of her.

At last the entire family was invited into the consul's office. An interpreter was present to translate for the family from German to English and vice versa. Two secretaries were also in the room.

Meeta was asked many questions about how she had managed to sustain this family during their escape and stay in Germany. Fortunately, Meeta had an excellent work record which demonstrated skill, consistency and responsibility. But the consul asked her a question she would never have imagined being asked of a woman. "Miss Kollist, if you were asked to fight in the American Army, what would you do?"

Though this question surprised her, a response came from her mouth that she never would have thought of had she known the question in advance. "A woman is a life giver, not a life destroyer." Her response was firm and her look unflinching as she spoke, but Meeta felt the tension her response caused. Her peripheral vision saw the interpreter and both secretaries look directly at her as she made the statement. The answer seemed to surprise the consul as much as it had Meeta.

After a brief pause, seemingly to collect his thoughts, he asked her, "Where is the father of your child?"

Meeta's response was once again firm and assured. "He is also processing for admittance into the United States. He has been very faithful in providing assistance both before and since the birth of his son."

With that the consul seemed satisfied and approval was granted.

Later that evening Meeta met one of the secretaries who had been present during the interview. She congratulated Meeta and then added, "You sure have luck." But Meeta knew it was not just "luck." The God she served had once again provided.

A few days later with suitcases in hand, the little family left on a train destined for Bremerhaven. Their destination was a resettlement center where they remained until the day they boarded the USNS *General S. D. Sturgis* that had a capacity for 3,000 people.

For Amalie and Meeta it was a happy yet sad occasion. They were leaving the European mainland—the only home they had ever known. Mother and daughter looked at each other as the ship pulled away from the harbor into the North Sea. Their tear-filled eyes told what their mouths could not express. What would the New World hold for them? Would it be welcoming or unfriendly? Was it really to be the "land of opportunity?" Or would it be a lonely, isolated place far from the customs and acquaintances they had known?

For Vello it was an exciting adventure. He stood on deck as the ship passed the Frisian Islands. Then the majestic "white cliffs of Dover" appeared as the ship approached England. After taking aboard another captain, the ship continued through the Strait of Dover and into the English Channel.

Finally, they entered the Atlantic Ocean, and all traces of land slowly disappeared, leaving only the monotonous rolling and dipping of the never ending sea. Water alone could not be observed too long, so the two children turned to exploration.

Hillar, now nearly four, enjoyed traversing the many steps, and he smiled as he scrambled up and down them. When his legs grew tired, he would sometimes use his hands and buttocks for the climb or descent. Together he and Vello explored the many decks until their curiosity had been satisfied.

The trip took place in the month of July, and good weather prevailed throughout. Some days found the ocean controlled by an unbelievable stillness that gave it the appearance of a lake. On one such day, Vello became particularly excited as he stood next to his aunt. "Look Ati! What is that?"

Meeta smiled at her nephew and picked up Hillar to be certain he wouldn't miss the wonderful display. "It's a group of porpoises giving us a show. They are very intelligent creatures that seem to like human beings." Hillar screamed with delight as he watched the marine animals jump out of the water, fly through the air and then dive back into the sea.

To the delight of the children, once in a while another merchant or sailing ship would be seen. They found it thrilling when the ships would exchange greetings by blowing their horns as they passed.

Nights aboard the ship could be enchanting as the children looked into the unknown darkness and enjoyed the twinkling lights shining throughout the ship. Even the sound of the ocean seemed to be more fascinating at night as it lapped against the sides of the vessel, and every breath brought with it the refreshing ocean air. Foggy days were interesting, too, when nothing but a damp hazy atmosphere engulfed them. The various faces of the ocean left their indelible mark on Vello and created in him an enduring love of the sea.

Approximately 10 days after leaving Bremerhaven they received their first glimpse of their new homeland. Fog bathed the harbor as the ship sailed past the most memorable sight to sojourners from foreign lands—the Statue of Liberty. The Kollist family stood on deck in the midst of the fog as they passed the pastel green lady holding a tablet in one hand and the torch of freedom in the other. She appeared dreamlike in the fog, and the family stared in awe as she passed into the hazy distance.

Suddenly triangular flags of many different colors were raised from the bow of the ship across the mast to the stern. Their display announced the ship's arrival and symbolized what those aboard had hoped for—entrance to the "land of the free." A number of tugboats shot water into the air heralding their arrival as refugees stood on deck watching the exciting display of welcome.

When the family disembarked, the children were seated on the luggage as Meeta and Amalie processed their paperwork. The first Americans the children met were Red Cross officials who greeted them in a strange language but provided them with donuts and milk. The children had never seen a donut before. Vello was a bit reluctant to taste it. Aboard ship he had been given a grapefruit and had found it to be the most bitter, detestable fruit he had ever eaten. It was promptly thrown overboard into the sea. But now Vello saw others eagerly eating these round pieces of dough with a hole in the middle and he took a small bite. His eyes brightened as he turned to Hillar. "This is good, Hillar. Try it. If you don't like it, I'll eat it." Both children decided this first food in their new country was delicious.

Soon a young man from the crowd appeared and identified himself as Eino Mägi, Pastor Eduard Mägi's son. He was a tall man in his late 20s with blond hair and spoke fluent Estonian. He told them he had recently completed his medical studies and was hoping to become a family practice physician in the United States. He carried the family's sparse luggage to his waiting convertible and then drove down Broadway.

The newcomers were entranced as they craned their necks to see the tops of the skyscrapers lining the New York City streets. Meeta looked at her mother and said, "The height of these buildings is amazing. And there are so many of them." They had seen cathedrals and churches, but these buildings were so different and so very "straight-up high."

Some apprehension was felt as they journeyed through the Queens-Midtown Tunnel and realized they were traveling underneath a river that was much wider than the mouth of the Pärnu River that led into the Pärnu Bay. Meeta kept eyeing the white tiles that lined the tunnel fearing that water might begin seeping through at any time. She was relieved when they emerged, yet another phenomenon greeted them as they entered the Long Island Expressway. Meeta had never seen so many cars traveling so close to one another at such high speeds. They turned onto a boulevard which led them to the Belt Parkway. Soon they exited onto a local road that paralleled the parkway and brought them to 153rd Lane, a gravel road.

The car passed about 10 homes and pulled up to the second to the last house on the right side of the street. This was to be their new residence in the Jamaica Bay area of New York City.

It was a grey, two-story stucco house. High wild hedges grew on the right side of the yard shielding it from view of the houses they had just passed. The house to the left was the last one on the street. Beside that house was a large sandy area about one-quarter of a mile wide beyond which was a chain-link fence surrounding Idlewild Airport.[48] On the opposite side of the street in front of their new residence was a large wetland area covered with six-foot tall cattails, their brown heads waving in the breeze.

Two other Estonian families were already living on the second floor of the house. Meeta and her family were directed to the downstairs apartment. It consisted of a living room and bedroom, each containing a potbellied stove fueled with coal, a kitchen, bath and a small room at the rear of the house which led to the backyard. There a clapboard three-car garage stood surrounded by an open field covered with high grass and wild flowers. The home provided a country setting in the outskirts of a congested city.

Vello found it especially exciting to sneak underneath the airport fence and walk within a hundred yards of the enormous intercontinental airplanes that were parked by the huge hangers. As Hillar grew, he enjoyed climbing and eating the fruit on the trees in the vacant lot to the right of their house. They both enjoyed eating from the raspberry bushes that lined a dirt road winding alongside the cattail field.

The boys found a treasure-trove of discarded 55-gallon drums. Vello and some neighborhood friends used one as a heater in an underground fort which they dug into the sand. They burned wood in it to keep their fort rooms warm when the weather turned cold.

Hillar and a friend lightly flattened two halves of a 55-gallon drum, placed them longitudinally next to each other, leaving a couple of feet between, and then placed a 2" X 12" X 5' board in the middle upon which they could sit. It became their "boat" whenever a section of a road beyond their backyard became flooded.

But if this was a fun time for the boys, it was not so for Meeta, who had to travel more than an hour by bus and train to and from Manhattan each day for her job as a bookkeeper at the Singer Sewing Machine Company. It seemed she would just return home in time to eat, go to bed and arise again for another day of work. During this time she was particularly thankful for the Sabbath. It was the one day of the week she could rest and not feel guilty.

She and the boys would attend the local Jamaica Seventh-day Adventist Church Sabbath mornings where Vello and Hillar became acquainted with additional friends. Sometimes the boys would spend Sabbath afternoons with these buddies at their homes. This afforded Meeta some time to quietly read, take a nap, or just sit and enjoy nature while seated on their back porch.

Life was not easy for Amalie either. She was totally unfamiliar with the

English language and struggled to learn enough to do the grocery shopping. The A & P grocery store was a good mile from their home. Shopping had to be done by foot and the items carried back to their house. Fortunately, Meeta was soon able to acquire a cart for her mother which made hauling the food easier but still required her walking.

The kitchen of their home contained a wringer washing machine, but the clothes had to be hung outdoors to dry. Amalie was now approaching 66 years of age and was expending quite a bit of energy to keep the house running, not to mention keeping an eye on two active boys.

Finances were tight with just one income in their household, which was difficult for Amalie to deal with. In her own country before the war began, she had a housekeeper and all of her needs amply provided. Now she was grocery shopper, chief cook, washer woman and babysitter with scant money to pay the bills.

Vello began third grade in the local public school the fall following their arrival in America. His first day in the school was an embarrassment for him as he entered with his *lederhosen*,[49] complete with suspenders and knee-high stockings that he was accustomed to wearing in Bavaria. As he entered the school, children stared at him and snickered. He found some cover behind his desk. However, when the children were called to the auditorium the first day for an introductory program, he sat bent over and tugged at his *lederhosen* in an effort to cover his knees. When he arrived home, he flatly stated, "I'm not going back to that school unless I have a pair of long pants like the other boys wear."

When Meeta arrived home from work that evening, he was promptly taken to a nearby clothing store where he was fitted for his first pair of long pants, his one and only pair, which he wore every day to school.

Clothing was not the only adjustment Vello had to make. He had learned some English during the summer while playing with his friends and going to church, but there were still many words he did not understand. Fortunately, an older Estonian boy living on the second floor of their home gave him assistance with homework that first year.

By 1951 Wasyl Myzak was becoming established in New York City and was living in Brooklyn. He had departed for the United States three months after Meeta and her family had left Germany. In January of 1951 Meeta was able to locate him by writing to the United States Displaced Persons Commission in Schweinfurt, Germany.

Ever the aggressive entrepreneur, Wasyl was making a living by doing tax returns at home. Mindful that this was a seasonal business, he contacted the Good Humor Ice Cream Company and secured a position with them for the summer months. His job consisted of manning a cart at Coney Island where he would sell ice cream. The two jobs provided enough income for him to eventually buy some rental property.

True to his commitment to Meeta, he regularly sent money to the family which was greatly needed and appreciated. He also purchased an accident and sickness insurance policy and made Hillar the beneficiary.

Hillar began kindergarten in the fall of 1952 in the local public school. His inquisitive mind produced frustration for his kindergarten teacher because he would often disassemble toys. When asked, "What are you doing?" His answer would inevitably be, "I want to see how this works."

Vello began attending his church's parochial school when he entered fourth grade. He also joined the church's Pathfinder Club, a group similar to the Boy Scouts, where he learned various skills and with whom he enjoyed camping.

In late March of 1956, a letter arrived from Meeta's cousin Anna Neemelaid of Malmö, Sweden. She had reestablished contact with the family for a few months, having obtained their address from Oskar who was once again employed in Sweden. Early in January she contacted Aunt Ann Kollist in Estonia and received a return letter with some news she wanted to share with the Kollist family.

Cousin Anna's letter brought a welcomed revelation to the family: "I wanted to send you the happy news about Ilse. I have enclosed the letter." The enclosure was from Aunt Ann who wrote: "I received a letter in January from Ilse. She is now music teacher in a kindergarten in Siberia and very much longs for a picture of Vello." It was a brief comment but enough. That evening Amalie greeted the rest of the family enthusiastically. "Ilse is alive!"

The news was encouraging. Still the family had no address, and further correspondence was necessary to discover her exact location. A picture of Vello was sent to Cousin Anna. She in turn was asked to forward it to Aunt Ann who had Ilse's address.

In May Oskar wrote sharing that he, too, had received news from Cousin Ann that Ilse was alive. Oskar warned, "We all must be very careful in writing over there [Siberia] so people are not harmed." With censorship of letters, those still being held could be accused of anti-government activities or espionage if some critical comment was noted in any correspondence arriving or leaving Russia. This caused the family to fear writing Ilse even after they had received her address.

Oskar included in his letter that he was by himself in Sweden. He and his family had immigrated to Australia from Sweden in 1946, but in 1955 he again began working in Sweden. Previously he had shared how he had thought his family would join him once he was established, but now he stated: "Ave doesn't want to come here. Life here is expensive. . . . Taxes are at least twice what we pay in Australia, and now again the fear of war nears one's horizon. . . . Sweden is preparing to defend itself. The defensive shelters against atomic war are built into the cliffs." At this time North and South Korea were filled with unsettled tension, China threatened taking over Taiwan, and the Cold War raged between the United States and the Soviet Union.

Meanwhile, the Kollist family was facing a personal dilemma regarding their housing. The house in which they had lived for nearly six years was in disrepair. It was slated by the city to be torn down with all of the houses in their subdivision for expansion of the Idlewild Airport. The previous winter the basement had flooded and their apartment was left with a foul odor. Two of the ceilings in the apartment were sagging. Additionally, the woman living in the apartment immediately above them showed signs of being mentally ill. Meeta petitioned the New York Housing Authority to help them find a suitable living situation and was placed on a waiting list for an apartment in the Rockaway Beach area.

One summer evening Amalie was seated on the small landing outside their apartment awaiting Meeta's arrival from work when the woman from the upstairs apartment approached her and began scolding her. "What are you doing just sitting here? Don't you have anything better to do?" Amalie replied, "I'm waiting for my daughter to come home." The woman then climbed the stairs to her apartment and began sweeping the stairs down to where Amalie was seated. When she reached Amalie, she took the dust pan full of dirt and threw it into her face. Amalie immediately rose and tried to clear the dust from her eyes asking, "Why did you do that?" The woman then hit her on the head with the dust pan, causing a bloody wound. Just then Meeta arrived, and the woman retreated to her own apartment.

This situation prompted Meeta to make another urgent appeal to the housing authority. Soon the family moved to an apartment on Rockaway Beach Boulevard one block from the ocean.

That fall Vello began his freshman year at his church's parochial high school, Greater New York Academy. Meeta enrolled Hillar, who was entering fourth grade, in the elementary school associated with it. This allowed the two boys to travel together on the three buses necessary to reach their destination.

Distinct personalities were developing in the two boys. Vello enjoyed studying languages and reading. Hillar excelled in math. When a city-wide ciphering bee was held, Hillar easily won.

Finances continued to be tight in the household. Meeta gave all her earnings to Amalie for food and expenses with the exception of a tithe which she believed belonged to the Lord. Amalie was not happy with that exception and repeatedly told Meeta, "In Estonia crooked partners took our money, then the government took our money, and now the church is taking it." Sometimes her anger became frenzied. "You're worthless. How come you can't make more money?" Meeta would retaliate with an appeal. "How can I? You tell me where I can earn more money. I don't know how. I'm doing the best I can do!"

Meeta understood how difficult life was for Amalie. She realized the disappointment her mother felt from losing a business that would have provided comfortable retirement instead of house work and pinching pennies in a foreign land. This was set against a backdrop of being separated from a daughter and son, the death of her husband, and the loss of almost all her possessions.

Despite understanding, sometimes Meeta felt like a beaten dog as she struggled to keep her own soul together. Life in New York was so different from what she had experienced in her country. She daily saw a concrete city that smelled of exhaust fumes. The subways were crowded, and everything was hurried. Commuting time was long, and she barely had enough time in the evening to recoup her strength before beginning another day. How she longed for the sweet smell of pine and linden trees and the fresh breezes that wafted from the Baltic Sea. She missed the evening walks at the close of a day and music. Would there ever be time for music again?

CHAPTER 30

True Relief
Siberia/Estonia 1948-1957

Significant changes began occurring for Ilse in 1948. Jefimia Maasik had been released from the settlement, so only she and Pikk remained in the apartment.

Ilse was placed in charge of stoking the boiler for the headquarters building of Kolpashevo. Coal was now used so she no longer had to fell and saw logs in sub-zero temperatures, but the work was dirty and very hot. The extreme heat precluded her from wearing the protective glasses that were given to protect her eyes because they became very hot on her face. Consequently, her eyes suffered from the heat and glare of the fire. She attributed her eye problems in later life to this experience. During the summer she worked in the hayfields.

She continued working in this manner until 1952 when she was transferred to the local hospital where she tended the heating system. In 1953 a second job, a part-time one, was added which she enjoyed very much. She began teaching music in the compound's kindergarten twice a week.

Joseph Stalin's death on March 5, 1953, gave hope to Ilse and many others in the settlement that they soon would be heading home, but once again disappointment reigned.

In early June of 1954 a letter arrived from Tutti. In it she included a picture of Amalie, Meeta, with her supposed husband and son, and Vello. Tutti explained that the picture had been sent to her by the son of Mrs. Vanakammer, a mutual friend, who had died a year earlier. The son had recently found the picture as he was sorting through his mother's things and forwarded it to Tutti because of her close association with Meeta and her family.

Ilse stared at the picture for a long while; so much needed to be assessed. Her mother looked old and shrunken with stooped shoulders. The transformation shocked Ilse. She next contemplated her son. If the picture had been taken a year earlier, Vello would have been 12. Ilse was amazed at how tall he appeared. She mused as she studied him. *He's a young man already and as tall as Meeta.* Then she stared at the man and boy standing next to Meeta. *Is this Meeta's husband and son? When did Meeta marry? The child beside her looks to be about five or six.*

As she continued reading the letter, she discovered that Mrs. Vanakammer's son had also gleaned information from his mother's things that "Jaak Kollist died about eight years ago." Ilse slumped into a chair. Her thoughts were a mixture of sadness, frustration and anger. *Papsi, my beloved Papsi is gone. What I had feared is happening. My loved ones are dying without my ever seeing them again. If only I knew how to contact them.*

January 1, 1955, brought some true relief for Ilse. She began working full time as teacher in the kindergarten of the compound. Her creative abilities were unleashed and found expression in artwork made to enhance the children's learning experience and make it more enjoyable. Some of the children's songs and poems mentioned oak trees. The children were totally unfamiliar with that type of tree, so to help them visualize it, she wrote Tutti: "Please send me some oak leaves. The children here have never seen such a tree." She also bought an accordion and found much joy in playing with and for the children.

Times were also changing in Russia as more communication outside the Soviet Union was permitted for those locked behind the Iron Curtain.[50] More and more of Ilse's friends were also being released from their assigned settlements. Lisette Silm, who had served two years in prison for attempting to escape in 1946, was released from the Maiga settlement on February 21, 1955. This produced great hope and encouragement that release for Ilse would be soon.

After the death of Joseph Stalin in 1953, suppressive control from the central government in Moscow began to decline. Now with the release of many deportees and a lessening of communication restrictions, she felt it was time to attempt to locate her family.

In January 1956 Ilse wrote to her Aunt Ann telling of her desire to find her family and expressed how she yearned to have a current picture of her son. Aunt Ann replied saying she did not know the location of Ilse's family but would do her best to try to find them for her. She also informed Ilse that Uncle Peeter, her husband, had died in 1952. Uncle Peeter was Jaak's brother. Another family member gone, thought Ilse. The news produced a greater urgency than ever to get in contact with her family.

During the summer things began to rapidly change for Ilse. Pikk, her last roommate, was released to return home to Lithuania. Ilse was given a full month and a half vacation and was able to upgrade her apartment. Now, in addition to a room, she had a separate kitchen and a small fore room. She also bought a bicycle so she could travel more easily in a wider radius. Sometimes she would go by bus to visit her long-time friend Hilda Pavelson who lived 50 kilometers away. Hilda worked as a saleswoman and store supervisor and was living well but, like Ilse, had not been released to return to Estonia.

By the end of July Ilse received a letter from Tutti who was now anticipating Ilse's soon release because so many who had been deported were returning. She wrote: "If you have the opportunity, you could come to the homeland. Everyone is coming who can get free. No one has starved, and surely you will find work." But she also cautioned her: "Finding an apartment is hard, but certainly through acquaintances one can be found. While searching, one can stay with friends. ... One place, I will declare, is to stay with me." Then she added, "You have been in Russia a long time. With the Russian language one can get along here because it is used everywhere."

In late summer Aunt Ann provided Ilse with the up-to-date picture of Vello, now 15 years old, that she had received from Cousin Anna. Ilse opened the letter and quickly turned the portrait face down. She struggled for composure before allowing herself to look at the child she had only known for three weeks. He was now a teenager, and she had missed it all—all the growing years of change and development. Two years had passed since she had seen a picture of him, and it had been a snapshot, not a portrait as this one was. Could she stand to look into his eyes as she viewed the picture? Who would he most resemble? Would he remind her of the husband she had lost? Would she like his looks?

Slowly she turned the picture over, her heart pounding as her eyes scanned the photo. He has a pleasant face, she thought as she took a deep breath. He was dressed in a suit, white shirt and tie and looked neat and trim. Yes, she thought, I could like this young man. His nose is like Peko's, but his features are his own, not really looking like either of us. As she stared at her son's face, emotions overpowered her. Tears began streaming down her cheeks and onto the letter that had accompanied the picture. My son is a stranger to me, she thought. This is the boy Peko and I longed to have. The child we could not bear the thought of losing by an attempted escape from Estonia to Finland. The child we lost anyway by remaining in Estonia. Peko was so proud of his son. Why, oh why has life treated us so? Tears came in rivers as all the losses of the past 15 years suddenly enveloped her. The weeping did not end that day. For several days thereafter, each time she looked at the picture, the emotions arose again.

Ilse eventually obtained the address of her family through correspondence with Aunt Ann, but at this time her aunt advised that the family was in the midst of a transition to a new residence. She assured Ilse that she would send the new address to her as soon as she received it from them. In correspondence with Aunt Ann, Ilse obtained the address of Cousin Anna. When she did not receive her family's new address from Aunt Ann, she wrote to Cousin Anna in the fall of 1956 requesting information about her family.

When Cousin Anna finally obtained the new address and sent it to her, Ilse pondered hard and rewrote drafts of introduction to the son with whom she yearned to have a relationship. By March 1957 she decided to send a carefully worded two-page letter written on the front and back side. One side was addressed to the family, the other to her son.

CHAPTER 31

Letter of Introduction
New York City 1957

Two months before Vello's 16th birthday, he received a letter from his mother:

Beloved Vello,

I have become acquainted with you through photographs. I received four new pictures from [Cousin] Anna and two from Aunt Ann. . . . Now I want to acquaint myself with you by letter. Judging by the pictures, you are a big boy for your age. . . . Learn as much as there is to learn. That is the only treasure a person can have that cannot be taken away from him. With that treasure you will be able to succeed in the world.

The letter went on to identify Kolpashevo and its location on the Ob River. She told of how, at the beginning of May, the first ships come from the South after the ice has melted. "In previous years I remember the whistles blowing on the arriving ships. Then half the city arrived on the shore to greet them. That was a great event years ago, but in the last few years it has changed, and people don't react to the event any longer."

Addressing the family at large, she expressed her delight at having received their address. Then she asked about what kind of house they live in and how they heat their living quarters. She shared: "We naturally heat with wood since we are surrounded by dense forests. Last year I prepared the wood myself in the forest, but this year I purchased the wood." Then she spoke of her apartment which is larger than what she had before, consisting of two rooms and a kitchen. "In the beginning of February we had great cold—as much as minus 50 degrees, but the apartment was warm. For you that seems very cold, but this is not so terrible. Naturally one has to dress warm. . . . In the winter the workers wear cotton or wool lined pants—both men and women. If it is more than minus 40 degrees then they don't work outside. On Saturday work time is shorter. Instead of eight hours, they work six hours but get a full day's pay."

She wrote of her work as music teacher in the kindergarten and added, "Meeta, if you were here, you would find work in music. I have learned to play the accordion." From her correspondence with Cousin Anna she had learned the name of Meeta's son and asked, "How old is Hillar? Is he attending school?" Next she mentioned that she had received a letter from Oskar who sent her a picture of his two daughters. Finally, she asked for details about Vello's personality. "Is he consistent with what he undertakes? Does he finish a task? Is he more like his father or mother?"

The letter was general in its content. The only words that came close to revealing personal feelings were those written to Vello in one brief sentence: "I have thought of you much through the years."

Having been warned by Oskar to be careful of what is written when corresponding with anyone in Russia, Meeta chose her words carefully when she responded, and Vello's first response was a brief note attached to hers that simply said, "Dear Mother, Our prayers have been with you, and we continue to remember you each day. Vello." It was short, but it was a first step.

That summer Vello began working for the Good Humor Ice Cream Company at the encouragement and good word of his "uncle" Wasyl Myzak. Vello carried ice cream in two dry-ice containers strapped over his shoulders up and down Far Rockaway Beach and sold his sweet, ice-cold treats to sunbathers. As he looked out into the ocean day after day, he decided that one day he would cross it to visit his mother.

Another letter arrived from Ilse in October. In it she described how things were changing and gave them another glimpse of life in Siberia: "I was on vacation for one and one-half months during the summer—42 days. . . . I went to swim in the Ob River. . . . In the beginning of August we had beautiful weather. . . . People here love cedar nuts [pine nuts], and in the fall every second or third person is chewing the nuts. I have learned to like them. The shells can be found thrown down everywhere, even in movie houses and stores. The clean-up crews scold the public for doing it."

She next explained that the apartment complex where she lives "provides a garden plot for each renter. We plant cabbage, tomatoes, and cucumbers. I have preserved cucumbers and cabbage with salt. The tomatoes are still on the vine today. Every establishment is ordered to give their workers land for growing potatoes, and I have planted 200 square meters."

Concerning Amalie she wrote: "Mamsi will soon have her birthday. I wish my beloved much good fortune and that her wishes be fulfilled." Then she addressed her mother directly: "Are you really 73 years old? Papsi at that age was quite youthful. One could not reckon he was that old. How do you feel? How is your health? . . . May the Heavenly Father give you many years to live so I can yet meet you in this lifetime."

CHAPTER 32

Old Friendships Renewed
Siberia/Estonia 1958

Ilse was officially released from custody on December 31, 1957, and on January 1, 1958, registered at the government office as a "rehabilitated person," which granted her the rights of a citizen of the Estonian Soviet Socialist Republic, albeit a notation appeared on her document indicating that she had been deported. The government promised her a double pension if she would continue working in Siberia, and this encouraged her to remain as a teacher in the kindergarten.

Ilse's friend Hilda Pavelson was released from custody in February of 1958 and returned to Estonia. Hilda's daughter, Luule, did not return with her. She had married a Russian and remained in the city of Vladivastok.

During the summer of 1958 Ilse took advantage of her vacation and her release to finally visit Estonia. Traveling by bus from the airport in Tallinn to her hometown of Pärnu, she felt emotions rising. The farmlands and forests of her beloved country were still lovely and little changed, but the towns she passed through revealed unpainted buildings, broken streets and walkways. She noticed, too, the people seated around her. Each sat stoically silent staring out the window or blankly forward. Faces were sullen and serious. She saw in their faces the same caution and fear she experienced in Siberia. Silence was safest in this world of suspicion.

Seeing friends and relatives deported without cause had left a pall of fear that one could immediately sense upon entering the country. Ilse had learned never to speak a word against the government, for one never knew who was an informer or where one would be lurking.

Approaching Pärnu she anxiously looked out the bus window for her first glimpse of the town where she had been born. Unlike the colorful houses she remembered, however, the homes were drab and weathered. Strange apartment buildings began coming into view, structures unfamiliar to Estonian architecture. Melancholy feelings surfaced as she observed the change that had come to her hometown.

Her ride ended at the bus station near the center of Pärnu, and Ilse was happy to see the familiar face of her long-time friend Tutti waiting for her as she disembarked from the bus. As Tutti had forewarned her, she was now a stout lady. The two middle-aged women embraced each other and mingled their tears. Tutti was first to speak, "Ilse, you, too, have become large around the middle as I have."

Ilse chuckled, "Yes, I have learned well how to eat."

Tutti's face became serious as she stared at her friend. "It has been 17 years since we have seen each other. It is hard to believe that we are finally together again."

Ilse, too, became serious. "This is a dream I feared would never happen, yet here we are, and I am really standing on Estonian soil." Ilse's eyes once again became teary as Tutti took her dear friend by the arm. "We must get a taxi now and take your luggage to my house. You surely need to rest and get something to eat."

"I am a bit weary from travel and am anxious to meet your husband and son. I believe he is now eight years old."

"Yes, his birthday was in April; he is his father's joy. As you know, we were married late in life and are enjoying parenthood, but it is difficult trying to juggle my work as a bookkeeper and still be a proper parent." She paused a moment and then added, "I am taking two weeks' vacation now to be with you. Tomorrow we can tour the town so you can see our former haunts."

Tutti's house was a modest home. She, her husband and son lived in the back portion of the house in three small rooms and kitchen. One of the rooms was used as a parlor where Ilse's bed was the couple's couch. In the front section of the home was what would have normally been the living room, but Tutti's aunt and father lived in this room. Tutti's father was suffering from dementia and spent most of his time in bed in an anteroom. All of them shared a small bathroom.

Tutti's husband was a congenial man, soft spoken and personable. But Ilse felt a special fondness for Tutti's son, Rein. Looking at him aroused her maternal desires for the son she would never see grow up. Rein was a well-behaved child and very courteous—just what Ilse would have wanted Vello to be. She witnessed the parental pride in both Tutti and her husband and recalled her own and that of Peko's for the son they both had wanted so badly.

The food that evening consisted of cucumbers, tomatoes, cheese, hard Estonian bread and apples. "Oh Tutti," said Ilse, these apples taste so delicious. I haven't had an apple since leaving Estonia." The statement surprised Tutti, and she quickly offered her another. Apples were served with a knife. Because no pesticides were used, sometimes a worm hole or a bad spot would have to be cut out. Apples were generally of a small size.

The following day Tutti had arranged for Ilse to meet with three of her classmates from high school. One of her classmate's appearance shocked Ilse as she saw how stoop shouldered she had become. She later commented to Tutti, "She reminds me of my mother." Still another classmate did not want to see Ilse because she "feared" her visit. Ilse had been deported, and some people feared that association with her could raise suspicions about them and jeopardize them and their families.

During this time, Ilse located Kristjan Sillaste who had been with her husband in the gulag and was recently released and returned to Estonia. She was shocked to learn from him, "Out of 500 men in the camp, only 30 had come out alive." He further said he felt he survived because he was a medic and lived in the dispensary where he had his own cot. "When patients became so ill they could no longer eat, I would get their portions of food."

The compound was surrounded by two barbed-wire fences with guard towers at each corner. Dogs paced in the area between the two fences. Each morning the camp held roll call, and then the inmates waited in line for a breakfast of watered-down soup and bread.

Sillaste said that most of the men were sent to the forest to cut trees and would work until the sun began to set. "Peeter had sciatica so was given the job of making birch-bark shoes. The men would sometimes work one to three months without a day off. The guards would tell them, 'We haven't brought you here for a vacation. We've brought you here to die.'"

When the men returned to the camp at night, they were given more watered-down soup and bread. They were so tired by then that they went immediately to sleep only to arise the next morning to begin the routine over again. Sillaste was expressionless as he spoke. Ilse felt certain his experience had left an indelible impression upon his character.

Sillaste assured her that her husband had not died of starvation. He had a box of dried bread which he obtained for payment from the other Estonian prisoners for translating documents they had received in Russian. When Peeter became ill, however, the doctor on the compound requested a suit from him in payment for treatment. Peeter was hoping to use that suit upon his release and would not give it up, so the doctor refused to treat him for pneumonia. Sillaste had drawn close to Peeter during their confinement and told Ilse that he buried him and made a wooden cross for his grave. Ilse was deeply grateful for his kindness toward her husband. Years later, when Sillaste died, she gave permission for him to be buried in the Kollist family gravesite.

Later that week Ilse and Tutti took a taxi past Jaak's former factory. Tutti cautioned Ilse not to mention that her family had once owned it while riding in the taxi. "The taxi driver could be an espionage agent, Ilse, so it is best to keep our conversation very general. The less he knows about you the better." Ilse was surprised to see that the Russians had added a third floor to the building and was told it was a shoe factory. Her childhood home next to the factory appeared rundown, and she noted that two small concrete structures had been built beside it.

How very much things have changed, she thought. Her mind panned over the years. She recalled friends and neighbors walking calmly in front of their home on quiet summer evenings as she and the other members of her family played the music of Chopin, Brahms and other great composers. It had been such a beautiful life. People then would smile and greet one another as they passed. Now people walked the streets like automatons looking beyond those who past as if they did not exist. Additionally, the Russian language was spoken everywhere.

The country had had an influx of Russians since the occupation, and it was the Estonians who were required to learn Russian. The Russian people made no attempt to learn even the most basic Estonian words; this created a problem for older Estonians who found it difficult to learn this new language with a Cyrillic alphabet.

One day as Ilse waited in line at the post office, an elderly Estonian lady tried to make herself understood by the Russian postal clerk who became extremely irritated at the lady's inability to communicate her need in Russian. Frowning at the woman, the clerk abruptly motioned dismissal with her hand. Ilse, usually placid, found herself suddenly saying in Russian, "This is a public institution! Why can't you learn basic Estonian words that would help these people?"

To Ilse the entire town of Pärnu looked dismal. Streets and buildings were pock marked and curbs broken. The paint on houses was peeling or they were painted dark green or grey. All paint was ordered through Moscow, and people had to accept what was offered.

Ilse looked closely at the apartment buildings being erected to accommodate the many Russian immigrants who were rapidly inhabiting her country. They were of a construction she had never seen before in Estonia but were common throughout Russia. These apartments were being built to replace homes destroyed by the war and were made of concrete cubes placed atop and beside one another until they were three and four stories high. The finished product looked like a large square box with many rooms. In her estimation, they were ugly with no aesthetic appearance.

Grocery shopping was a time-consuming ordeal of lines. One had to wait in the bread line, then in another line for dairy, yet another line for produce, and finally the check-out line. Every store was government owned with workers paid a set wage. Clerks did not try to satisfy a customer. If one saw something they wished to purchase, the sales person would pick up the item closest to him regardless of whether it was flawed. The customer was obliged to take it or decline purchasing it without the option of another choice.

Quality products were hard to find, so customarily when one passed a store with a long line extending from it, he would get into it regardless of what was being sold. A long line indicated that whatever was being sold had to be worthwhile. People could purchase whatever it was and later trade it for something they really needed or wanted.

Thankfully, the beach in this resort town of Pärnu had not changed. The water was clear as ever and reminiscent of wonderful times swimming with girlfriends from school. The sand was as white as ever also, and the sun felt comforting as she and Tutti sat on a low stone wall basking in its warmth. Tutti saw Ilse looking pensively at the Baltic Sea and asked, "What are you thinking, Ilse?"

"You'll laugh when I tell you," Ilse chuckled.

"That's okay. These days we need a good laugh."

Ilse smiled and then said, "Do you remember how Papsi used to ride his bicycle down to the beach whenever there was a concert in the shell behind us?"

Tutti's face broke into a broad smile. "Yes, he would never think of missing a summer concert, and then at the end of summer he would say, 'I'm glad summer is over. I'm so tired of attending concerts.'" They both laughed out loud together at the recollection.

Ilse looked endearingly at Tutti. "It is so good to be with someone who remembers those wonderful days and can appreciate them with me. Old friends truly are better than gold."

All too soon the two weeks ended, and Tutti had to return to work. Ilse then traveled by bus to Tõstamaa, a town about an hour's ride west from Pärnu, where Hilda Pavelson was living in a house that her mother owned.

Tõstamaa was a quiet little village near the sea with but one general store. Its biggest attraction was a former manor house once owned by a German baron but now serving as a museum during the summer and a high school during the rest of the year. The entire setting was the perfect place to relax and enjoy the beauty of the forest and farmland surrounding the village. Hilda worked as a saleswoman in the general store and sold everything from fishing items and food to clothing.

Hilda's mother, Miina Schön, was a delightful, easy-going woman in her 70s with a lovely sense of humor. She giggled as she told Ilse, "When Hilda returned from Siberia to live with me, she threw out all the old stuff I had: an old table, some old lamps and several other things I had been accustomed to for years. I told her, 'I'm getting worried. Are you going to throw me out, too?'"

Hilda improved her mother's three-room home before Ilse arrived by arranging to have the outhouse attached to the dwelling so there was no longer need of going outdoors to use the facility. It was still not a flush toilet, but certainly more convenient to use. She also painted the house and refreshed it for her mother.

While Ilse was visiting, she helped the family prepare for winter by canning items picked from their backyard vegetable garden. It was common for anyone who owned land to utilize it for growing food. Fresh produce was limited. Even when it could be purchased, the travel time to a distant market was a deterrent. In addition to the vegetables grown, the family had raspberry bushes yielding a rich harvest that could be made into preserves.

Ilse enjoyed reminiscing with her dear friend Hilda and her mother while they worked together. A feeling of comradery existed that only a shared project can produce. Ilse felt a part of the family and at one with the fertile land of Estonia that was producing such abundance. It was so different from the hard labor she had encountered in Maiga and Kolpashevo where she had struggled to get enough from the ground to survive.

One evening as Hilda and Ilse sat together on the front steps of the house after having put up the last jar of raspberry preserves, they began to recount the years and the similar paths their lives had taken.

"Remember the car trip we took together with our husbands back in the summer of 1938?" asked Ilse. "Peko and I had just been married for a few months, and everything was so new and exciting as we traveled to Poland, Czechoslovakia and on to Austria and Hungary. What a trip of a lifetime that was, Hilda."

Hilda's face was bathed in the orange hew of sunset as she smiled at the thought. "That was a wonderful trip, Ilse. We four always did get along well together. Volli and I felt so comfortable with you and Peeter."

Ilse's face grew suddenly serious. "It seems the best of times in this life always have a cloud of gloom overshadowing them, Hilda. Remember the barriers that were being erected on the border of Czechoslovakia to deter the German troops from entering?"

Hilda's face now grew sullen as she spoke. "Yes, the fear of an approaching war was in the air." She paused and then added, "That telegram we received from your parents while in Budapest was unnerving. It simply said, 'Unrest everywhere. Come home immediately.'"

"I remember that well," said Ilse. We had planned to go to Yugoslavia but cut our trip short and headed home. That night from the second-floor room of the inn where we stayed, we watched a crowd gather on the street below. They were in an uproar and spoke excitedly with one another. The atmosphere seemed filled with electricity."

"That was truly frightening," said Hilda. "Especially since we could not understand what they were saying." Ilse nodded agreement and Hilda continued. "But what really made us uneasy was the next morning as we crossed the Carpathian Mountains. Remember the driver who approached us saying that he had not found gasoline?"

"That was scary," said Ilse. "We feared if we continued we might find ourselves stranded in some remote area. Fortunately, we did find gas and travelled to Warsaw where we spent the next night."

Hilda creased her brow as she spoke, "But the following night in Königsberg, Poland, was an eye opener for all of us when our waiter in the restaurant asked us where we had been traveling. When we mentioned Czechoslovakia, he said, 'Oh, the Czechs are a malicious people.'"

"Yes," said Ilse, "and when I said, 'That is not true,' he said, 'If you don't believe it, I will bring you a journal. You will see how badly they treat Germans.' Then he returned with an article complete with pictures that told of how the Czechoslovakians were forcing Germans living in Sudetenland[51] to eat dog food and live in attics."

Hilda frowned as she spoke. "I have thought of that often throughout the years, Ilse. Those were lies propagated by the Germans as an excuse for the annexation of Sudetenland. The amazing thing was that the waiter in that restaurant was convinced this was true because he had read it in a German periodical."

"Reasoning with him was useless," said Ilse, "and trying to tell him that we had just been there and had seen no such thing did not change his mind."

Hilda shook her head as she spoke, "The German propaganda machine was terrific. Unfortunately, most people believe whatever they read in print."

Now both women were in a serious mood as Ilse relived their history. "It is interesting that our lives have taken such similar turns, Hilda. All four of us were deported—for what we will never know. You were separated from your daughter for a time, and I have been separated from my son since that awful day. Your husband and mine ended up in the same concentration camp together, and both died there. Now once again you are separated from your daughter, and we two are once again together."

Shadows of night had begun to fall as Hilda responded. "It has been quite a journey, Ilse. One I would not like to travel again—at least not the portion that consisted of the last 17 years. But tell me, why don't you consider returning to Estonia for good now?"

"What would I come home to, Hilda? I have no immediate family here. Mamsi, Meeta and Vello are in the United States. Oskar and his family are in Australia, and my husband is dead. If I continue working in Kolpashevo until I retire, I will receive a double pension. I might as well take advantage of that. I surely feel entitled to some compensation for all the years of life that have been stolen from me. Besides, I enjoy working with the kindergarten children. They are now my children. Each child reminds me of what I missed as my son was growing up without me. I vicariously raise him each time I instruct one of those little ones."

Hilda reached for her friend's hand and gave it a sympathetic squeeze. "I understand what you're saying, Ilse, but don't you miss your homeland?"

"Oh, yes, more than I can say. It was what I longed for during the past 17 years. And seeing it again tears at my heartstrings even though it has changed dramatically. One day I will return, Hilda, but it will be after I retire."

CHAPTER 33

The End of an Era
New York City 1958-1959

The summer of Vello's junior year of high school he found employment as a foreman in a bicycle shop keeping a record of all incoming shipments for the warehouse. He also worked in a machine shop making metal parts. During his senior year, however, he attended Blue Mountain Academy in Hamburg, Pennsylvania, a Seventh-day Adventist church-operated boarding school. There he was able to work for Harris Pine Mills, a furniture factory, making dressers. Laymen had developed this industry in order to help those attending the academy to work their way through school. Vello began work there in the summer of 1959 and was able to work throughout his senior year. Financially, he saw this as a wonderful opportunity for completing school without any debt. An added benefit was that the school was in a lovely country setting in the midst of a mountain range, and he found the youth there very accepting and encouraging.

That summer, however, brought health problems to both Meeta and her mother. As the summer progressed, Amalie felt weak and dizzy and complained of stomach pain. Meeta wanted to take her to the doctor, but Amalie resisted. "Let's wait. Perhaps this will solve itself. We don't have enough money for doctors. Let's wait until the next pay period." So it went from pay check to pay check.

Meeta was experiencing intestinal problems that required surgery. Fortunately, her employment covered her for health insurance. She entered the hospital on August 2 and was operated on August 4. Vello hitchhiked home from the academy the following Friday to be with the family.

On Saturday Vello, Hillar and Amalie visited Meeta in the hospital, but Amalie was feeling quite ill. Meeta noted her mother did not look well and asked, "Mamsi, how are you feeling?" Amalie responded weakly, "I have bad pain in my stomach today." Meeta became very concerned and said to Vello, "Take Mamsi to the hospital emergency ward." This time Amalie did not refuse.

Amalie's initial examination revealed a soft mass just under the skin in the area of her liver. She was admitted for further testing into the Queens General Hospital as a charity case. Glucose and three pints of blood were given to her. Then a tube was placed through her nose into her stomach which made it difficult for her to speak. Meeta was released from the hospital two days later.

On August 19, while Meeta was visiting her mother, the doctor called her aside to say it would be necessary to operate to determine what was wrong with Amalie.

The surgery was scheduled for the following day at 8:00 a.m. Vello was back at work at the academy, but Hillar and Meeta took the 90-minute ride to the hospital utilizing trains and buses and arrived about noon.

When Meeta located the doctor, he was very sad as he greeted them. "Your mother has cancer, and it has spread so far that no surgery can remove it. All the vital organs are affected by the disease." The news hit Meeta like a bullet to the chest. Her response came weakly, mechanically. "How long does she have to live, Doctor?" The doctor looked down at the floor and then at Meeta before responding. "If she recovers from this operation, maybe two or three months." He paused and then said in an empathetic tone, "I'm terribly sorry we can't do more for her healing, but we will do everything possible to make her comfortable."

Meeta reentered her mother's hospital room and sat beside her as she slept. Amalie's hands lay atop the sheets; Meeta looked at them through new eyes. Her fingers were knobbed from arthritis, and the veins protruded like tree roots. Tears welled and spilled down Meeta's cheeks as she thought of the countless hours those hands had washed dishes, mended and laundered clothes and prepared meals for the little family. Now the differences of the past seemed so insignificant. What mattered were the sacrifices her mother had made—even neglecting her own health because of the lack of finances. There are no better days to look forward to for Mamsi, she thought. This is her life.

That evening Meeta wrote both Oskar and Ilse apprising them of their mother's current situation. Oskar had permanently returned to Australia in early 1957 and was now reunited with his family.

On Friday evening, August 28, Vello once again hitchhiked home from the academy. The next day he visited his grandmother in the hospital. She was seated in a chair, stooped shouldered and weak as he entered. After exchanging greetings Amalie said, "Vello, I'm so very thirsty. I have such a desire for lemonade. Would you please see if you can find some for me?" Vello knew a small store across from the hospital that he felt would carry it, so he hurried down to the first floor and out the front door. When he returned with the drink she took a sip, but no sooner had she done so it came back up.

When Vello returned home from the hospital, he shared what had happened with his Aunt Meeta. "Ati, it was so hard seeing Mamsi unable to enjoy lemonade today." His youthful face reflected pain as he spoke. "Today I prayed that a cure for cancer might be found before she dies." Meeta looked with sympathy at her nephew. She knew how much loss this young man had already experienced in his life, but words could not allay his sorrow and she remained silent.

On September 2, 1959, Amalie passed away. The funeral service was held in the Jamaica Seventh-day Adventist Church. Ever the supporter, Wasyl Myzak and about 15 other friends were present for the service. However, because of the distance to the cemetery only Wasyl, Meeta, Hillar and Vello were present for the graveside commitment.

Meeta knew their lives would never be the same. Hillar and she would now be alone with Vello away at boarding school. This would be Hillar's first experience with death and the loss of a family member. How difficult would this loss be for him? He, now 12, would have to arrive home from school to an empty house with no supper awaiting him. He would have to shoulder some of the household chores while she continued to earn a living.

CHAPTER 34

A New Beginning
Takoma Park, MD/Estonia 1960-1969

Vello was elected class pastor by his Blue Mountain Academy graduating class of 1960. It was a different role than what he had envisioned for himself, but it provided a seed that unwittingly germinated as he entered college. When he began his junior year at Columbia Union College[52] in Takoma Park, Maryland, he decided to major in theology.

During that school year Meeta lost her job at Singer Sewing Machine Company. Vello now had a car and was working part time at a college-owned shop assembling furniture. On a weekend trip home he encouraged his aunt. "Ati, this could be an opportunity for you. Why not move to Takoma Park? It's where our church's world headquarters is located along with a publishing house, college, hospital and three large churches. You would certainly be able to find employment in one of those institutions. We could find housing together, and I wouldn't have the extra expense of dorm living. Besides, Hillar is now in his second year of high school and Takoma Academy[53] is right there for him."

Meeta stared at Vello pondering his words before she responded, "Do you think we could find housing?"

"That won't be difficult," said Vello with certainty in his tone. Vello had been selling Christian books that summer and learned that the art of selling often involved turning negatives into positives. "Many church members there have rental apartments to house newcomers to the area. I'm certain I can find us something."

Meeta contemplated his words as he continued. "Look, Ati, this would be your chance to get away from this concrete city you don't like. Takoma Park is just outside Washington, D.C., but it is a small bedroom community with large trees and lovely homes. Sligo Creek runs through it with a beautiful stream of water flanked by ferns, mosses, and rocks. You'd love it there."

Vello's sales pitch was too much for Meeta to resist. She agreed that if he could find a place for the three of them, she would be willing to move.

Vello found an upstairs apartment in a two-story home on Boyd Avenue. He was able to get the trucker of the college-owned furniture company to move his aunt and cousin to Takoma Park on a return trip after making a delivery in New York City. And Meeta found employment as an elevator operator at the Washington Sanitarium and Hospital.[54]

Hillar entered Takoma Academy in the midst of his sophomore year and worked as a janitor for the school. In summer and on holiday vacations he worked with a crew painting residential and commercial structures. His mathematical mind and interest in science prompted him to consider becoming a doctor until he saw a movie of an actual operation.

Both young men worked their way through high school and college. In the fall of 1965, Vello entered the seminary at Andrews University in Berrien Springs, Michigan. Hillar graduated from high school that year and entered Maryland University in College Park, Maryland, to work toward a degree in engineering.

Both Vello and Ilse had been corresponding through the years, and it was their longing to one day finally meet. While at the seminary Vello had become a citizen of the United States. His country of birth was now one of 16 republics ruled by the Soviet Union. Without US citizenship he would not have dared return to Estonia because he feared possible detainment.

Early in 1968, Vello's last year of seminary, he began contacting travel agencies to obtain information on the best possible flights to Estonia. Ilse waited anxiously for details of her son's possible visit.

One day in June as she listened to Voice of America, the only accurate communication in that controlled environment, she heard a reporter say, "Vello Kotter has graduated with a Master of Divinity degree from Andrews University." Her mother's heart could not believe what she was hearing, albeit she was not excited about her son deciding to be a minister. Both she and her brother Oskar had advised him to go into some type of business where he could make some significant money. But to think that the news of his completed degree came at the very time she was listening seemed providential.

After graduation Vello began his first pastorate in South Boston, Virginia, and settled into the parsonage. The first item placed on the wall of his home office was a picture of the Tallinn harbor, the entry place for all foreigners coming to Estonia. Looking daily at the picture gave him the incentive to prepare the details of the trip.

The year 1969 marked the 100th anniversary of Estonia's Song Festival. This was an event celebrated every five years and drew thousands of people from within Estonia. The festival featured choral groups and traditional dancers from towns and villages throughout the country. Choirs and dancers would practice locally and then combine once they arrived in Tallinn for the event. There they merged into a mass choir of 25,000 and coordinated 7,000 dancers.

The 1969 celebration was one of the first in Soviet Estonia that allowed great numbers of foreigners to visit. With this event to open the way, both Vello and his mother felt certain this was the most likely time for permission to be granted them. Their supposition became reality, and the long hoped for date of meeting was set for June 25, 1969.

The plan was that Ilse would travel from Kolpashevo to Tallinn and meet with Vello at the harbor where his ship was to dock. She traveled largely by train and arrived in Tallinn the second week in June. She was housed by a friend named Helmi whom she had become acquainted with during their detainment in Siberia.

Vello began his trip on June 22 from Washington National Airport, Washington, D.C., connected in New York and arrived in London the following morning where he spent the day sightseeing. At 6:25 a.m. on June 24 Vello took a taxi to the West End Terminal in London to await his flight to Helsinki, Finland.

It was late afternoon when Vello landed in Helsinki, and he scurried to get his luggage. A taxi took him to the harbor where he rushed to purchase a ticket on a ferryboat that would leave for Tallinn the following morning at 10 o'clock. He found a room in a nearby hotel and promptly fell fast asleep.

His sound sleep, however, was all too soon aroused by bright sunlight streaking across his face. He sat straight up in bed and looked about him. The room was filled with light as bright as noonday. The clock next to his bed said 2 o'clock. His heart began to pound, and he felt sweat rising on his forehead. "Oh no," he said aloud. "I've overslept!" He quickly reached for the telephone on the nightstand and called the front desk. As soon as the clerk answered, he blurted out, "What time is it?"

The clerk politely responded, "It's 2:00 a.m."

Vello breathed an audible sigh and continued, "Oh, thank heavens." He paused and then added, "It's so bright I thought I had overslept and that it was 2:00 p.m."

The clerk laughed and calmly consoled him, "Sir, you are in the land of the midnight sun. This time of year we only experience about two hours of dusk. Why don't you tell us what time you wish to be awakened? We will give you a call to be certain you don't over sleep"

Vello thanked the clerk and asked to be awakened at 7:00 a.m. But now sleep evaded him. He tossed restlessly until 6:00 a.m. when he finally gave up the struggle and arose to ready himself for the day. The hotel provided a continental breakfast that Vello ate heartily. He had always found his appetite increased when he was anxious.

Ilse was unable to sleep well the night before she was to meet her son. She confided in her hostess the next morning to gain some relief. "Helmi, I can't begin to express how nervous I am about meeting Vello. I have longed for this day for so many years, and yet now I'm fearful of the meeting. He is no longer the little baby I held in my arms. How do I respond to an adult child who has come from my body but who is really now a stranger to me?"

Helmi listened intently. "I can only tell you that it was a bit like that for me when I returned from Siberia. My son had been away visiting a relative when they came for my husband and me. He was only eight years old. When I was released in 1952, my son was 19 and he had become a man. Fortunately, he did have some recollection of me, but it was still quite strange to be reunited. It took a few days to acclimate to one another again, but we now have a very good and loving relationship."

Ilse's brow furrowed as she spoke, "But my son has no remembrance of me. We truly are like strangers to one another. What do I say to him when we meet? Should I hug him . . . kiss him? I feel it will be so awkward to do either."

Helmi's kind blue eyes looked sympathetically at her friend. "Ilse, when the moment comes, your response will be automatic. He, too, will be feeling apprehensive about meeting you for the first time. When it happens, you will both muddle through as best you can."

Vello had prearranged to meet Pastor Haikonen, a Seventh-day Adventist pastor serving in Helsinki, at 8:00 a.m. At that time the Bible was not readily available to Christians in Soviet Estonia. Some Christian organizations were actually smuggling Bibles into Russian occupied countries. Pastor Haikonen had agreed to take Vello to a bookstore where he could purchase Estonian Bibles. Vello hoped to get the Bibles through customs and give them to the pastor of the Tallinn Seventh-day Adventist Church when he arrived. He already had brought with him a Russian language Bible to distribute. Now he purchased two Estonian New Testaments and put them into his travel bag.

The day was warm and sunny. At 10:00 a.m. Vello boarded the ferry. He was a bit concerned when an attendant began taking all the passports from those who were boarding but was told this was standard procedure for anyone entering Soviet Estonia. He was assured that passports would be returned as they disembarked. Vello loved the sea and climbed to the deck of the ship where he could best enjoy the three-hour trip ahead of him.

That morning was a tense time for Ilse. She was unusually quiet as she pondered. All she knew for certain was that the long years of waiting would come to an end that day. The thought of how they might end caused apprehension. How would her son relate to her? How would she relate to him? What if he didn't like her? What if she didn't like him?

She and Helmi planned to meet Ilse's long-time friend Hilda Pavelson and her daughter Luule. Luule had divorced her Russian husband and now lived in an apartment in Tallinn. Hilda had traveled to Tallinn from her home in Tõstamaa to be with Ilse for this grand reuniting of mother and son, and Luule offered to be chauffer for the occasion. She drove a red four-door Russian made Zaparovich. The four of them met at noon. Ilse stopped at a kiosk to purchase flowers to present to her son upon his arrival, a custom in Estonia when one greeted a visitor.

They journeyed to the harbor and arrived shortly before 1:00 p.m. The ship was due to dock at 1:30. As they approached the chain-link fence behind which they were to stand, they could see a good number of people had already begun to gather.

Ilse looked timid as she spoke to the ladies. "I must admit my stomach feels a bit squeamish. This waiting is so difficult."

* * *

Vello stood and scanned the distant landscape of Tallinn. As the ship drew closer, he began to see some of the church towers that appeared in the picture he had hung on the wall of his home office. Then he noticed three small ships coming directly toward them. He waved his arms in greeting but noticed that no one else was waving. The man next to him said, "Those are Russian patrol boats." Vello noticed that one of them had its gun turret pointed directly at their vessel. He now realized they were patrolling the Estonian coast to prevent anyone from trying to escape. The thought brought a shiver of reality to him. He had read about Communism and its oppressive government, but to see it in action was depressing.

Vello stared at the boats as he replied to the man beside him. "I think this will be a real learning experience. Those of us who have lived in a free society take our freedoms so much for granted."

While the ferry docked at the Tallinn harbor, Vello noticed a crowd of hundreds of people standing behind a chain-link fence next to the customhouse waiting for friends and family to disembark. He surveyed the crowd knowing somewhere in that crowd was the mother he had never met.

One by one names were called, and people began leaving the ship. An hour passed and Vello pondered why it was taking so long for him to be called. He knew his passport revealed Estonia as his place of birth and that his birth year was 1941, the year of a mass deportation. Were the authorities taking this extra time to check his family history? The waiting was torturous.

During the second hour of waiting, he finally heard his name over the loudspeaker. He was relieved to receive his passport as he started down the gangplank. Only a fraction of the people remained standing behind the fence. He walked along its length peering into their faces but could not identify anyone who looked like the pictures he had seen of his mother.

Vello stepped in line at the customhouse and waited as people slowly moved inside. His mind swirled. What if the government had censored his letter and his mother had never received the information regarding the day of his arrival? His whole bearing registered dejection. He had addresses of relatives in the city. Perhaps he could at least contact them. But that was not the purpose of his coming.

The line slowly moved forward until Vello stood under the extended roof of the customhouse. The roof shaded him from the glare of the sun, and he removed the sunglasses he had been wearing. Almost immediately he heard a soft woman's voice call reticently, "Vello," from behind the fence about six feet from where he was standing. He turned and looked into the face of his mother. She stood holding the bouquet of flowers in her hands and instantly began to cry. He wanted to cry, too, but at the same time a feeling of joy surged through him and he called out, "Ema!" the Estonian word for "mother." Vello stood as tall as he could to show his mother the full stature of his six-foot-one-inch frame. The fence was still between them, but he began taking pictures of her in order to capture the moment of a lifetime. He vaguely noticed some ladies standing behind her smiling profusely. The air was filled with excitement, but there was one more hurdle to surmount—customs.

Once inside the customhouse a Russian guard began going through his luggage. As Vello opened his large suitcase, the guard noticed the Russian Bible in plain sight on top of his clothing. The guard asked in English, "Is this your Bible?" Vello replied, "Yes."

The guard looked questioningly at him with a stern face. "Can you read this?" Vello shook his head and said, "No."

The guard took the Bible in his hand and left his station. In a few minutes he returned with a long yellow form. On it he wrote Vello's name, passport information and checked other items on the form. The guard's face was void of any expression, and Vello became worried that he might be detained and not allowed to see his mother. After completing his work, the guard handed the document to Vello for his signature and informed him that the Bible would be returned to him upon leaving Estonia. Vello breathed deeply and took his suitcase and travel bag from the counter. As he turned to leave, he realized that in the excitement of finding the Russian Bible the guard had overlooked checking his travel bag containing the two Estonian New Testaments he had purchased in Finland.

Vello left the customhouse through a door opposite the one he had entered. It led to the area behind the fence where his mother waited. As he stepped outside, his mother stood just a mere five feet away. Behind her were three strange women grinning broadly.

Ilse took a step forward as he approached, and Vello's luggage slipped from his hands. Instinctively, they both reached out to embrace one another. It seemed the right thing to do but at the same time artificial and strained. The embrace, however, introduced a beginning—a new beginning.

＊

EPILOGUE

Meeta Kollist spent the last years of her life in North Carolina living near her son Hillar and his wife Rita. Hillar had become a dentist and established his own practice in Sylva, North Carolina. He provided his mother with a lovely manufactured home, surrounded by mountains, and bought her a piano. His three children, Wendy, Ryan and Heather, gave her much joy during her retirement. When Wasyl Myzak finally secured a legal divorce, he proposed marriage to Meeta several times, but she repeatedly refused because they could not find a common ground on religious beliefs, and Meeta did not want a spiritually divided home. For a number of years she served as church pianist in her local congregation. She died in 2004 shortly before her 94th birthday.

Ilse Kotter retired from her work as a kindergarten teacher in Kolpashevo, Russia, in 1971 and returned to Pärnu, Estonia, on May 28 of that year. Though she had applied and was placed on a waiting list for an apartment in 1969, she was unable to obtain one until early 1973. Upon her return to Estonia she found accommodations by living with various friends until her apartment was available. She was not permitted to leave Estonia for a visit to the United States until November of 1977 and spent the next year with her son Vello and his wife Bonnie in America. During that time she reunited with her sister Meeta, whom she had not seen since 1941. She also shared time with Meeta's son Hillar and his family. After her year's visit, however, she chose to return to her beloved Estonia. Upon her return she began giving piano lessons and became the pianist of a local orchestra. As a result of receiving independence, the Estonian government returned the building that was once Jaak Kollist's leather tannery to Ilse Kotter and her brother Oskar Kollist who still resided in Australia. Though empty and in disrepair, they leased portions of the building to several different businesses, hired a general manager for the day-to-day decisions and slowly began refurbishing the structure. Oskar remained in Australia until his death in 2001 at the age of 89. Ilse continued directing the facility in Estonia until her death in 2006, three months before her 92nd birthday.

Vello Kotter, as V. Eric Kotter, continued ministering throughout the East Coast from Florida to Maine. He obtained a Master of Public Health degree from Loma Linda University, Loma Linda, California, in 1981 and a Doctor of Ministry degree from Andrews University in Berrien Springs, Michigan, in 1985. In 1991 he conducted a series of religious meetings in Tallinn, Estonia, where his mother Ilse came forward to publicly recommit her faith in Jesus Christ. During that series of meetings Estonia declared its freedom from the Soviet Union. Vello and his wife felt privileged to be present at that dramatic time. The story of that miraculous period of Estonian history was chronicled in the motion picture entitled *The Singing Revolution*.

The Pärnu homestead in 1937 from the opposite side of the Sauga River.

J. Kollist Pärnu Leather Company in 1936.

Employees preparing hides for tanning.

A new addition was added to the leather factory in 1941. This picture was re-covered in the sand after looters stole the contents of Amalie's suitcase as the family fled Neumarkt Oberpfalz, Germany. This is the only picture the family had of that addition.

Ilse and Peeter Kotter were married on April 23, 1938.

Frozen Ob River in Kolpashevo.

Work in the hayfields of Siberia was done by hand.

Kolpashevo during the spring thaw.

Kolpashevo: Ilse lived in an apartment in this building from mid-October 1943 to July 1, 1945, with six other women. It also included a shoe repair shop, a seamstress workroom, the commandant's office and two rooms housing men.

Meeta Kollist in 1941.

Liina Jansen, the woman who
aroused Meeta's interest
in studying the Bible.

Jaak Kollist loved to ride his bicycle
to the Pärnu concerts.

Oskar Kollist in 1930.

During the winter of 1943/1944 German soldiers, who often saw Vello walking, called him *Das Kind mit dem Stock* (the child with the cane).

Hillar Kollist at three years of age in 1950.

Wasyl Myzak, Hillar and Meeta Kollist, Vello Kotter and Amalie Kollist while in Germany in 1948.

Amalie Kollist, Vello Kotter, Hillar and Meeta Kollist in 1956.

Hillar Kollist and Vello Kotter in 1956 with their dog Ruffi in the New York City multiple-family house by the Idelwild Airport.

Ilse Kotter (with accordian) standing among fellow teachers and her
Kolpashevo kindergarten class in 1957.

Wasyl Myzak, Meeta and Hillar Kollist and Vello Kotter at the cemetery
following graveside services for Amalie in 1959.

Vello and Ilse Kotter in 1969 when they met for the first time following 28 years of separation.

The refurbished factory in 1996, five years after it was returned to Ilse Kotter and her brother Oskar Kollist.

NSVL PROKURATUUR

**EESTI NÕUKOGUDE
SOTSIALISTLIKU VABARIIGI
P R O K U R Õ R**

Tallinn, Mitšurini 7   Telefon 452-26

ПРОКУРАТУРА СССР

**П Р О К У Р О Р
ЭСТОНСКОЙ СОВЕТСКОЙ
СОЦИАЛИСТИЧЕСКОЙ РЕСПУБЛИКИ**

Таллин, ул. Мичурина 7   Телефон 452-26

№ ¹⁴/15к   9 aprillil 196 6 .a.

Õ I E N D

    Käesolev õiend on antud kod.   K o t t e r, Ilse
Jaagu tr., sünd. 1914.a. selles, et tema oli 1941.a.
8.juunil Eesti NSV-st administratiivkorras välja saade-
tud Tomski oblastisse, kus ta viibis 1954.aasta novemb-
ri kuuni.

    Eesti NSV Ühiskondliku Korra Kaitse Ministeeriu-
mi ja Eesti NSV Prokuratuuri määrusega " " aprillist
1966.a. on kod. K o t t e r, Ilse väljasaatmine tunnis-
tatud põhjendamatuko ning teda on rehabiliteeritud.

    NSV Liidu Ministrite Nõukogu 17.juuli 1959.a.
määruse p.1 alusel kuulub Ilse K o t t e r i suhtes
kohaldamisele NSV Liidu Ministrite Nõukogu 8.septembri
1955.a. määruse "Põhjendamatult kriminaalvastutusele
võetud ja hiljem rehabiliteeritud kodanike tööstaažist,
nende töölepaigutamisest ja pensioniga kindlustamisest"
sätted, väljaarvatud kahe kuu palga kompensatsiooni väl-
jamaksmine.

                     Eesti NSV prokuröri asetäitja
                     3.klassi riigiõigusnõunik
                     /K.Kimmel/

This document states that Ilse Kotter was deported without cause or criminal
charges. Her rights as a citizen have been reinstated and her pension has been
certified. Though this document states that she was officially released in
1955, in actuality, she was not informed of this until two years, three months
and 23 days later.

1973 — V. Eric Kotter (Vello), his mother Ilse and wife Bonnie stand near the house where he and his parents lived at the time of the deportation.

After years of submitting requests, the Soviet government finally permitted Ilse to visit the United States in 1977 where she reunited with her sister Meeta after 36 years of separation.

Ilse and Vello Kotter and Meeta Kollist shortly after Ilse's arrival in the United States in 1977.

Bonnie and V. Eric Kotter with Ilse Kotter during her year-long visit to the United States in 1977/1978.

END NOTES

[1] Good night in Estonian.

[2] People's Commissariat for Internal Affairs, predecessor of the Committee for State Security (KGB).

[3] Capital of Estonia.

[4] Good evening.

[5] Forest Brothers: Estonian patriots who conducted guerilla warfare against the Communists.

[6] A Medieval tower in the heart of Tallinn that flew whatever flag signified the controlling power of the period.

[7] The Czar's Army.

[8] In Greek mythology Dionysius hung a sword suspended by a single hair over the head of Damocles, a courtier.

[9] Small fish similar to sardines.

[10] Estonian equivalent of Mr.

[11] Collective farms where members were to be paid a share of the farm's products and also profits according to the amount of time worked.

[12] Dough stuffed with a meat or vegetable mixture and then baked.

[13] Four degrees below zero Fahrenheit.

[14] Minus 51 degrees Fahrenheit.

[15] Raun, Toivo U., *Estonia and the Estonians*, Second Edition, 1991, Hoover Institution Press, Stanford University, Stanford, California, p. 18.

[16] I Timothy 6:16.

[17] Three Wisemen's Day is the day the Russian Orthodox Church celebrates the coming of the Magi to see the Christ child.

[18] Deuteronomy 18:10-12.

[19] I Samuel 28:5-19.

[20] Daniel 2:34, 35.

[21] Daniel 2:41.

[22] Raun, p.158.

[23] A gentleman would scrape one foot backward while simultaneously bowing the head and offering his hand.

[24] There is the child with the cane.

[25] The required daily workload.

[26] Raun, p. 159.

[27] Estonian for "long."

[28] Raun, p. 159.

[29] Ibid.

[30] Vienna, My Delight!

[31] Are you from Vienna?

[32] Job 1:21.

[33] A root plant that grows wild.

[34] A Norwegian figure skater and film star, she was a three-time Olympic champion in the 20th Century.

[35] Hitler's last reserve soldiers.

[36] Top administrator.

[37] Similar to a money order.

[38] Dreaming.

[39] Exodus 14:14.

[40] *Source Book for Bible Students*, Review and Herald Publishing Association, Washington, D.C., 1922, p. 604.

[41] Matthew 15:3.

[42] Deuteronomy 4:12,13.

[43] Jeremiah 31:33; Ezekiel 11:19, 20; 36:26, 27; Psalm 37:31; Romans 8:4; 2 Corinthians 3:3; Hebrews 8:7-10.

[44] Hebrews 4:4-10.

[45] Romans 6:2, 3; 1 Corinthians 11:23-26.

[46] John 1:1-3, 14; Exodus 20:8-11.

[47] Named after U.S. Secretary of State George Marshall, it was a plan that provided $13 billion dollars aid for European countries to rebuild schools, repair factories, restore towns and improve farming following World War II.

[48] Now Kennedy International Airport.

[49] Short leather pants.

[50] The ideological and physical boundary separating the free West and Communist countries during the Cold War.

[51] Sudetenland was an area of Czechoslovakia on the northwestern border settled largely by Germans that Germany annexed in March of 1939 by means of the Munich Pact.

[52] Now Washington Adventist University.

[53] A Seventh-day Adventist high school.

[54] Now Washington Adventist Hospital.